Action Anthropology and Sol Tax in 2012: The Final Word?

Edited by Darby C. Stapp

Contributors:
Joan Ablon
John H. Bodley
Marianna Tax Choldin
Douglas E. Foley
Susan Tax Freeman
Robert E. Hinshaw
Solomon H. Katz
Joshua Smith
Darby C. Stapp
Albert L. Wahrhaftig
Tim Wallace

JOURNAL OF NORTHWEST ANTHROPOLOGY

Composed by Northwest Anthropology LLC, Richland, Washington. For back issues and catalog of prices contact Coyote Press, P.O. Box 3377, Salinas, CA 93912. www.californiaprehistory.com.

POLICY

Journal of Northwest Anthropology, published semiannually by Northwest Anthropology LLC, in Richland, Washington, is a refereed journal and welcomes contributions of professional quality dealing with anthropological research in northwestern North America. Regular issues are published semiannually with additional memoirs issued as funds are available. Theoretical and interpretive studies and bibliographic works are preferred, although highly descriptive studies will be considered if they are theoretically significant. The primary criterion guiding selection of papers will be how much new research they can be expected to stimulate or facilitate.

SUBSCRIPTIONS

The subscription price is $40.00 U.S. per annum for individuals, payable in advance, $60.00 for institutional subscriptions, and $30.00 for students with proof of student status. Remittance should be made payable to ***JONA.*** Subscriptions, manuscripts, change of address, and all other correspondence should be addressed to:

Darby C. Stapp, ***JONA***
P.O. Box 1721 • Richland, WA 99352-1721
(509) 554-0441
email: dstapp@pocketinet.com website: northwestanthropology.com

MANUSCRIPTS

Manuscripts can be submitted in electronic files in Microsoft Word sent via e-mail or on CD. An abstract will accompany each manuscript. Footnotes will be avoided and if used at all will be assembled at the end of the text. Questions of reference and style can be answered by referring to the style guide found on the website or to *Journal of Northwest Anthropology,* 37(1):101–130. Other problems of style can normally be solved through reference to *The Manual of Style,* University of Chicago Press, 16th edition (2010). All illustrative materials (drawings, maps, diagrams, charts, and plates) will be designated "Figures" in a single numbered series and will not exceed 6 x 9 inches. All tabular material will be part of a separately numbered series of "Tables." Authors will receive one free reprint of articles, Memoirs, or full-issue monographs. Additional reprints may be produced by the author; however, they must be exact duplicates of the original and are not to be sold for profit.

CONTENTS

Figures

Title page photograph—

Sol Tax in Algeria on a Beloit College archaeological excavation in 1930 while an undergraduate at the University of Wisconsin-Madison.

ABSTRACT

Action Anthropology and Sol Tax are both important chapters in the development of contemporary anthropology and applied social science. Although unknown or forgotten by most, both continue to be revered and applied by a group of intellectual descendants who will not let die either the man or the approach to helping communities. In 2010 and 2011, former students, colleagues, the two Tax daughters—both academic professionals—and others came together to explore the relevance of Action Anthropology and Sol Tax to applied social science today. In reflecting on the history of the man and the intellectual tradition that he inspired, the authors document the many contributions made by Tax and his student-colleague cohorts. Using examples from contemporary applications, the contributors also demonstrate the present-day power of the ideas and approaches developed over the first 75 years.

Time will tell whether *Action Anthropology and Sol Tax in 2012: The Final Word?* will close this important chapter in the development of applied social science research. Regardless, the tenets of Action Anthropology, detailed and explicated throughout this volume, will continue to provide a foundation for all applied scientists interested in social justice, indigenous decolonization, and improving the human condition.

FOREWORD

The impressive set of contributions contained herein will permit future generations to more fully understand the foundational influence and current relevance of Sol Tax in bringing anthropology out of the museum and universities and into the non-academic, international world of the mid-20th century. As Tax confronted the world of his time, he led the way in using anthropology to define, confront, and provide solutions to a world of problems not unlike those we now see again in the 21st century. These following contributions make clear that Tax and his work are as relevant today as they were in his time.

The contributions in this work show the profound influences that were exercised during Tax's productive career. My familiarity with Sol Tax began as a graduate student during my years at the University of Oregon, and my first impressions of him were that he was a very energetic innovator and an expert on American Indians with an activist orientation that he termed "Action Anthropology." As my career progressed during the 1960s I became ever more aware of the many areas in which Tax was active. My first direct encounter with him was while I was teaching at George Washington University, when S. Dillon Ripley, Secretary of the Smithsonian Institution (1964–1984), recruited Tax to form the Smithsonian Center for the Study of Man, where I also first met Sam Stanley, Tax's able, long-term assistant. By 1968 Sam and I were working together on an American Anthropological Association (AAA) Symposium on American Indian fishing rights for the Annual Meeting, a record of which I helped organize and later published in Vol. 2, No. 2 of *Northwest Anthropological Research Notes* (now the *Journal of Northwest Anthropology*).

In 1966–1967 Tax and the leadership of the National Congress of American Indians (NCAI) assigned me the task of analyzing the "Indian Resources Development Act of 1967." This bill turned out to be another veiled federal attempt to further the termination objectives of certain Western congressmen. In steep contrast to the Bureau of Indian Affairs (BIA) summary of reports and recommendations, my report was used by the NCAI to demonstrate that there was wide opposition to termination and a strong need for many increases in support, promises made as early as those made by Commissioner of Indian Affairs John Collier in the Indian Reorganization Act of 1934.

There were 1,950 distinct tribal recommendations for increasing support of all kinds, including strengthening of tribal self-determination and sovereignty for the 150 tribal groups that submitted recommendations.

My 1967–1968 experience with the Seattle AAA symposium, which focused on American Indian fishing and hunting rights, gave me a firsthand look at Tax and his mode of operation. It became apparent that he was extremely active and moved quickly from one project to another, whether it was his Iowa Meskwaki and Oklahoma Cherokee projects; his service under President Lyndon B. Johnson (LBJ) as an advisor on Indian affairs; his United Nations Educational, Scientific, and Cultural Organization (UNESCO) work; his editorial direction of *Current Anthropology* in the 1960s and 1970s; or his organization of the Ninth International Congress of Anthropological and Ethnological Sciences that promoted anthropology as an international discipline. Stemming from his earlier Meskwaki project, one of his most enduring contributions to American Indian affairs was his organization of the 1961 American Indian Chicago Conference, which brought together some eighty tribes that resulted in an evolving consensus seen in the Mission Statement from the conference described as the "Declaration of Indian Purpose." In retrospect, I believe the Chicago conference helped set the stage for numerous Indian policy reforms led by the Kennedys, LBJ, Nixon, Carter, and more recently by Clinton.

Of considerable significance was Tax's recruitment and involvement of NCAI individuals in his projects, especially D'Arcy McNickle and Vine Deloria Jr. I had encountered McNickle as a graduate student but came to know him and Vine in 1969 professionally at the University of Colorado. They were instrumental in resisting the lingering termination fever in the West. At that time I was becoming more familiar with ongoing covert attacks on John Collier's Indian Reorganization Act of 1934. Tax also, as much as any anthropologist, was central to the struggle to revive the John Collier reformist agenda expressed in Franklin Delano Roosevelt's "Indian New Deal." Tax worked primarily with D'Arcy, who had served in Collier's administration, and came to depend importantly on him, as had Collier. D'Arcy once informed me that his position in Chicago's Newberry Library was created by Tax. Tax's close association with the NCAI and Vine Deloria Jr. is not well known, nor is Tax's support for D'Arcy's American Indian Development Corporation, which hosted numerous National Indian Youth Council workshops and conferences in Boulder, Colorado, and elsewhere.

Earlier, the 1965 AAA meeting in Denver had made me aware of the University of Chicago spirit of activism that eventually led to my 1969 acceptance of a position in anthropology at the University of Colorado, Boulder, based on advice of my professors Homer Barnett and David Aberle. During the 1965 AAA meeting I had already been introduced to other of Tax's Chicago activist associates, among whom was Edward Spicer, who developed an impressive applied program at Arizona and who was influential in the development of the Society for Applied Anthropology (SfAA).

On coming to the University of Colorado in 1969 I found myself surrounded by influences that were obviously traceable to the University of Chicago and to Sol Tax. An important source of activism was Gilbert White, another Chicago whirlwind, who was serving as director of the Institute of Behavioral Science. He is one of the most well-known geographers in the world because of his work on flooding and natural hazards. Under White's direction, and that of Omer Stewart of the anthropology department, I became editor of the SfAA's journal, *Human Organization*, and later elected SfAA Treasurer. Part of Gilbert's support was his provision of an office for me and funding for editing and printing *Human Organization*. Incidentally, it was at this time that most of us were also heavily influenced by Kenneth Boulding, who provided powerful theoretical and methodological foundations for activist undertakings in the Institute of Behavioral Science.

From this rich environment, based heavily on Chicago figures such as Sol Tax and Gilbert White, we all drew strong encouragement for applied anthropological research among American Indians. Gilbert quickly engaged me in a study of the acceptance and impacts of birth control among the Blackfeet and Shoshone-Arapaho, which led to various other applied projects. Omer Stewart's example of using anthropologists as expert witnesses on behalf of American Indians was yet another example of the activist orientation I encountered at Boulder.

I think it's useful to draw from a characterization of Action Anthropology and applied anthropology by John W. Bennett from his 1996 *Current Anthropology* article. In his characterization of Sol Tax's Action Anthropology, he says that applied anthropology in the United States emerged as a mixture of New Deal humanitarian liberalism. Tax wanted to free anthropology of attachments to establishment organizations and academic institutions in favor of voluntary academic projects in which anthropologists intervened in solving the problems of local communities.

It is possible to argue that this orientation is viable and morally more justified than some of the applied activity we have come to expect from contemporary applied anthropologists. While Action Anthropology has diminished in the discourse of contemporary applied anthropology, I am convinced that the action orientation motivation preferred by Tax is preferable, especially for university anthropologists. There can be no question, however, that applied anthropology itself has become institutionalized as a separate subfield and continues to expand from its institutional base, not only in some universities but also in various governmental organizations as well as independent entrepreneurial organizations. I'm uncertain what Tax might say about this development, but I suspect he might see at least some of contemporary applied anthropology as morally compromised when considered in light of his own orientation in Action Anthropology.

In closing, I wish to call further attention to Collier's and Tax's associate, D'Arcy McNickle. I was witness to D'Arcy's successful defeat of federal termination that was being proposed for the Salish-Kootenai of the Flathead Indian Reservation by Senator Watkins and his congressional allies who were still seeking to enforce House Concurrent Resolution 108 in the 1960s. D'Arcy also helped appoint me as editor of the Plateau volume of the *Handbook of North American Indians*. D'Arcy and I, with Vine Deloria Jr., sat on the planning committee with Bill Sturtevant for the *Handbook*, all of which was initiated by Sol Tax and his Smithsonian Center for the Study of Man. D'Arcy's life has been well-chronicled by Dorothy Parker in 1994 in *Singing an Indian Song: A Biography of D'Arcy McNickle* (University of Nebraska Press). As a role model, he, like Sol Tax, requires careful review by those of us who choose to give voice to the voiceless and power to the powerless, as seen in the following contributions to this celebration of Sol Tax.

Deward E. Walker Jr., PhD
Professor of Anthropology and Ethnic Studies
University of Colorado, Boulder
June 2012

PREFACE

In 1998, while attending the Society for Applied Anthropology (SfAA) Annual Meeting in San Juan, Puerto Rico, I heard a presentation by Nancy O. Lurie on Sol Tax, Tribal Sovereignty, and the American Indian Chicago Conference. The presentation was remarkable to me because it described a professional orientation, Action Anthropology, that sounded surprisingly familiar to what I, my colleague Michael Burney, and others were pursuing in the American West: using our anthropological training to help indigenous peoples control their own heritage resources, on their own terms, with their own people.

There was one big difference, however. Whereas Action Anthropology had forty years of history and a body of method, theory, and assessment, we had little more than our own trial and error to guide us. Trained in the anthropological subdiscipline of archaeology, we had been thrust into a world where we were working day to day with living people, namely Native Americans—work for which we had had no training, little coursework, and no mentors. We were in new territory and making it up as we went along, with little more than common sense and political expediency to guide us. It was on-the-job training.

Upon returning from Puerto Rico, I called Michael, sent him Nancy's paper, which would later be published in *Human Organization*, 58(1), and we set out to learn as much as we could about Action Anthropology and its chief architect, Sol Tax, by digging into the massive literature. These readings inspired us to develop a symposium on Action Anthropology and cultural resource management the next year at the SfAA meeting in Tucson, Arizona, with Nancy Lurie as discussant; the session papers were later published in the *High Plains Applied Anthropologist*, 20(1). The Action Anthropology readings also led us to reflect on what we had been learning from our work with tribes and to document our thoughts in a book, *Tribal Cultural Resource Management: The Full Circle to Stewardship* (2000). Over the succeeding decade, we continued on our quest, applying to our work the teachings from Action Anthropology.

Finding Action Anthropology and learning about the efforts of its first- and second-generation practitioners was important, because it provided a solid foundation from which we could work. Once we had Action Anthropology to ground us, the work was not necessarily any easier; but the uncertainty, struggles, and stress over every decision subsided. Action Anthropology did not give us the answers, but it gave us a process and a set of values from which to move forward.

The idea to gather Action Anthropologists and revisit the approach and the contributions of Sol Tax began during the planning stages for the 71st annual meeting of the Society for Applied Anthropology to be held in Seattle, Washington. A session called "Learning from Sol Tax in 2010" was proposed, sponsored by the Sol Tax Award Committee, and a call for participation was issued. Soon, a group was formed comprising professionals who had worked with Sol Tax or were inspired by him.

The group engaged in numerous discussions via email for the months preceding the meeting. The four-hour session was then held on April 1, 2011, at the Grand Hyatt in Seattle. Presentations were followed by discussions with audience members, many of whom brought their own questions, experiences, and perspectives. A podcast of this session is available at the SfAA website (www.SfAApodcasts.net/2011/05/01/). Following the session, buoyed with new information and new perspectives—and anchored by the Action Anthropology tenet to share what had been learned—a commitment was formed to assemble the material and make it available to others.

Figure 1. Participants in the Learning from Sol Tax in 2010 Symposium, Society for Applied Anthropology Annual Meeting, April 1, 2011, Seattle, Washington. Left to right: Michael S. Burney, Albert L. Wahrhaftig, Joshua Smith, Susan Tax Freeman, Darby C. Stapp, Joan Ablon, Sandy Lane, Marianna Tax Choldin, Robert A. Rubinstein. (Photograph by Tim Wallace.)

This edited volume is the result. All of the presentations made in Seattle are included, supplemented by additional material solicited to round out the book, comments from the audience, and historical items of interest (such as the syllabus for the first Action Anthropology class taught by Sol Tax at the University of Chicago in 1958). Former students of Sol Tax contributing chapters are Joan Ablon and Albert Wahrhaftig, both students at the University of Chicago in the late 1950s, and Robert Hinshaw, who studied under Tax in the 1960s. Family members contributing chapters are Susan Tax Freeman and Marianna Tax Choldin. Individuals contributing chapters, who have been influenced by Sol Tax and Action Anthropology, are John Bodley, Doug Foley, Sol Katz, Joshua Smith, Darby Stapp, and Tim Wallace. Others contributing in the discussions before or during the Seattle session include Michael Burney, Sandy Lane, Nancy Lurie, Jay Miller, David Rice, Sally Robinson, and Robert Rubinstein.

Many people helped in the production of this volume. I thank Richard Badalamente, Julia Longenecker, Dave Payson, Kara Powers, Barbara Scott, and Diana Stapp.

Finally, to help distinguish the many discussions pertaining to Action Anthropology from those pertaining to applied anthropology, I have capitalized the terms Action Anthropology and Action Anthropologist. Typically, neither would be capitalized.

Darby C. Stapp, PhD
Northwest Anthropology LLC
Richland, Washington
June 2012

INTRODUCTION

Darby C. Stapp

This memoir is for the many applied social scientists and other professionals working in complex cultural settings. It is especially for those professionals working with indigenous peoples and other groups competing to survive in the modern world. The contributions in this volume provide insight from three generations of anthropologists, all of whom have actively worked in multicultural settings in order to understand and improve conditions. The book adds to the professional literature concerning applied anthropology, Action Anthropology, and other contemporary approaches to collaborative community practice.

Action Anthropology

The focus of this book is Action Anthropology, a methodological and theoretical approach to collaborative community service and research pioneered by Dr. Sol Tax and 75 years in the making. Action Anthropologists help indigenous and underrepresented communities solve problems. A fundamental precept of Action Anthropology is that decisions affecting a community are best made by that community. Action Anthropologists, therefore, will work with a community to define problems and issues, to develop alternative solutions, and to implement the chosen plan of action. The emphasis on all of these is to "work with the community," which means listening to its leaders and members, and collaborating with, rather than directing them.

Action Anthropology emerged from the University of Chicago in the 1950s, where its chief architect, Dr. Sol Tax (1907–1985), trained and influenced generations of applied social scientists. Its roots are traced to the university's anthropology field school at the Meskwaki Indian community, near Tama, Iowa—commonly known as the Fox Project.

The initial goal of the Fox Project, which ran from 1948 to 1958, was to understand the processes of acculturation that were taking place in the late 1940s and to intervene in those processes in order to help the Fox community improve the quality of their everyday lives. In time, the students realized that assimilation into American society was not going to be the endpoint for this group of American Indians. Before long, Tax and his student colleagues turned their attention to issues of self-determination and cultural persistence. Rather than study the community, these anthropologists began to develop and recommend actions that might improve conditions for the Meskwaki. The term Action Anthropology was soon in use.

Tax explained his vision for Action Anthropology in 1958:

> All we want in our action programs is to provide, if we can, genuine alternatives from which the people involved can freely choose—and to be ourselves as little restrictive as is humanly possible. It follows, however, that we must try to remove restrictions imposed by others on the alternatives open to Indians and on their freedom to choose among them. We avoid imposing our values upon the Indians … (Tax 1958:18).

This approach was revolutionary. While hard to imagine in this day and age of collaboration, anthropology was quite different fifty years ago. The majority of anthropologists at that time were pure researchers, not interested in applying their knowledge directly to help people. Those few anthropologists who did work in applied settings served largely as government administrators implementing programs from the top down; allowing communities to identify problems and propose solutions, much less make decisions, was not the typical approach.

Action Anthropology developed further during the 1960s and 1970s, assisted by increasing recognition and acceptance of cultural diversity by Western societies. Examples of work conducted include the 1961 Chicago American Indian Conference, the 1950s and 1960s Colorado workshops for Indian youth, and projects designed to assist various North and Central American indigenous communities. Before long, Action Anthropologists were involved in projects associated with health services, education, native languages, economic development, and resource access and protection. Workshops, meetings, and gatherings of all sorts became major aspects of the action process.

In addition to helping indigenous and disadvantaged communities, Tax insisted that a fundamental goal of Action Anthropology was to learn from its experiences and contribute to the understanding of culture and intercultural relations. A body of method and theory would be needed, and this would be accomplished by analysis and dissemination of results to colleagues. Much of this was accomplished by producing reports and publishing in professional venues such as *Current Anthropology* and *Human Organization.*

In 1974, a conference held in Panajachel, Guatemala, brought Sol Tax and many of his colleagues together to share and assess their contributions. Many of the papers from that conference were later included in a Festschrift (celebratory publication) honoring Sol Tax (Hinshaw 1979). Other insights into Action Anthropology are found in Rubinstein (1986), Bennett (1996), Foley (1999), Stocking (2000), Daubenmier (2008), and Smith (2010). A Festschrift prepared for Tax's student/colleague Robert K. Thomas also provides important material (Pavlik 1998).

Action Anthropology as a distinct approach continues today, primarily practiced by both academics and non-academics who have direct intellectual ties to Sol Tax, or who discovered the approach through the professional literature. Articles still appear, with "Action Anthropology and Pedagogy: University-Community Collaborations in Setting Policy" in *Human Organization* (Lane et al. 2011) a recent example. Those who identify themselves as Action Anthropologists are passionate about its distinctiveness. For some it is a method; for some it is a process; for some it is a professional orientation; and for some, a way of life. In addition, the influence of Action Anthropology can be seen throughout the popular community-based approaches of today, identified by names such as collaborative anthropology, engaged anthropology, and participatory action research.

The Tenets of Action Anthropology

Action Anthropologists recognize general guidelines, principles, and assumptions for conducting applied work in intercultural settings. Each situation is unique and demands unique responses. Settings are dynamic, confusing, emotional, sometimes ethically challenging, and often involving conflicts at all levels. Tenets provide the professional an anchor, helpful for tolerating and dealing with the ever-present ambiguity that typically characterizes these complex cultural work settings.

To assist professionals working in complex intercultural settings, nine "Tenets of Action Anthropology" were developed during the 2010–2011 effort. The group began with the operating principles distilled by Robert Hinshaw (1979:vii), who built upon those described by Tax (1975), and agreed on the following nine tenets:

1. We serve at a community's discretion and direction.
2. We recognize that we can never fully know a community and its needs; but to

the extent we can, it takes time, and we therefore temper our bias for action by avoiding premature choices and responses.

3. We work collaboratively with a community to develop alternatives for improving conditions.
4. We respect the right and ability of a community to make choices affecting its future and the freedom to make its own mistakes.
5. We are open and truthful.
6. We promote community sustainability and capacity building, and we strive to work ourselves out of a job.
7. As professionals, we learn from our experiences and use them to improve our method and theory.
8. We recognize that our source of funding can present conflicts of interest, and we confront this problem by insisting on professional independence.
9. We share what we have learned with the community, our professional colleagues, and others, as appropriate, to improve the human condition.

While pages could be written about each of these tenets, we think it best to keep them simple and let them radiate in the reflections, stories, and recommendations found in the following pages.

The Need for This Book at This Time

The last quarter century has seen a dramatic increase in support for cultural groups in North America and around the world. Individuals, volunteers, and professionals from various backgrounds have been thrust into action—working for government agencies, corporations, humanitarian groups, religious institutions, and various nongovernmental organizations—to provide assistance and pursue ways to improve conditions for indigenous groups, minorities, refugees, and displaced peoples.

Much of this work proceeds with little understanding of the people at risk or the situation at hand. Expertise is often not available, and there is rarely time to do proper study, even when funds are available. Individuals are needed who have an understanding of the cultural dynamics that affect patterns of behavior under changing conditions—especially when different cultures collide.

This is a serious problem. Complex cultural settings are widespread. War, famine, technological and economic development, and natural disasters are ongoing processes that continue to bring groups in contact that have different beliefs, values, languages, social structures, economic systems, and expectations. There is an ever-present need for cultural specialists who can mediate among groups, develop and explain alternatives, and help groups implement their choices.

Anthropology is but one of several disciplines that teach those committed to helping communities in areas such as health services, education, economic development, and resource protection. Anthropology is especially valuable, however, because it brings special expertise to our global challenges, namely an understanding of culture, cultural dynamics, and intercultural dynamics. For over a hundred years, anthropologists have been building methods and theories for understanding why groups behave as they do, why we differ, and how we deal with differences when forced to be together. For more than 50 years, Action Anthropologists have been learning how to put this knowledge to work.

Any professional working with other cultures will learn from the perspectives and experiences of Action Anthropology.

Organization of this Memoir

The memoir begins with a timeline of Sol Tax's life and a reprint of his 1994 obituary. Joan Ablon then describes the man, his characteristics, and some of his accomplishments. Albert Wahrhaftig then describes one of the first Action Anthropology projects, the 1960s Carnegie Corporation Cross-Cultural Education Project conducted in Oklahoma with the Cherokee Nation. Next, Robert Hinshaw provides his perspectives on Sol Tax and his University of Chicago colleague, the applied geographer Gilbert White. Additional perspectives on Sol Tax and his life are then provided from his two daughters, Marianna Tax Choldin and Susan Tax Freeman.

The next set of papers focuses on contemporary perspectives and applications of Action Anthropology. Joshua Smith first places Action Anthropology in the context of collaboration and decolonization movements in anthropology. Doug Foley then contributes a chapter based on his research on the Fox Project and his perspective on Sol Tax's contribution to contemporary anthropology. Next, Tim Wallace describes the influence that Sol Tax and Action Anthropology have had on the trajectory of his career, much of which has focused on Guatemalan communities. Robert Hinshaw returns to contribute a contemporary piece based on his life of serving and learning, also in Guatemalan communities. Albert Wahrhaftig also makes a return appearance, sharing his thoughts regarding his trip back to Cherokee country 40 years after his initial work there. I then describe the 2011 American Indian Tradition Food Summit held in Seattle, which was inspired by the 1961 American Indian Chicago Conference. John Bodley next presents a chapter on his research concerning small-scale societies, which was inspired by one of Sol Tax's last articles, "Anthropology for the World of the Future: Thirteen Professions and Three Proposals," which appeared in 1977 in *Human Organization*.

The volume concludes with a chapter by Solomon Katz, who provides a perspective on anthropology today and its value in addressing global problems. Throughout the collection, there are comments from the Seattle symposium (Stapp 2011), vignettes, and items of historical interest.

References Cited

Bennett, John W.
1996 Applied and Action Anthropology: Ideological and Conceptual Aspects. Special issue: Anthropology in Public, *Current Anthropology*, 37(1):S23–S53.

Daubenmier, Judith. M.
2008 *The Meskwaki and Anthropologists.* University of Nebraska Press, Lincoln.

Foley, Douglas E.
1999 The Fox Project: A Reappraisal. *Current Anthropology*, 40(2):171–191.

Hinshaw, Robert E., editor
1979 *Current Anthropology: Essays in Honor of Sol Tax.* Mouton Publishers, New York.

Lane, Sandra D., Robert A. Rubinstein, Lutchmie Narine, Inga Back, Caitlin Cornell, Alexander Hodgens, Monique Brantley, Rachel Kramas, Kathleen Keough, Brandon O'Conner, William Suk, Eric Morrissette, and Mary Benson
2011 Action Anthropology and Pedagogy: University-Community Collaborations in Setting Policy, *Human Organization*, 70(3):289–299.

Lurie, Nancy O.
1999 Sol Tax and Tribal Sovereignty. The 1961 American Indian Conference. *Human Organization*, 58(1):108–117.

Pavlik, Steve
1998 *A Good Cherokee, a Good Anthropologist: Papers in Honor of Robert K. Thomas.* UCLA American Indian Studies Center, Los Angeles, California.

Rubinstein, Robert A.
1986 Reflections on Action Anthropology: Some Developmental Dynamics of an Anthropological Tradition. *Human Organization*, 45(3):270–279.

Smith, Joshua
2010 The Political Thought of Sol Tax: The Principles of Non-Assimilation and Self-Government in Action Anthropology. In *Histories of Anthropology Annual*, Volume 6:129–170. University of Nebraska Press, Lincoln.

Stapp, Darby

2011 Learning from Sol Tax 2010, Parts I and II, www.SfAApodcasts.net/2011/05/01 (accessed September 18, 2012).

Stocking, George

2000 Do Good, Young Man: Sol Tax and the World Mission of Liberal Democratic Anthropology. In *Excluded Ancestors, Inventible Traditions: Essays Toward a More Inclusive History of Anthropology,* edited by Richard Handler. *History of Anthropology,* 9:171–264.

Tax, Sol

1953 *Penny Capitalism: A Guatemalan Indian Economy*. Institute of Social Anthropology, Publication No. 6. Smithsonian Institution Press, Washington, D.C.

1958 The Fox Project. *Human Organization,* 17(1):17–19.

1977 Anthropology for the World of the Future: Thirteen Professions and Three Proposals. *Human Organization,* 36(3):225–234.

Sol Tax Career Timeline

1907 Born in Chicago, Illinois.
1926 Starts at the University of Chicago, but transfers to the University of Wisconsin–Madison.
1927 Withdraws from studies due to Hillel Foundation activities.
1927 Protests the imprisonment of Gordon Brown (who wrote the poem "America").
1928 Re-enters the University of Wisconsin. His first anthropology course is with Ralph Linton.
1930 Spends four months in Algeria on an archaeological expedition and two months in France with the American School of Prehistoric Research.
1931 Attends field school on the Mescalero Apache Indian Reservation in New Mexico directed by Ruth Benedict and Harry Hoijer.
1931 Re-enters the University of Chicago.
1932–1934 Conducts fieldwork for both his master's thesis and his dissertation.
1933 Summer: Travels among Wisconsin tribes to gather comparative information.
1933 Marries Gertrude Katz.
1934 Hired by Robert Redfield to study communities in Guatemala for comparison to the communities Redfield studied in Mexico; researcher with the Carnegie Institution of Washington.
1934 Finishes dissertation (approved in 1935). "Social Organization of the Fox Indians."
1935 Mostly out of the United States.
1937 Invited with Gertrude to Meskwaki powwow as honored guests.
1934–1941 Conducts fieldwork in Guatemala, leading to writing of *Penny Capitalism*.
1942–1944 Teaches anthropology in Mexico City.
1948 Members of the first University of Chicago field school arrive in Tama.
1949 Social Science Research Council holds its Seminar on Social Sciences and Values at the University of Chicago in the spring. Tax enters the debate with his paper: "Can Social Science Help to Set Values or Offer a Choice Between Alternative Value Systems?"
1950 Robert Rietz goes to Fort Berthold, North Dakota, to help relocate members of the Three Affiliated Tribes displaced by the construction of Garrison Dam.
1951 Signs a statement on peyote that appears in *Science* after *Time* magazine prints an article quoting the anti-peyote sentiments of Arizona Public Health Commissioner Clarence Salisbury.
1951 Coins the term "Action Anthropology."
1951 Persuades the AAA to adopt a resolution that great and irremediable harm and injustice could result from the government's assimilationist policies. It calls for an independent commission to study Indian policy and come up with new one based in humanitarian and scientific principles.
1952 Makes speeches and publicly promotes the idea that Native Americans are not being assimilated into the mainstream.
1953 Begins term as editor for the *American Anthropologist*, serving until 1956.
1954 Organizes a conference on Indian policy under the sponsorship of the Wenner-Gren Foundation for Anthropological Research.
1954 Begins a scholarship program for Meskwaki youth: the Fox Professional Education Scholarship Program.
1955–1958 Serves as chairman of the University of Chicago anthropology department.
1955 Showcases Action Anthropology at the meeting of the Central States Anthropological Society.
1955 Tax, Fred Gearing, and Reverend Galen R. Weaver of the American Missionary Association of the Congregational Church come up with the idea of a summer workshop for Indian college students.
1956 Fred Gearing directs the first workshop at Colorado College in Colorado Springs in July and August, focusing on Indian policy; 259 students attend between 1956 and 1966.

1957 At the meeting of the Central States Anthropological Society, Tax calls "Termination" undemocratic because its forced assimilation violates the American tradition of allowing a community to live as it wishes. Instead, Tax proposes a policy of self-determination under which tribes would run their own programs and services, with funds provided by the federal government.

1957 In a speech to the National Congress of American Indians, Tax calls out "Termination" as destructive and backs the NCAI call for economic development of Indian land; he emphasizes the right of Indians to be consulted on Policy. NCAI reprints and distributes Tax's speech, "Termination Versus the Needs of a Positive Policy for American Indians."

1957 Organizes AAA Symposium: Values in Action. Symposium papers are published in *Human Organization* (Spring 1958).

1958 Appointed president of the American Anthropological Association.

1958–1959: Travels throughout the world to hold 26 conferences to enlist scholars in launching the journal, creating an international network of colleagues and friends who would communicate through the journal *Current Anthropology*. Pushes for greater use of the social sciences in the design and implementation of economic-development projects.

1960 Accepts a position with UNESCO on a panel responsible for U.S. participation in the United Nations' educational, scientific, and cultural organization.

1960 Attends the National Congress of American Indians in Denver and proposes that they hold a national conference whereby all self-identifying Native Americans could participate; his idea for the conference and that they should draft their own Declaration receives strong support (especially from D'Arcy McNickle and Helen Peterson).

1961 Turns the Colorado summer workshop over to D'Arcy McNickle, director of American Indian Development Corporation.

1961 Organizes the American Indian Chicago Conference, June 13–20, 1961, a turning point in American Indian political activity.

1962 Pursues a grant from the Carnegie Corporation that includes the establishment of a newspaper called *Indian Voices;* publication begins with a mailing list based on AICC conference registration.

1962 Awarded the Viking Fund Medal for outstanding anthropological achievements.

1962–1967 The Cross-Cultural Education Project, supported by the Carnegie Corporation of New York: addresses myriad social and political problems during its five-year research focused on literacy and education in the old Cherokee capital of Tahlequah, in eastern Oklahoma.

1966 Appointed by President Lyndon B. Johnson to a White House Task Force on Indian Affairs. Tax sends everyone a copy of the Declaration of Indian Purpose (from the AICC). He pointes out there are no Indian members. The task force goes public with recommendations.

1966 Serves on an advisory committee to the National Study of American Indian Education, a three-year study financed by the U.S. Office of Education. The report's central conclusion is that Indians should be given the authority and responsibility for education in their communities.

1969 The National Indian Youth Council assumes sponsorship of the summer workshop and renames the program the Clyde Warrior Institute in American Indian Studies.

1969 Asked to support the occupation of Alcatraz, Tax advocates for transferring the island to Indian control for use as an educational and cultural center. Tax loans $10,000 to a Chicago group that begins carrying out sit-ins and other protests in support of the Alcatraz occupation.

1974 Tax plays a crucial role in the founding of the Native American Educational Services Inc., the first Indian-run institution of higher education to offer bachelor of arts degrees.

1974 Festschrift conference for Sol Tax is held in Panajachel, Guatemala, organized by Steven Polgar.

1977 Meets with anthropologists at the University of South Florida, and inspires the development of *Practicing Anthropology.*

1976 Appointed emeritus professor at University of Chicago.

1977 Receives SfAA Malinowski Award for Outstanding Contributions to Applied Anthropology and gives address at its annual meeting in San Diego, California.

1979 The Sol Tax Festschrift is published, edited by Robert Hinshaw and including the papers presented at the 1974 Panajachel gathering.

1986 Participates in oral history interview conducted by Robert Rubinstein at the request of the Wenner-Gren Foundation. Five hours of video are produced.

1995 Passes away following a heart attack.

2002 Society for Applied Anthropology (SfAA) names Distinguished Service Award after Sol Tax.

2011 "Learning from Sol Tax in 2010" session at SfAA Annual Meeting in Seattle.

SOL TAX OBITUARY 1995

George Stocking Jr.

The following obituary of Sol Tax appeared in the March 1995 *Anthropology Newsletter* (p. 43), written by George Stocking Jr., well known for his interest in the history of anthropology. A more detailed obituary was produced by Sol Tax's colleague Sam Stanley, which appeared in *Current Anthropology* (1996).

SOL TAX, 87, innovative kinship analyst and economic anthropologist, facilitator of "Action Anthropology" and the modern Native American movement and organizer of international anthropology, died of a heart attack on January 4, 1995. Tax was born in Chicago in 1907, child of an immigrant family with a strong rabbinical tradition. He grew up in Milwaukee, where he absorbed the reformist spirit of a city with a socialist mayor, and at twelve served as editor of the *Newsboy's World.* "I was a Walter Mitty, and had constant dreams of glory ... somehow or other saving the troubled world." The means he discovered was anthropology, to which he was introduced by Ralph Linton at the U of Wisconsin. From the beginning, Tax's anthropology was, like Linton's, embracive: in 1930 he went with Beloit's Logan Museum Archaeological Expedition to North Africa; in 1931 he participated in an ethnological summer field program among the Mescalero Apache led by Ruth Benedict. By that time, Tax had become convinced that "pure science" must provide the prior knowledge for effective social reform, and for almost twenty years he "dropped everything but anthropological research."

Undertaking graduate study at the U of Chicago, Tax was introduced to social anthropology, serving as Radcliffe-Brown's research assistant in the study of Native American kinship. He did fieldwork on the Meskwaki (Fox), reservation near Tama, Iowa; augmented by comparative and historical research, to produce his doctoral dissertation on "The Social Organization of the Fox Indians" (1935). He was also strongly influenced by the "folk culture" approach of Robert Redfield, who in 1934 recruited him for fieldwork in highland Guatemala under the auspices of the Carnegie Institution. Accompanied by his wife, Tax worked there during seven years, focusing on issues of economics and worldview, which he was later to treat in his innovative study of *Penny Capitalism* (1953).

After a year as visiting professor at the Instituto Nacional de Antropología in Mexico, Tax returned to Chicago in 1943 as Research Associate (retaining until 1946 his position as tenured scientist at the Carnegie Institution). Appointed Associate Professor in 1944, he was instrumental in developing a new three-year graduate curriculum in the four-field tradition. Promoted to professor in 1948, Tax served for five years as Associate Dean of the Social Sciences Division, and was chair of the Department of Anthropology (1955–58).

Around 1950, the focus of Tax's anthropological activities shifted from "pure" research toward the social welfare, editorial and organizational interests of his youth. When graduate students in a summer field school at the Fox reservation expressed concern in 1948 that their work should somehow treat the problems faced by returning Indian veterans, Tax worked with them to establish a program of "Action Anthropology"—which differed from "applied anthropology" in seeking to facilitate goals set by the Indians themselves, rather than by any outside individual or agency. Convinced that assimilation was not inevitable, Tax became an active opponent of the government's "termination" policy and in 1961 coordinated the American Indian Chicago Conference, where 800 Native American leaders formulated a "Declaration of Indian Purpose" and the American Indian Youth Council was founded.

During the 1950s Tax was active in the professional propagation of anthropology on a national and world scale. He edited a number of volumes produced from major symposia, including the *Heritage* of *Conquest* (1949), an appraisal volume of the "Anthropology Today" conference (1952) and three volumes from the Darwin Centennial (1959). During a stint as editor of the *American Anthropologist* (1953–56), he doubled its capacity and in 1958 was elected president of the AAA. In the late 1950s he traveled worldwide on behalf of the Wenner-Gren Foundation, meeting with anthropologists behind the Iron Curtain and in Third World countries, to organize *Current Anthropology* (in the grass-roots spirit of Action Anthropology) as "an open-ended international journal." He served as editor until 1974 and was in this period perhaps the most widely known anthropologist in the world. In 1973 he organized and presided over the Ninth International Congress of Anthropological and Ethnological Sciences in Chicago, editing the resulting 91-volume *World Anthropology Series.* Although he retired that year, Tax continued active as emeritus professor and in the Library-Anthropology Resource Group—one of a number of bibliographical and biographical resources he promoted. He is survived by his wife Gertrude Katz Tax, his daughters Susan Tax Freeman and Marianna Tax Choldin, and three grandchildren. His papers are preserved in the Sol Tax collection of the Regenstein Library at the University of Chicago. See also Tax's autobiographical "Pride and Puzzlement" in the *Annual Review* of *Anthropology,* 1988.

CHAPTER 1

SOL TAX, PIONEER IN PARTICIPATORY RESEARCH

Joan Ablon

What I wish to do in this opening chapter is to present to those who did not know him a sketch of some of the personal characteristics and philosophy of Sol Tax, this amazing man, the most remarkable person one could ever hope to meet. Sol was a shortish, handsome man, an ever-moving ball of exuberant energy (Figure 2). He was a whirling dervish with his hand in innumerable pots, and regarded every problem or issue a challenge to be productively and positively conquered. Sol, like Zeus with ideas springing forth from his head, had more original ideas in one week than most people have in a year or even a lifetime. He was radically different in most ways from his colleagues at Chicago or indeed from any other important figures in the field at that time. He was, so to speak, always swimming upstream. I was Sol's research assistant in the late 1950s and for all of my years at Chicago, and I tried to keep up with Sol and his wife Gertrude as best I could until the end of their lives.

First, and perhaps most importantly, you must transport yourselves back to almost 60 years ago to understand the enormity of the difference from the anthropology of that time to our field today. The field then was of ridiculously narrow scope as compared to today. Any application of anthropology was considered vulgar, and the finer features of the relationships of the mother's brother and appropriate social expectations in an African tribe, or types of fishing knots in the Marquesas were ideal topics for graduate study. The University of Chicago—then a very formal, impersonal, and elitist institution—offered an extreme example of this pure, "Blue Lagoon," mentality. To understand the great difference between what Sol proposed in Action Anthropology, you must understand that in the 1950s, applied anthropology most often served as a handmaiden to governments or companies. For a gross example, "Tell us about the people of Bikini and how we can get them to allow nuclear testing there!"

Sol was the most work-driven person I have ever known, and he inspired and even demanded this orientation for all who were close to him. His enormous amount of daily activity allowed little time for discussion of even urgent affairs. At one point, a male research assistant and I worked in an anteroom to Sol's office. We each kept heaps of administrative or research papers we needed to talk to him about. When he would burst through his door to leave his office, we would both expectantly jump up and ask where he was going. If he were going anywhere but to the men's room, I had priority to walk (run) along with him and go through papers. If he were going as far as the bookstore, it was real luck; once we even went to get the brakes on his car fixed, and I got to work through a huge mass of accumulated materials! I even read him my dissertation proposal as he mowed his lawn, running up and down the rows beside him as Gertrude periodically brought us orange juice for sustenance!

Figure 2. Sol Tax, ca. 1950s, during his early years at the University of Chicago.

Sol was the only faculty member who was at all caring about students and approachable about personal issues, except perhaps for Clark Howell, the most junior member, a paleoarchaeologist, and not into social anthropology at all. Other faculty avoided students as much as possible outside of class, and one bragged to me that there were three doors and a secretary between him and any hapless petitioning student! I and others could talk to Sol about our insecurities, and he assured us that even he, at that time probably the most well-known anthropologist in the world (besides Margaret

Mead, whose newspaper and magazine columns kept her in the public eye), also had his moments of self-doubt. I have told many of my students about these sessions with Sol, and they have always found this very helpful.

During the years he was chair, he would hold an afternoon tea in his home for new students before classes began. We sat there on his living-room floor in awe, watching the members of this world-famous faculty as they chatted and called each other by their first names. That day presented a small aura of warmth, which we all badly needed. We were continually reminded by others of the faculty that most of us would not make it, and they were right. (Seven of us finally finished from 42 entrants!) Sol was so generously supportive of his students' interests that he sometimes sent them to another faculty member who might have more appropriate research directions for them. Sadly, many faculty even today are so jealous of their students that they fight over student allegiances.

In great contrast to his colleagues, Sol was very open to new ideas, and vitally involved with the social and political problems of the city of Chicago, the country, and the world—poverty, housing, race, and the multiple problems of the Hyde Park neighborhood in which the University was situated. The University was essentially a white island in a black ghetto—hostile, and with good reason. Sol was the only faculty member who focused on these larger issues and he offered a course to the public on Wednesday evenings called "Anthropology in the Modern World," which filled a university auditorium each week. Sol appeared often on television to discuss current problems. He was so relaxed doing this that I recall once that as he chatted about some important issue he was casually eating potato chips.

As an aside, I recall Sol got regular correspondence from a man in prison who sent weird missives to him written on long rolls of toilet paper. (I can't remember whether they were handwritten or typed.) He welcomed these communications and gave them the same time and attention as he did to the other 50 or so items that would come daily.

Because of his eye and heart for the significant, he often attracted students with a variety of interests who had backgrounds or current positions in social work and other humanistic areas. Some of these wonderfully talented persons closest to him who I came to know well were Robert Rietz, then director of the Chicago American Indian Center and past superintendent of the Fort Berthold Indian Reservation; Leonard Borman, who had worked with Kalmuk immigrants in Philadelphia and went on to found the Evanston Self Help Center; and Steven Polgar, a man of many interests who left academia for a while to become national research director of Planned Parenthood in New York, but who later returned to academia. Another close associate was Bob Thomas, a Cherokee Indian, who did remain in academia.

These men were all mature persons who followed interests not in keeping with the university's academic traditional topics and, most importantly, essentially did not publish—or if they did so, it was in social work or literatures other than anthropology. My own publications by and large were not written for anthropologists, but instead for my research subjects and their families, as well as the health, genetics, and welfare professionals who worked with them. This pattern of publication was clearly discussed in Robert Rubinstein's excellent analysis of why Action Anthropology was not carried on as a well-known distinctive tradition in our field (Rubinstein 1986). However, my hours of conversations with Robert Rietz and Bob Thomas instilled in me an intuitive understanding of Indians that I believe many of my other non-Indian colleagues who have worked with Indians their whole careers have never had. (Once I went to the bathroom in Rietz's apartment and found an Indian sleeping in his bathtub, a common occurrence I was told.)

Tax's interest in the world around him led him to organize meetings on many problem topics of the day. Al Wahrhaftig, Nancy Lurie, and I worked with him on the remarkable American Indian Chicago Conference in 1961, when 500 Indians from hundreds of tribes descended on the University, stayed in dorms, and wrote up a "Declaration of Indian Purpose," which they formally presented to President John Kennedy in 1962. The positive relationships and movements which resulted from this Conference cannot be overestimated. To illustrate how much of an anathema Sol's activities were to the rest of the faculty, during the Chicago Conference, I witnessed his colleague Fred Eggan, whose scholarship I greatly admired and who had worked with Hopis for 30 years or more, approach Sol and say, "Sol, when are you going to come back to anthropology?" At that time, practical current problems of Indians were not on the traditional agenda of anthropologists!

To carry this example further, in 1963 I was writing up my dissertation research on relocated American Indians in the San Francisco Bay Area. Fred Eggan was on my dissertation committee, and when I presented him with the first three chapters of my dissertation, after reading them, he suggested that I might want to switch to sociology because there had never been an urban thesis in the department! I was dumbfounded. At that time, the turf determined the discipline. Furthermore, in the 1980s a Chicago graduate who came to the University of California at San Francisco for a postgraduate fellowship told me that when he had presented his thesis proposal on the Metropolitan Community Church in Chicago to the faculty, it was negatively received and he was told there had never been an urban thesis in the department since Joan Ablon's, some twenty years before! He won approval for the topic only because Sol Tax, with whom he had not worked, defended his choice and clearly argued that it was a legitimate topic. (As a further aside, in the 1970s, Fred Eggan introduced me to his new wife, saying, "Joan used to be an anthropologist, but now she works in a hospital.")

Incidentally, I wrote the paper on the American Indian Chicago Conference for Sol's Festschrift volume (Hinshaw 1979) because some of his colleagues at our wonderful 1974 meeting in Panajachel to celebrate Sol's work did not think my ongoing research in a San Francisco Catholic Parish was appropriate enough for inclusion, still too much like social work (Ablon 1979)!

Sol's vital concern with world problems and the field of anthropology and anthropologists around the world led not only to his conceiving and organizing many conferences on urgent topics such as war and peace, etc., but led him also to the idea of the journal *Current Anthropology*. He called me in one day as I sorted through the ordinary huge pile of mail that came in each day and he said, "Look, how many letters do you think the scholar in Burma gets in a month? Maybe one." That need was his inspiration for *Current Anthropology*. To carry out his planning for the journal, he utilized his Action Anthropology philosophy and traveled around the world to engage scholars in every corner to ask them what *they* needed and wanted. And so *Current Anthropology* was born. One of his prominent colleagues disparaged this to me and thought the whole idea and his "running around" was an aimless exercise.

It was perhaps Sol's fame in organizing so many conferences and editing volumes of the proceedings resulting from these that led to his image and reputation as an entrepreneur, more a businesslike activity than scholarly. His earlier years of excellent research work were forgotten. Contributing to this image was the fact that he tended to eschew jargon and communicated in direct, clear language.

One of the most important elements of Sol's thinking was that people had to have the freedom of choice, even if ultimately, their choice proved to have negative consequences. It was their own decision. He elucidated this elegantly in his presentation for his daughter Susan's high school graduation: "Freedom to Make Mistakes." Surely this was an aberrant philosophy at the time, and perhaps still is. An example of his flexibility and openness to the decisions of the populations he worked with was a complex arrangement he made to film a meeting of the Native American Church to use as a defense in court, should this possibility come up. At that time, the use of peyote was totally illegal and wrongly portrayed as leading to orgies and violence. Sol arranged, with great difficulty, for a camera crew to attend a meeting in a remote spot (meetings had to be carefully hidden then). The camera crew had to leave their vehicle and carry the heavy equipment of the time to the meeting site. As the assembled participants of the peyote meeting discussed the proposed filming, only one person felt the ceremony would be degraded and hence ruined and made useless for him. In keeping with the Indian necessity for consensus and total agreement, the leader sadly told Sol the film could not happen. Sol quickly understood and told the grumbling camera crew to pack up and carry everything back. The leader was embarrassed, but Sol assured him he understood this perfectly. [A letter published in *Science* in 1951 by Tax and other prominent anthropologists arguing for the use of peyote by American Indians is included at the end of this chapter.]

There are various opinions circulating in professional circles today about whether Action Anthropology has died or has been resurrected or incorporated as a current approach in applied anthropology. If you heard Steven Schensul's very fine presentation at the Society for Medical Anthropology Business Meeting at the American Anthropological Association in November 2010, in my view you heard essentially straight Action Anthropology. I see Action Anthropology as Sol envisioned it as very much alive.

I will close with the wording of my dedication of my first book: "For Sol Tax, teacher of social conscience, who has broadened the horizons of Anthropology."

References Cited

Ablon, Joan

1979 The Indian Chicago Conference. In *Current Anthropology: Essays in Honor of Sol Tax*, edited by Robert E. Hinshaw, pp. 445–456. Mouton Publishers, New York.

Hinshaw, Robert E., editor

1979 *Current Anthropology: Essays in Honor of Sol Tax*. Mouton Publishers, New York.

Rubinstein, Robert A.

1986 Reflections on Action Anthropology: Some Developmental Dynamics of an Anthropological Tradition. *Human Organization*, 45(3):270–279.

COMMENTARY FOLLOWING JOAN ABLON'S PRESENTATION

Jay Miller, Susan Tax Freeman, Joan Ablon

April 1, 2011
Sol Tax Symposium

Jay Miller. I just wanted to say something on Fred Eggan's behalf. After the Fred Eggan memorial during the American Anthropological Association meeting in Chicago, a reception was held afterward at Sol's house. I remember Sol saying that Fred was like an older brother to him, who always challenged him. I wanted that on the record.

Susan Tax Freeman. Do remember that in 1959, the huge and heavily published Darwin Centennial Conference was basically his doing. Also—and I think this fact has probably been forgotten—in 1973, on Copernicus' 500th birthday, my father got the university to produce a humongous cake and have a ceremony on the Midway Plaisance, the park on the South Side of Chicago.

Joan Ablon. In a paper Sol wrote, "Pride and Puzzlement: A Retro-Introspective Record of 60 Years of Anthropology" in the *Annual Review of Anthropology* (1988), he almost casually described many different conferences and events as, "well we did this and I decided to do that and that worked well," and it went on citing examples. However, the organization of these events, like the organization for the American Indian Chicago Conference, was unbelievably complex. In the case of the Chicago Conference, groups met for months and months all over the country on different reservations to choose representatives. Some didn't want representatives and, in fact, the traditional Hopis refused to send a representative, so Sol sent me as a personal representative to the Hopis a few months later so they would not feel that the traditionalists were being left out. Sol's casual descriptions in this article almost belittle the work and the energy, not to speak of the vision, that went into these truly monumental efforts, as Susan has mentioned. I would suggest people read this wonderful article.

STATEMENT ON PEYOTE IN SCIENCE *MAGAZINE*

Weston La Barre, David P. McAllester, J. S. Slotkin, Omer C. Stewart, Sol Tax
Science, *Volume 114, pp. 582–583, November 30, 1951*

In connection with the current national campaign against narcotics, there has been some propaganda to declare illegal the peyote used by many Indian tribes. We are professional anthropologists who have made extensive studies of Peyotism in various tribes. We have participated in the rites and partaken of the sacramental peyote. We therefore feel it our duty to protest against a campaign which only reveals the ignorance of the propagandists concerned.

Briefly put, the propagandists argue that Peyotists are simply addicted to a narcotic and intoxicant, which they use orgiastically.

Peyote is a small, carrot-shaped, spineless cactus which, in the U.S., grows in the Rio Grande Valley. The top of the plant is usually cut off and sun-dried, forming the peyote button. When taken internally, it appears to have remarkable mental and physical effects, although these have not been thoroughly studied.

According to Webster's *Dictionary*, a narcotic is a drug that "allays sensibility, relieves pain, and produces profound sleep;" an intoxicant "excites or stupefies." According to Merck's *Manual*, the symptoms of drug addiction are increased tolerance and dependence. On the basis of our experience, we would say that peyote seems to have none of these effects. It does not excite, stupefy, or produce muscular incoordination; there is no hangover; and the habitual user does not develop any increased tolerance or dependence. As for the immorality that is supposed to accompany its use, since no orgies are known among any Indian tribes of North America, the charge has as much validity as the ancient Roman accusation of a similar nature against the early Christians.

Actually Peyotism is a religion, with a national intertribal organization incorporated under the name of "The Native American Church of the United States." Its modern form, developed about 1870, is Christianity adapted to traditional Indian beliefs and practices. The basic tenets of the Native American Church are given in its articles of incorporation:

> The purpose for which this corporation is formed is to foster and promote religious believers in Almighty God and the customs of the several Tribes of Indians throughout the United States in the worship of a Heavenly Father and to promote morality, sobriety, industry, charity, and right living and cultivate a spirit of self-respect and brotherly love and union among the members of the several Tribes of Indians throughout the United States...with and through the sacramental use of peyote.

The belief is that God put some of his Holy Spirit into peyote, which he gave to the Indians. And by eating the sacramental peyote the Indian absorbs God's Spirit, in the same way that the white Christian absorbs the Spirit by means of the sacramental bread and wine. Peyote is used by Peyotists in two ways: spiritually and medically.

The traditional practice of many Indian tribes was to go off in isolation to contemplate and fast until a supernatural vision was achieved. This is now replaced by a collective all-night vigil in which, through prayer, contemplation and eating peyote, the Peyotist receives a divine revelation. For the Peyotist, this occurs because he has put himself in a receptive spiritual mood and has absorbed enough of God's power from the peyote to make him able to reach God. A scientific interpretation might be that the chemicals in peyote diminish extraneous internal and external sensations, thus permitting the individual to concentrate his attention on his ideas of God and, at the same time, affecting vision and hearing so that these ideas are easily projected into vision.

The all-night rite is highly formalized. One man functions as priest, with the help of three assistants. During the rite they pray for the worshipers at fixed intervals, while the other men and women pray to themselves in low voices. Early in the rite everyone takes four pieces of peyote; later, anyone may take as many more as he or she thinks proper. Most of the time is occupied in having each man, in rotation, sing four religious songs that correspond to hymns sung in white churches. Peyote is also considered as a catholicon, or cure-all. If a sick person is spiritually clean, the Holy Spirit in the peyote will help him get well.

We can state categorically that these two circumstances—spiritual and medical—are the only ones under which peyote is eaten by members of the Native American Church.

Finally, something should be said of the communion meal eaten toward the end of the all-night rite. It usually consists of water, corn, fruit, meat, and sometimes candy; these symbolize the major foods important to the Indians, and they pray to God to give them adequate amounts. According to the antipeyote propagandists, the fruit and candy are eaten to get over a "peyote hangover"!

It will be seen from this brief description that the Native American Church of the United States is a legitimate religious organization deserving of the same right to religious freedom as other churches; also, that peyote is used sacramentally in a manner corresponding to the bread and wine of white Christians.

Weston La Barre, Duke University
David P. McAllester, Wesleyan University
J.S. Slotkin, University of Chicago
Omer C. Stewart, University of Colorado
Sol Tax, University of Chicago

CHAPTER 2

THE CARNEGIE PROJECT: ACTION ANTHROPOLOGY AMONG THE OKLAHOMA CHEROKEES

Albert L. Wahrhaftig

The Carnegie Corporation Cross-Cultural Education Project among Cherokee Indians in eastern Oklahoma from 1963 to 1966 directed by Sol Tax with Robert K. Thomas as Field Director, was a significant episode in the history of Action Anthropology. It has never been adequately reported, although there has been discussion of it in a few publications (especially Treat 2003:49–56; Cobb 2007; and Wahrhaftig 1998). A graduate student researcher during the project, I am the only significant participant still living, and am grateful for this opportunity to add to the history of the Carnegie Project with particular attention to the relationship between Sol Tax and Robert K. Thomas on the one hand, and on the other to Action Anthropology's commitment to "the freedom to make mistakes."

After much debate during the period when the tenets of action were first formulated, those involved concluded that anthropologists can participate with the people they are studying to assist them with things they might want to do to enhance their way of life, even, perhaps, in a way that had not previously occurred to them. That is, Action Anthropologists may help the people they study to perceive alternatives that had not occurred to them before, or that had not been available to them, but must do so without being so powerful as to inflict on those studied the anthropologist's choice among possible alternatives. From observing the choices made anthropologists may learn a great deal about the values of the people they study and about how they deal with innovation and modifying their adaptation. Of course, there will be times when the people studied make choices that the anthropologists involved consider disastrously bad, but if people can't make mistakes, they are deprived of the opportunity to learn from their own experience. Thus, the freedom to make mistakes is essential.

Thinking about the cross-cultural and cross-class relationship between Sol Tax and Bob Thomas during the Carnegie Project, it occurs to me that this notion of the freedom to make mistakes applies not only to the relationship between the Carnegie Project's Action Anthropologists and the Cherokee Indians with whom they became involved, but also to the anthropologists themselves: Sol Tax, a Jewish American anthropologist, and Bob Thomas, Tax's Cherokee Indian anthropology student and, later, colleague.

Shortly after World War II, Robert K. Thomas, GI Bill benefits in hand, enrolled in the University of Arizona as a geography major. There he discovered anthropology and Edward Spicer with whom he had a lifelong relationship, first as teacher and later as friend and colleague. With Spicer's encouragement, Thomas engaged in fieldwork among the traditional Cherokee Indians of Eastern Oklahoma and wrote a master's thesis (Thomas 1953) on the Redbird Smith Movement, an effort by Cherokees at the end of the 19th century to revitalize their sacred practices and community. Thomas brought an encyclopedic knowledge of American Indians gained through extensive reading and equally extensive travel through contemporary Indian communities to the University of Chicago's doctoral program in anthropology. There, Sol Tax set Thomas, together with Sam Stanley, to work developing a current map of American Indian populations (Tax 1956). Not only did Tax have a great respect for Thomas's knowledge of American Indian life, he also came to trust Thomas's insights and the originality of his thinking. In turn, Thomas was impressed by Tax's conviction, quite unorthodox at the time, that the "melting pot" assimilation of culturally distinctive minority groups such as American Indians into the general population of a larger society is not inevitable and in fact is perhaps rare. It was Thomas who participated with Tax in the development of Action Anthropology and the evolution of its commitment to learning by helping.

From the American Indian Chicago Conference to the Carnegie Project

Sol Tax and his students in the field had seen the destructive consequences of the then current policy of terminating federal responsibilities to American Indian tribes whenever and wherever possible. An opportunity for a change in federal American Indian policy was provided by the 1960 election of President John Kennedy. As an alternative to the customary appointment of a "blue ribbon" committee of highly placed American Indian tribal and Bureau of Indians Affairs (BIA) bureaucrats charged with recommending changes in Indians policy to each new administration, Tax thought why not have Indians themselves have a say in the matter. Which Indians? Why not all of them? Why not bring to Chicago as many of them as wished to come for two weeks of deliberation, feasting, and powwow, culminating in production of a declaration of the policy they desire? The fulfillment of this notion was the American Indian Chicago Conference (AICC), itself an Action Anthropology project (Lurie 1970, 1999; Ablon 1979). The Carnegie Project was a child of the AICC.

The AICC, it seems to me, was "very Sol Tax" and consistent with his rational and liberal commitment to anthropology as an instrument for making the world a better place, often based on the optimistic assumption that by bringing people together to talk things over good results will follow. Tax never hesitated to organize such gatherings on a grand scale, as exemplified by his organization of the Darwin Centennial Conference; Another example is his organization of the Ninth International Congress of Anthropological and Ethnological Sciences, "planned from the beginning not only to include as many of the scholars from every part of the world as possible but also with a view toward the eventual publication of the papers in high-quality volumes" (Tax 1978: vi), and the resulting publication of the encyclopedic World Anthropology series and his creation of *Current Anthropology*.

Bob Thomas was among those Tax enlisted to help him develop what became the AICC. Although Thomas signed on and agreed in principle that Indians should have a say about federal Indians policy, he also forecast that Tax was "headed for big trouble." He doubted that "country Indians" who tend to identify in terms of their tribe and home community and who do not necessarily picture themselves as "American Indians" would come in great numbers, and even if they did come they were likely to be overwhelmed by the more politically sophisticated and assimilation minded tribal and Bureau of Indian Affairs (BIA) bureaucrats who supported the existing policy. Thomas expected the conference to divide into factions with Indian traditionalists expressing dissent in the customary way, that is, by withdrawal, taking their unvoiced opinions with them and leaving an open field for those who would turn the conference's declaration into a highly assimilationist document. In some ways, the American Indian Chicago Conference was a success, but in many ways Thomas's predictions were correct.

Non-Indians served the conference only as coordinators and were allowed to be observers.[1] Planning was turned over to an all-Indian Steering Committee, all the deliberations of which, as well as the results of regional planning conferences in Indian Country, relevant correspondence, and any other relevant bit of information were printed and periodically mailed to a ceaselessly growing list of Indians throughout the nation so they could be informed and contribute their suggestions and opinions. As recipients added more names and addresses the resulting mailing list grew to include 5,000 Indian individuals and groups.

During and after the conference Tax became aware that Indians perceived the periodic mailings from the conference as a sort of American Indian magazine for American Indians and wanted him to find a way to continue it. Foundations Tax visited had no interest in sponsoring a magazine for American Indians until he hit on the Carnegie Foundation. Carnegie was supportive of experimentation in ways to enhance the capacity of linguistically subordinate groups seeking entry into a world that requires competence in the language of the nation in which they are embedded. The notion that an American Indian magazine could be a vehicle for increasing the American Indian literacy in English was appealing, especially if it incorporated the new educational technologies such as programmed education and "teaching machines" that were then much in vogue. Carnegie funded Tax's proposal and the Carnegie Corporation Cross Cultural Education Project was established. Tax recruited Bob Thomas to create a magazine that would be a device for increasing American Indian literacy in English.

When it came to the Carnegie grant, Thomas once again had strong doubts. He was convinced that Tax had made an unrealizable commitment and felt an obligation to, as he put it, "save Sol." There is, of course, no single American Indian language, so a bilingual format was not feasible and a magazine in English was not likely to appeal to those Indians most lacking in English literacy. Moreover, Thomas argued that although such a magazine could be produced (and it was, in the form of *Indian Voices,* edited by Thomas but lacking a programmed education component), it would be useless for purposes of research. Instead, Thomas proposed a project to be located in the old Cherokee Nation, addressed to the Cherokee-speaking population there. Among the Cherokees it would be possible to test the proposition that speakers of an indigenous language will more quickly become literate in a second, national language if they first become literate in their own language. Tax was persuaded both by the merits of the argument and because he knew how much Thomas wished to return to Oklahoma and be among his own people. As good professors do, Tax supported his former student. Thomas, in supporting a project he considered questionable, and Tax, in turning the reins over to Thomas, each were in effect practicing the "freedom to make mistakes."

The Carnegie Project in Eastern Oklahoma

Because Cherokees had evolved their own literacy in the early 19th century, using Sequoyah's invention of a Cherokee syllabary; and because by the mid-19th century, Cherokees were not only near universally literate in Cherokee but also more literate in English than whites in the neighboring states of Arkansas and Missouri; and because by the 1960s, Cherokee educational attainment had declined so far that they had become the least schooled of American Indian tribes, the Oklahoma Cherokees were an appropriate people among whom to work. Clearly, if Cherokee literacy retrogressed during a century in which American educational technology progressed, then more than tinkering with such gadgets as programmed education and teaching machines would be required to affect the situation.

Thomas hypothesized that Cherokees had retreated from schooling and literacy because of negative definitions of literacy and education that were themselves the product of inequities in social structure. For nearly a century, Cherokees had lived in the environment of a "myth of Cherokee assimilation" continually foisted on them by a white population that insisted that the Cherokee language and Cherokee culture are things of the past, the remnants of which would disappear in the present generation (Wahrhaftig and Thomas 1969). Following the abrogation of the independent Cherokee Nation in Indian Territory and the creation of the State of Oklahoma in 1907, Cherokees maintained the integrity of their traditional culture and communities by staying as far away as possible from white people and white controlled and assimilation-minded schools and by keeping a low profile (which, of course, led credence to the myth of Cherokee assimilation). Hence the rapid decline of Cherokee educational attainment and English literacy.

Since the thrust of the Carnegie Project was to test the proposition that people will more rapidly become literate in a national language if they first become literate in their own language, no such test can be possible if people have no interest in becoming literate in their own language. Therefore, the initial task was to redefine the cultural meaning attached to Cherokee literacy by demonstrating to Cherokees that their language, just as much as English, is neither old fashioned nor obsolete and can deal fully with all the requirements of the modern world. Accordingly, the project hired an initial staff of Cherokees to produce and distribute a newspaper entirely in the Sequoyah syllabary and to produce, for the first time, a weekly Cherokee-language radio news program with the expectation that Cherokees might take these over, incorporate them into their traditional way of life, and perhaps create further innovations.

At this point, a clarification of my use of the term "Cherokee" is critical. In eastern Oklahoma just who is and who is not a Cherokee is an exceedingly difficult issue (Strum 2002), and a very serious one. Indeed, I have argued that those who control the definition of "Cherokee" hold the key to political and economic power in eastern Oklahoma (Wahrhaftig 1978). When the Carnegie Project entered eastern Oklahoma, Cherokee affairs were directed by a Principal Chief appointed by the Secretary of the Interior and a Cherokee Executive Committee personally appointed by the Principal Chief, all of whom where federally recognized as members of the Cherokee tribe because they could trace descent from an individual named on a Roll of Cherokee Citizens that was completed and closed in 1907. Though proud of their trace of "Cherokee blood" none of these individuals spoke Cherokee or had ever had any involvement with the social and cultural activities of traditionally living Cherokees. Referred to locally as "mixed bloods" they were assimilated within the mainstream of Oklahoma society while also enjoying legal entitlements to Cherokee benefits and social prestige as "original citizens" of the State. The term "fullbloods" designated identifiably Indian persons living for the most part "back in the hills." These were the Indians, soon to vanish. In this narrative, my use of the terms "Cherokee" and "Cherokees" refers exclusively to this culturally traditional population. The term "Cherokee government" refers to institutions dominated by people Cherokees referred to as "those white men who say they are Indians."

Did Sol Tax realize that Action Anthropology research among the Cherokees might touch off a frenzy of community rebuilding activity, something much more "activist" that the forward advancement of individuals that Americans normally conceive of as the results of improved education? To this day I wonder about that. Did Bob Thomas expect that the project's activities might touch off a social movement much like that which took place in Redbird Smith's time? I wonder about that too. I do know that Thomas stuck to conducting the project as carefully constructed anthropological research. At the same time, I think such a byproduct couldn't have pleased him more. In any case, just as the Carnegie Project was an offspring of the American Indian Chicago Conference, so too was local opposition to the Carnegie Project.

The deeply conservative W.W. Keeler, federally appointed Principal Chief of the Cherokee Tribe, had long been suspicious of the involvement of Sol Tax and the "pinko University of Chicago" in national Indians affairs. He delegated the Cherokee Tribe's attorney, Earl Boyd Pierce, to infiltrate the AICC Steering Committee and be his eyes and ears. In both the planning sessions and the actual conference Pierce was disruptive and did everything in his power to derail anything that even implied that Indians should be anything other than loyal subjects of the BIA. Thomas warned Tax that the Carnegie Project was going to engender a fight in eastern Oklahoma between what Earl Boyd Pierce came to call "Sol Tax's forces" and the Cherokee government-BIA establishment. Thomas was right. Tax was unfazed.

That said, what exactly did the Carnegie Project do? Thomas was convinced that Cherokee educational regression was the result of Cherokee withdrawal from white-dominated society and, in particular, from the Oklahoma school system after the traumatic 1907 dissolution of the Cherokee Nation. With no Cherokee constitution, laws, court records, newspaper, and schools employing the Cherokee syllabary, there was little requirement for Cherokee literacy. Written English was increasingly viewed as the tool through which white people stole Cherokee property. Only by redefining the value, for Cherokees, of Cherokee literacy, demonstrating that it could contribute to contemporary Cherokee well-being and survival, Thomas thought, could Cherokee literacy be increased. Accordingly, the Carnegie Project set about producing examples of the use of Cherokee literacy (as well as spoken Cherokee) as a vehicle for becoming informed about and contending with current events of interest to Cherokees. Cherokees were hired to produce and distribute a newspaper in syllabary. Other Cherokees were hired to produce Cherokee radio programs. Willard Walker, a linguist, was recruited to produce a Cherokee [literacy] Primer employing programmed education principles (Figure 3; Walker 1965). With it, any Cherokee speaker could, through visual referents, learn the syllabary a character at a time. Later a Cherokee reader with stories printed in both Sequoyan and in English was made available (Figure 4; Spade and Walker 1966). Using these the project offered Cherokee literacy classes in Cherokee communities and in public schools while supporting uses of written Cherokee in an increasing number of places. Signs in syllabary (including "A Cherokee speaker works here") were produced for local businesses. Eventually even the Oklahoma driver's license manual was produced in Cherokee syllabary.

(a)

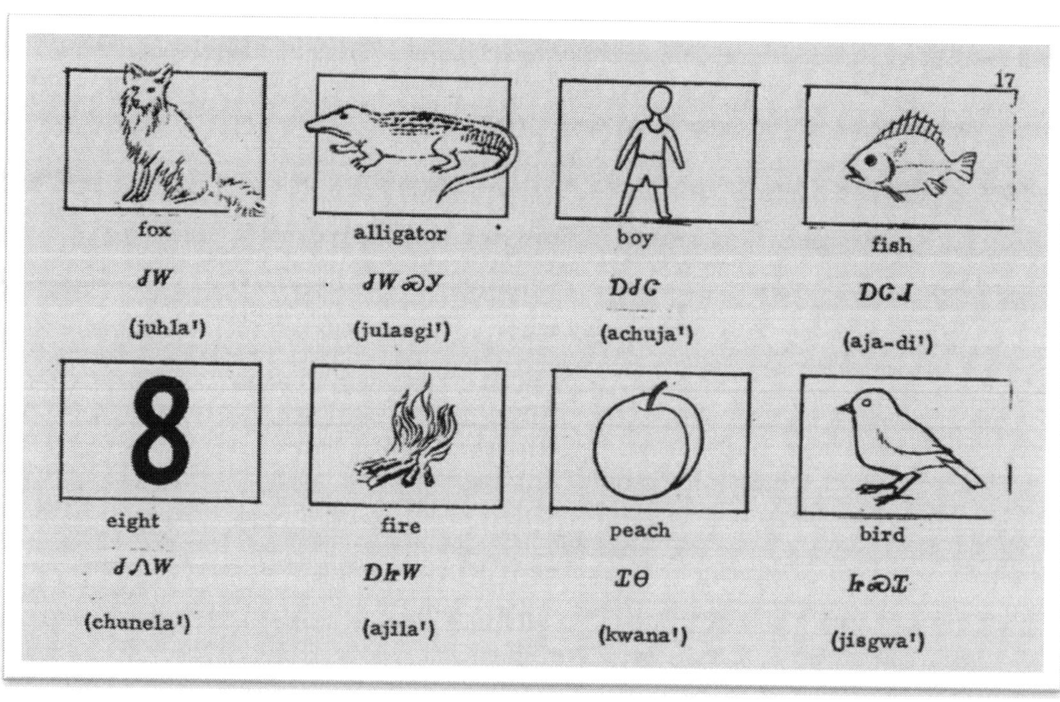

(b)

Figure 3. Example of the Carnegie Project's primer using the Cherokee Syllabary invented by Sequoyah. a) cover; b) page 17 (Walker 1965).

Meanwhile, I did baseline research to determine the size of the Cherokee population, and the number of largely Cherokee-speaking communities (Wahrhaftig 1968), and later a survey to determine the actual degree of Cherokee educational attainment, the percentage of Cherokees monolingual in English, bilingual, or monolingual in Cherokee and other significant socioeconomic factors (Wahrhaftig 1970). The results were first published in a Cherokee syllabary—English edition distributed free to Cherokee speakers (Wahrhaftig 1966). This information, together with the new syllabary publications, Cherokee radio programs, and other project activities began to filter through Cherokee communities and to energize the Cherokee population.

It is understandable that Cherokees had internalized the myth of their own assimilation. Virtually every family I surveyed had members living and working in Tulsa, Dallas, Ft Worth, Chicago, or even Los Angeles, so consequently every family experienced a sense of loss that seemed to confirm the myth that the Cherokees were "dying out." Eastern Oklahoma was economically depressed and the rate of Cherokee outmigration to jobs elsewhere was high. However, with the Cherokee population viewed as a whole as I was able to do and publish in my report to Cherokees, it was clear that the Cherokees' high rate of natural increase offset their high rate of migration. My research informed that some 9,500 Cherokees lived in 74 identifiable Cherokee communities and at least 12,000 Cherokees lived within the boundaries of the former Cherokee Nation. Their population was as large as ever it had been. The Cherokees certainly were not dying out.

While this new information and these new activities were having their impact, the powerful local establishment made every effort to convince Cherokees and the public at large that the "Carnegie people" were communists intent on spreading unrest and promoting disloyalty, and to harass the project's researchers and employees. Their inability to suppress the project's activities only served to demonstrate to Cherokees that there was in fact more elbowroom for autonomous Cherokee activities than Cherokees had supposed.

It was important that what the Carnegie Project did be produced by Cherokees for Cherokees. The project hired whatever Cherokees they could. Necessarily, those first hired had to speak both English and Cherokee and be willing to work with "outsiders" (and with the very people the gossip spread by the local establishment was calling "communists"). Those who first came forth tended to be somewhat marginal Cherokees and not necessarily very competent. Given the freedom to make mistakes, they certainly did and things got off to a slow and shaky start. However, just as Thomas predicted, when Cherokees began to see some value in the project's goings on, people who were more at the heart of Cherokee society, often elderly and sometimes traditional religious leaders with prestige and important responsibilities in their home communities, began to appear and quietly took over from the original employees. Then things really began to happen.

I recall what Daniel Littlefield (1971) called the "utopian dreams of the Cherokee Fullbloods" together with my experiences on my first afternoon in Cherokee country. Thomas and I went to the local Indian bar for a beer and were approached there by an old and rather boozy white (I thought) guy who kept talking about what I heard as "the seven claims." He kept telling Thomas that "we can get our lands together and start working together, start small and it will grow." Unfamiliar with the local accent and the fact that some Cherokees are fair skinned, I thought this fellow was talking about some sort of lawsuits. It turned out that he was Alex Smith, a Cherokee and the head of the Cherokee Seven Clans Society's ceremonial ground, talking about how Cherokee communities could confederate and rebuild the kind of life they had in the Cherokee Nation "before the State come in." As Littlefield documented, ever since they lost their Nation, thoughts of restoring Cherokee autonomy have remained as a substratum in the Cherokee mind.

As the activities of the Carnegie Project began to demonstrate Cherokee as a viable contemporary language and as Cherokees began to conclude that they could express themselves even in the context of a society bent on their assimilation, their "utopian dreams" began to become actualities. Cherokees became activists. They launched a protest over Oklahoma State interference with Cherokee treaty rights to hunt and fish without external regulation (Steiner 1968). To assure themselves that all Cherokees were in accord with that effort, a secret Cherokee organization[2] arose with minutes and a declaration of the purpose of the organization produced and distributed in syllabary. In this and related activities it was evident that Cherokees were beginning to define literacy as a valuable, even essential, tool, and as this organization evolved its activities spread to searching county records to document continuing thefts of Cherokee lands, instances of welfare abuse, and other grievances, *activities that increasingly demanded literacy in English.* Meanwhile, at the level of their home communities, Cherokees began to organize Cherokee literacy classes on their own, usually in association with their Cherokee Indian Baptist churches or with their non-Christian ceremonial grounds, and they embarked on a variety of other local projects. It was apparent to me that Cherokees were sewing roots much like those from which the former Cherokee Nation grew[3] (Wahrhaftig and Lukens-Wahrhaftig 1979).

As Action Anthropologists we learned a lot.[4] Thomas's assumption that the decline in Cherokee educational attainment was an artifact of their involvement in a society bent on their assimilation was validated. It was apparent that a redefinition of the value of Cherokee literacy as an instrument of their survival in the contemporary world led to an increased value attached to Cherokee literacy and, as hypothesized, increased involvement of Cherokees with Cherokee literacy led to increased involvement with literacy in English.

Sol Tax visited Oklahoma several times and was pleased both with the direction of the project's research and with the resulting ferment in Cherokee communities. He witnessed the many efforts of the local establishment to destroy the project and to discredit him both locally and nationally and he saw that Action Anthropology research activity could have radical consequences and pose a critical threat to those who hold power over the population studied. Simply put, the Carnegie Project messing around with literacy touched off a nativistic (cf. Linton 1943) social movement among Cherokees. I didn't forecast that outcome. I don't know if Thomas and Tax did or did not. All I know is that as a trio raised in the University of Chicago's anthropological tradition, and well aware of the Malinowskian functionalist dictum that a change in one part of a system will affect all parts of the system, we should have guessed that would happen.

Action Anthropology and the Freedom to Make Mistakes

In terms of how the "freedom to make mistakes" applies to anthropologists I think we learned from at least two mistakes of our own. Our research and activities were based on two implicit and erroneous assumptions. For one, we tended to assume that the individual learner is the significant unit in Cherokee literacy acquisition. For another, we conceived of the attainment of literacy as a strictly secular accomplishment. What subsequently became clear is that the context of Cherokee literacy in the 1960s was, and probably still is, both communal and sacred.

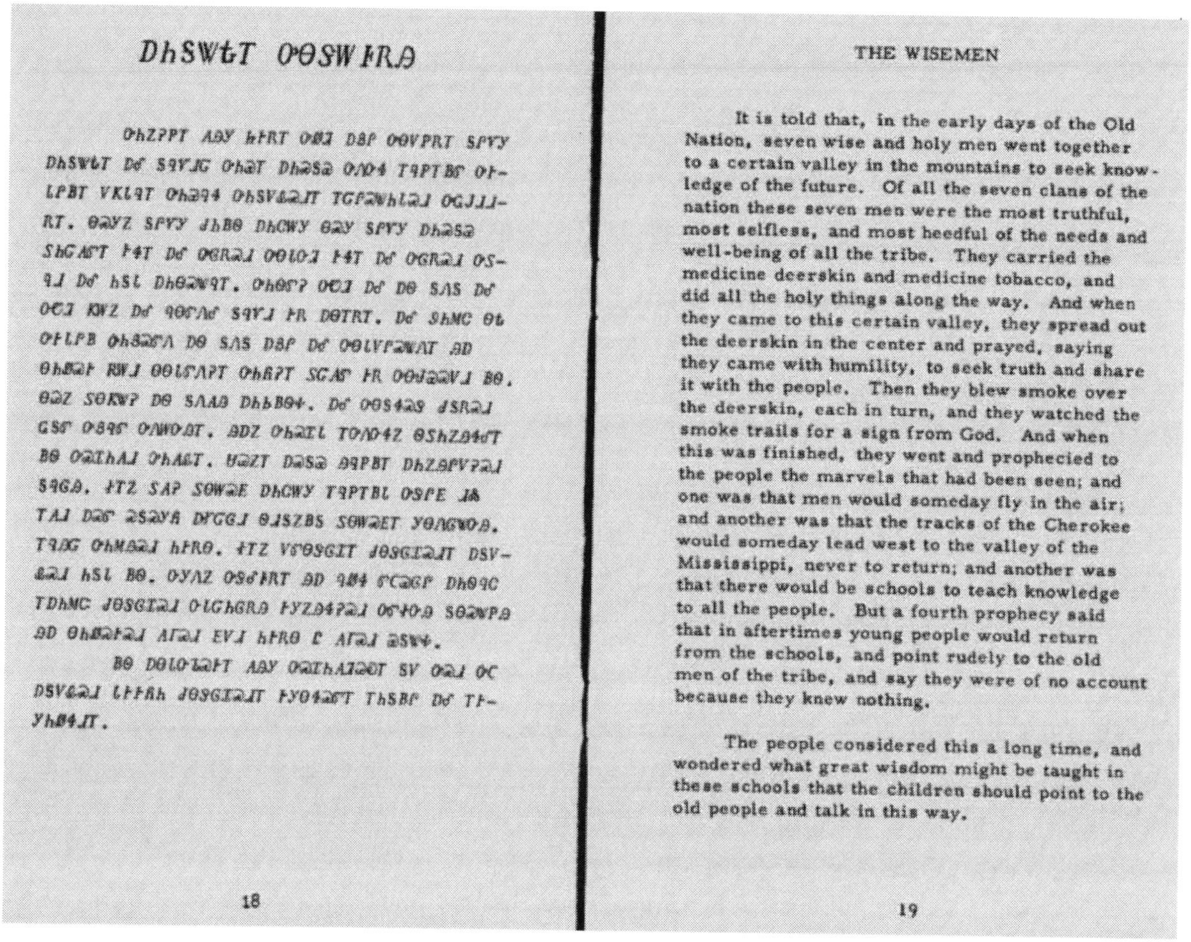

THE WISEMEN

It is told that, in the early days of the Old Nation, seven wise and holy men went together to a certain valley in the mountains to seek knowledge of the future. Of all the seven clans of the nation these seven men were the most truthful, most selfless, and most heedful of the needs and well-being of all the tribe. They carried the medicine deerskin and medicine tobacco, and did all the holy things along the way. And when they came to this certain valley, they spread out the deerskin in the center and prayed, saying they came with humility, to seek truth and share it with the people. Then they blew smoke over the deerskin, each in turn, and they watched the smoke trails for a sign from God. And when this was finished, they went and prophecied to the people the marvels that had been seen; and one was that men would someday fly in the air; and another was that the tracks of the Cherokee would someday lead west to the valley of the Mississippi, never to return; and another was that there would be schools to teach knowledge to all the people. But a fourth prophecy said that in aftertimes young people would return from the schools, and point rudely to the old men of the tribe, and say they were of no account because they knew nothing.

The people considered this a long time, and wondered what great wisdom might be taught in these schools that the children should point to the old people and talk in this way.

18 19

Figure 4. A Cherokee story from a reader, in Sequoyan and English.

When Willard Walker was developing the Cherokee Primer, I think he and I dreamed of hundreds of Cherokees sitting in solitude in their leisure hours, trekking their way through it step by step to quickly become readers of Cherokee. The day the Primer came off the press, I rushed back to the small Cherokee settlement at Lyon's Switch where I was living in the home of Jasper Smith, an accomplished and prestigious Indian doctor, and excitedly presented him with a copy, telling him that this little book would make it possible for any Cherokee-speaker who wished to do so to learn to read Cherokee. After paging through it for a very few moments, Jasper set it aside, stating quietly but emphatically "It won't do no good." More than a bit taken aback, I pressed Jasper for further elaboration of his negativity, but all he found it sufficient to say was "A good man won't need it," leaving me to ponder the rest. Having pondered, I think I can explain Jasper's response.

By the 1960s the use of publications in syllabary had, with the exception of the Cherokee New Testament and the Cherokee Hymnal, had been extinct for decades and the use of handwritten Cherokee was restricted almost entirely to sacred contexts. One remaining important use of syllabary manuscript was recording by Indian doctors in personal notebooks the "sacred formulae" that they use in curing (and, it is sometimes said, in conjuring). To avoid pollution and, perhaps, inadvertent discovery by unqualified persons, these notebooks are never kept in the home. As a rule they are sealed in mason jars and buried in some appropriate spot or tucked into a hollow in a tree trunk. When the author dies (and conceivably even before) someone may chance to discover a "medicine book." Cases of this are known and when that happens there are possibilities for danger to innocent people, for a person with evil intentions who can read can use this medicine to part lovers, to injure persons, and to cause all manner of serious mischief. What Jasper was saying was that supernatural forces protect the Cherokees by not permitting a person who is not "good" to become literate and cause harm. The converse of his statement is that if a person is "good" s/he will have no need for a device such as a schoolbook in order to become literate. Indeed, when I asked Cherokee-literate Cherokees how they learned to read and write syllabary, they described an event in which literacy was instantaneously revealed to them. It was a "gift from God." To Cherokees, literacy is a sort of Grace that emanates from an external and sacred source.[5]

This leads to understanding how seemingly innocuous research about literacy led to a social movement. Cherokee literacy is a matter connected with the sacred and, as I have discussed elsewhere (Wahrhaftig 1979) the Cherokee syllabary is itself one of the array of symbols that express Cherokee identity. Moreover, Cherokees are a people who live under prophecy, and therefore a people for whom the future is known, the only question being whether has it arrived. In times of crisis Cherokees divine what the future has in store for them, as happened at the turn of the century when it became apparent that white people were going to dissolve the Cherokee Nation. At that time, the principal medicine men of each of the seven Cherokee clans gathered to receive a set of prophesies. Now, only some older Cherokees know the prophecies in detail, but virtually every Cherokee is familiar with the following anecdote that stands as a metaphor for the whole: The seven diviners gathered at a remote place, bringing with them a dipper and a bucket of drinking water, and spent the night. During the night, one of them carelessly kicked the bucket over and spilled all the water, yet when they gathered to go home in the morning, the bucket was full again. That symbolizes the

Cherokee future. The Cherokees will go down, down, down in numbers and in power just as water drained from the pail until, like the drops remaining in the bucket, only a few "real Cherokees" are left. From them, the Cherokees will rise again, free of white people.

For secular people, the future is unknown and unknowable, but people who live under prophecy know what the future holds for them. For them, the question is whether the prophesied time has arrived, and the answer is sought in omens. That in spite of the efforts of powerful white people doing their best to suppress them, suddenly Cherokees were visibly doing new things and getting away with it—pressing law suits, speaking in Cherokee openly on the radio, restoring their communities in various ways, conducting secret meetings in the woods—and getting away with it could only be a sign that Cherokees are turning the corner, that their restoration is under way. I remember visiting at that time the elderly head medicine man of the Redbird Smith Ceremonial Ground on a frigid winter day. A flu epidemic was raging and I hoped to learn how he was treating it. To my surprise the old man was absolutely gleeful. He had been listening to the radio and recited to me an inventory of recent disasters: a big cyclone in western Oklahoma had done millions of dollars of damage, there were riots at McAlester Penitentiary in which buildings had burned and lives had been lost, and the flu was serious among the white people. All of this he took to be signs that the white world was, as prophesized, collapsing. "It won't be long now," he said. That was the Cherokee mood then, I think, for under prophecy a worldview in which "we are dying out" can instantaneously flip to one in which "We are on our Way. Let's get going, guys," with an associated sudden release of energy and activity.

If nothing else, the Carnegie Project taught us to be cautious about secular assumptions inherent in anthropology and in the end we had to admit that as misguided, racist, and sometimes crooked as they were, the Cherokee government's W.W. Keeler and Earl Boyd Pierce were, when it came to their accusations that we were stirring up trouble, righter than we thought.

Notes

1. As Assistant to the Coordinators of the AICC, I witnessed meetings of the Steering Committee and the Conference itself; collected and sorted all incoming mail pertaining to the Conference, answering some of it myself; and was present during many of the conversations between Tax, Thomas, and others.
2. At first called The Five County Northeastern Oklahoma Cherokee Organization, the organization later changed its name to the Original Cherokee Community Organization (OCCO). Summoned to the first meeting, I was incorporated as the organization's English language secretary. As the organization was to be kept as a secret, especially from white people, there was initial debate over appointment until those present resolved that Jews are not white people but rather are like "a tribe of Indians from the other side of the water." Soon, Andrew Dreadfulwater joined me as the Cherokee language secretary.
3. I would like to be able to say that these activities expanded and endured, but in fact the efforts of Cherokee to join their communities and rebuild their autonomy were contained by competing efforts of the local establishment. During my first and brief revisit to Cherokee country in 2002, I found that in the communities I had surveyed a generation ago, a new generation had simply replaced the generation I knew, many living in the houses in which their parents had lived. The government of the Cherokee Nation had grown into an enormous bureaucracy which was clearly the dominant political and economic institution in the region, but within that institution there was a cell of traditional yet very sophisticated Cherokees who were working with the population I call "Cherokee" in this essay. These few were clearly bearing the "utopian dreams of the Cherokee Fullbloods."
4. Charlie Starr was a Cherokee who drifted from one Cherokee Indian Baptist Church to another, tuning their pianos and playing in exchange for room and board. Charlie pasted blank paper over each page of his copy of the Cherokee Primer. He then ruled staves across each page and in "old time" shape notes copied Cherokee hymns under which he inscribed the lyrics in Syllabary. When Thomas saw what Charlie had done by turning the "new" Primer into something uniquely Cherokee, he was convinced that the Carnegie Project was a success. I note here that Charlie had learned piano tuning along with his very adequate English while in prison. When I found elderly Cherokees who spoke good English, they had often learned it while incarcerated.
5. If only "good" Cherokees could become literate in Cherokee and if literacy is acquired through revelation, did Cherokees participate in Cherokee literacy classes? Because, I think, such classes were generally on sacred grounds such as churches and ceremonial grounds and were officiated by respected elders and thus under traditional controls.

References Cited

Ablon, Joan
1979 The American Indian Chicago Conference. In *Currents in Anthropology: Essays in Honor of Sol Tax*, edited by Robert E. Hinshaw, pp. 445–456. Mouton Publishers, New York.

Cobb, Daniel M.
2007 Devils in Disguise: The Carnegie Project, the Cherokee Nation, and the 1960s. *American Indian Quarterly*, 31(3):465–490.

Linton, Ralph
1943 Nativism. *American Anthropologist*, 45(2):239–248.

Littlefield, Daniel F. Jr.
1971 Utopian Dreams of the Cherokee Fullbloods: 1890–1930. *Journal of the West*, 10:404–427.

Lurie, Nancy O.
1961 The American Indian Chicago Conference. *Current Anthropology*, 11(5)478–500.
1970 An American Indians Renascence? In *The American Indian Today*, edited by Stuart Levine and Nancy O. Lurie, pp. 329–328. Penguin Books, London.
1999 Sol Tax and Tribal Sovereignty. *Human Organization*, 58(1):107–117.

Spade, Rev. Watt and Willard Walker
1966 *Cherokee Stories*. Carnegie Corporation Cross-Cultural Education Project of the University of Chicago, Tahlequah, Oklahoma.

Steiner, Stan
1968 *The New Indians*. Harper and Row, New York.

Strum, Circe
2002 *Blood Politics: Race, Culture, and Identity in the Cherokee Nation of Oklahoma*. University of California Press, Los Angeles.

Tax, Sol, Sam Stanley and Robert K. Thomas
1970 The North American Indians: 1950 Distribution of the Aboriginal Population of Alaska, Canada and the United States. Map, University of Chicago Department of Anthropology. In *The American Indian Today*, edited by Stuart Levine and Nancy O. Lurie. Originally published in 1956. Penguin Books, London.
1978 General Editor's Preface. In *American Indian Economic Development*, edited by Sam Stanley, p. *vi*. Mouton Publishers, New York.

Thomas, Robert K.
1953 U.S. GovernThe Origin and Development of the Redbird Smith Movement. Master's thesis, University of Arizona, Tucson.

Treat, James
2003 *Around the Sacred Fire: Native Religious Activism in the Red Power Era*. Palgrave Macmillan, New York.

Wahrhaftig, Albert L.
1966 *The Cherokee People Today*. Carnegie Corporation Cross-Cultural Education Project. Tahlequah, Oklahoma.
1968 The Tribal Cherokee Population of Eastern Oklahoma. *Current Anthropology*, 9:510–518.
1970 Social and Economic Characteristics of the Cherokee Population of Eastern Oklahoma. *Anthropological Studies* No. 5. American Anthropological Association, Washington, D.C.
1978 Making Do with the Dark Meat: A Report on the Cherokee Indians in Oklahoma. In *American Indian Economic Development*, edited by Sam Stanley, pp. 409–510. Mouton Publishers, New York.
1978 We Who Act Right: The Persistent Identity of Cherokee Indians. In *Currents in Anthropology: Essays in Honor of Sol Tax*, edited by Robert E. Hinshaw, pp. 255–270. Mouton Publishers, New York.
1998 Looking Back to Tahlequah: Robert K. Thomas' Role Among the Oklahoma Cherokee, 1963–1967. In *A Good Cherokee, A Good Anthropologist: Papers in Honor of Robert K. Thomas*, edited by Steve Pavlik, pp. 93–104. UCLA American Indian Studies Center, Los Angeles.
2002 Literacy as a 'Gift' Some Observations About Cherokee Literacy and the Sacred. Unpublished manuscript in possession of the author.

Wahrhaftig, Albert and Jane Lukens-Wahrhaftig
1979 New Militants or Resurrected State? The Five County Northeastern Oklahoma Cherokee Organization. In *The Cherokee Indian Nation: A Troubled History*, edited by Duane H. King, pp. 223–246. The University of Tennessee Press, Knoxville.

Wahrhaftig, Albert and Robert K. Thomas
1969 Renaissance and Repression: The Oklahoma Cherokee. *Trans-action*, 6:4:42–48.

Walker, Willard
1965 *Cherokee Primer*. Carnegie Corporation Cross-Cultural Education Project of the University of Chicago. Tahlequah, Oklahoma.

VIGNETTE: JEWS ARE INDIANS FROM THE OTHER SIDE OF THE WATER

Albert A. Wahrhaftig

On the night of November 20, 1965, I drove James Draper, a representative of the Department of Justice's Community Reconciliation Service,[1] to a meeting with so-called "fullblood" Cherokees at Briggs School house in rural Cherokee County, Oklahoma.

A few weeks previous, Cherokees, especially Cherokees from Bull Hollow deep in rural Delaware County, convinced that their treaties guaranteed them the right to hunt eternally on their lands without restriction, were resolving to oppose Delaware County law enforcement officials who arrested them for hunting out of season and without hunting licenses. Their proposal was to gather a group of hunters, go hunting together and, as they put it, "see who wants to stop us." They sent a delegation to solicit an opinion from Robert K. Thomas. Bob was convinced that a confrontation between armed and bellicose Cherokees and armed and hostile sheriffs was likely to result in a disastrous shootout and suggested that they first wait while he sought someone "from Washington" who could brief them on their treaty rights. James Draper was the "someone from Washington" and the November 20 meeting was the result.

When we arrived at the schoolhouse, I sent Mr. Draper in. I wished I could also enter to and observe what I expected could be a pivotal moment in the Cherokees' increasing unrest about their status and rights in Oklahoma, but it was the Cherokees' meeting. I had not been invited.

About an hour later, I was asked to enter the school. When I did, I saw that Fines Smith was seated at the teacher's table while all the other Cherokees were seated in student desks facing him and Mr. Draper sat was off to one side of the room. Fines was employed at the Carnegie Cross-Cultural Education Project as my interpreter when together we conducted a survey of the traditional Cherokee population and settlement pattern. Together we had canvassed five northeastern Oklahoma counties interviewing dozens of informants. Fines gestured to me to sit next to him and instructed me to write down whatever he told me in English. Long discussions took place in Cherokee. When a consensus was reached, Fines would dictate it in English, I would write it down, and the next discussion would commence. Obviously, I was functioning as a secretary.

Among the things decided in discussion were that these were important matters. All Cherokees should be informed of them, and all Cherokees should have opportunity to participate in discussion of them. Therefore, all present were encouraged to spread the news about this meeting and the determination to do something about Cherokee complaints, but to discuss only in Cherokee. They threatened that "anyone who talks about this in English better watch his backyard." Thus, the Cherokee language was used to maintain secrecy from whites, none of whom were fluent in Cherokee and breach of this secrecy was going to merit major punishment. They then agreed to have meetings in each of the five northeastern Oklahoma counties to be followed by a general meeting at which, having consulted throughout "fullblood" territory, a decision about action could be made. I was thus witness to the birth of an underground Cherokee resistance organization!

I never was able to learn much Cherokee, but I did know more than a few words, so when Willy Proctor from Bull Hollow stood to speak, I recognized that he was talking about English, about writing, about paper, and about me, *dihanulv*, "the moustache" as Cherokees called me. A long discussion using those same words with considerable frequency ensued, a consensus was reached, and I was offered no translation. The group proceeded to the next matter at hand.

After the meeting, Fines and I had a conversation. I told him that I believed that Willy Proctor and those who spoke after him had objected to having a white man involved in their meetings, especially since they had just threatened anyone who spoke about them in English. I told him that I would like nothing better than to be an observer of these events, but that I recognized that this was Cherokee private business and that I would agree with what I perceived as their desire that I stay away. Fines said that I had it all wrong.

Apparently, Willy Proctor had said that he knew me, that he knew I worked well with Fines, and that I could help Fines (who had been designated their Chairman) by being his secretary. The second man who spoke objected, pointing out that I was a white man, but the third speaker opined that I was not a white man; I was a Jew. The following long discussion had to do with whether Jews are white men or not. The consensus was that Jews are not white men. They are like a tribe of Indians from the other side of the water, and, as they have a language of their own, a homeland, and a sacred history attested in the Bible, they are unlike white men who have none of these. On these grounds, I continued to serve as the English language secretary of what came to be known as the Five County Northeastern Cherokee Organization and later as the Original Cherokee Community Organization.

[1] I think the Community Reconciliation Service was at that time under the Department of Commerce and later was switched to the aegis of the Justice Department, but I'm not sure about that.

CHAPTER 3

FAITH IN SCIENCE AND GOVERNMENT: APPLYING KNOWLEDGE FOR HUMAN BETTERMENT BY CHICAGOANS SOL TAX AND GEOGRAPHER GILBERT WHITE

Robert E. Hinshaw

It is my understanding that the Society for Applied Anthropology (SfAA) 2011 Seattle session on Sol Tax and Action Anthropology was prompted in part by concern about the "soul" of applied anthropology—if not about anthropology's future as a viable discipline—and in part to understand and rectify the discipline's neglect of Tax's role in reframing what he termed its "therapeutic" praxis. How encouraging it is that this moving and shaking is largely at the hands of anthropologists, such as Darby Stapp and Joshua Smith, who were not his students nor even personally acquainted in some instances! The youngest of the latter, Joshua Smith, enters the fray in timely fashion, concerned to document Tax's role in establishing the university norm in American anthropology of a four-subfield amalgam of physical anthropology, linguistics, archaeology, and social/cultural anthropology (ethnology).

Also of concern at these SfAA meetings is assessing and perpetuating awareness of Tax's seminal role in heightening North American awareness of the cultural persistence and self-determination insistence among native peoples—everywhere—with regard to their assimilation. All of these concerns share Sol's deepening conviction that distinguishing between pure and applied anthropology is unwise, if not senseless, in the face of the deepening challenges we face. Among such challenges, the SfAA meetings highlighted those in the northwestern U.S./Canada of native peoples' rights to—and their wise stewardship of—natural resources, especially water.

Gilbert White

One purpose of this chapter—beyond those mentioned above—is to introduce into the literature the influence upon Tax's career of a University of Chicago associate from 1955–1969, geographer Gilbert White (Figure 5). As a global ecological pioneer in natural resources management—of water in particular—White would champion that Northwest agenda as fully as would Tax. But White's influence lay less in topical focus than in how both men behaved as scientists.

Anthropology and geography fortuitously were housed in close proximity at Chicago with Tax and White regularly crossing paths and exchanging ideas—soul mates in intellectual breadth and public-minded citizenship. With their wives Gertrude and Anne—all comparably motivated by religious upbringing to make a difference with their lives—they worked unceasingly on Hyde Park and inner city social issues while thinking and networking ever more globally.

Figure 5. Gilbert White in the early 1980s.

To grasp how either man managed to "matter" so distinctively both at home and abroad, not only as scientist but also as public servant and mentoring "mensch," it behooves us to know the other. I had known White for a decade before he introduced me to Tax … on the occasion of my exploratory visit to the University. With no anthropology courses yet in my background, but convinced by reading Ralph Linton's *The Study of Man* (1936) that anthropology was my destiny (the book that also led Tax into the discipline), White supported my choice of anthropology over geography and urged my working with Tax. Sharing with White membership in the Society of Friends, he already was anticipating that my scruples would prevent my signing of the loyalty oaths requisite in that McCarthy era for garnering federal funding for doctoral study/research. White knew that Tax would sympathize and assist in obtaining financial assistance … as Tax promptly did, inviting me on board as his teaching assistant in the night classes he regularly taught in downtown Chicago. (Between White and Tax my wife subsequently was kept busy typing doctoral dissertations in anthropology and geography as we struggled—with three children—to make ends meet.)

Even during that introductory interview with Tax, I learned of Tax's own agenda: to find a student with knowledge of Spanish and an interest in Mesoamerica to revisit his research in Guatemala. He had long assumed that daughter Susan—aspiring to a career in anthropology—would follow in those footsteps. But she had left Chiapas to pursue research in Spain, where she later met her future husband, the archeologist Leslie Freeman. White, knowing all of this—including my familiarity with Spanish from its teaching on the secondary level—had prepared Tax for our meeting. Serendipitously, it was decided from the outset of my sojourn at Chicago that I would work with Tax—fulfilling my youthful dream of becoming a Mesoamericanist. Although in childhood I had envisioned digging in Mayan ruins, by 28 my conscience was arguing for saving the world instead! Nonetheless, I have visited one or more Mayan archeological sites virtually every year since. My gratitude to both men is immense.

Despite their shared convictions and parallel careers, I doubt that Tax was as outspoken with regard to rights and expectations of scientists and the subjects of their study (for example, when he addressed anthropologists as president of the American Anthropology Association in the late 1950s) as White was upon assuming presidency of the Association of American Geographers in 1961. Chiding his profession for squabbling over what was and wasn't appropriate scholarship and praxis for geographers, White urged the question: "Is what we do significant, and do we have the competence to do it?" White contributed to a firestorm of disciplinary self-doubt and rethinking that contributed to the demise or reorganization of geography departments at many major American universities (including disbanding the department at Chicago and dividing subfields among sister disciplines). Anthropology faced similar challenges in that era, joining sociology and/or social work—even geography. I participated in such regroupings at universities in Illinois (Carbondale) and Colorado (Denver). Departments with the four traditional subfields (for example, Beloit College—under whose auspices Tax experienced his first foreign fieldwork—and Chicago) may thereby have benefitted in weathering that storm. Until reading Joshua's paper (Smith 2010), I hadn't thought about Tax's role in establishing/protecting our U.S. four-subfield consciousness of anthropology.

The Legacy of Action Anthropology and the Humanizing of Fieldwork

I have not kept abreast of the spate of publications over the past two decades addressing Tax's and other actionists' legacies with respect to the humanizing of fieldwork (equally for researchers and their subject colleagues-in-learning). Foley's assessment in his review of Daubenmier's helpful appraisal mirrors my own: "Tax never gave the (Fox) project his sustained attention and intellectual leadership ... he was right in theory, if not in practice" (Foley 2009). But we, as well as Tax, have Rubinstein to thank for analyzing in Guatemala his contributions to a range of efficacious fieldwork procedures (Rubinstein 1991). No question but that many of his students have been more faithful to his ideas about responsible learning/helping in the field than to his practice of documenting and sharing "everything" that he thought and did. Of this I am as guilty as is anyone, especially of my doings toward century's end. In a nutshell, I convinced myself that time is running out too rapidly in our human experience to warrant business as usual in a host of arenas ... science included with respect to its purism (as opposed to its applications in addressing our challenges). Not that I am any less committed to "mattering"—not in the least. But decreasingly can I abide endeavoring to do so in the United States.

Others have observed that, while Tax's influence among North American anthropologists admittedly declined over the last half of his career, his international visibility/influence strengthened rapidly and dramatically. The same shift in influence here and abroad characterized Gilbert White's career, and at about the same time beginning in the 1960s. White's trajectory was just as rapid and dramatic ... even as White let his successes go to his head no more than did Tax. For all the descriptors that they share in common, the most endearing were their essential humility and empathy: their penchant for listening to and learning from all whom they befriended. They also were admirably compassionate, abhorring injustice and violence at all levels, in all contexts. The influence of the war in Vietnam—and the University of Chicago trustees' forthright support of U.S. policy there—was the cause of White's abrupt change in career direction. In very public manner, after coordinating faculty protest of University policy, White left Chicago in 1969 for Colorado (despite his deep love for the University; He had been born in its Hyde Park shadow and having enjoyed all of his education there commencing with the University's Laboratory School). Both Tax and White had publicly deplored the University of Chicago's role in development of the bomb that devastated Japan a quarter century earlier, but neither had permitted that to compromise their loyalty to the University during the era of Robert Maynard Hutchins' liberal leadership. I had listened to Tax's anguished recollections of World War II—the Holocaust—and would eventually listen to White's recollections of his Quaker service in Vichy France and subsequent imprisonment under the Nazis, before he became president of Haverford College (where I first made his acquaintance as a student 1951). But unfortunately I have no memory of comparably querying Tax regarding the impact of Vietnam on his subsequent thinking and priorities. It is noteworthy that White's field service in Europe and Tax's anthropological fieldwork in the U.S. exempted both from military service.

Pertinent to Tax's priorities subsequent to the 1960s, is his letter written to me when he was a Fellow at the Center for Advanced Study in the Behavioral Sciences at Stanford (see Figure 6 at end of this chapter). In this letter he presented his vision for an International Center for the Study of Man, to be housed at the Smithsonian:

> There would be some 30 interdisciplinary Fellows and graduate student junior Fellows who would come for one, two, or three year terms to work on basic problems in the human sciences, and on the social problems which suggest their importance. A series of conferences would suggest subjects for limited-time task forces; a task force might consist of—say—ten or 12 people who would become Fellows for the periods in which they would be in residence; if a task force took five years, its Fellows would be in residence together for three to six months initially, then do research with their students anywhere, returning together at least for a period near the end, for developing conclusions and a publishable report. I imagine at least one such task force being organized each year, so that several would eventually be working simultaneously. The Fellows in residence at any time would of course be in communication with those who comprise the other task forces (Tax 1970:1).

White had just commenced chairing the U of Colorado's similarly interdisciplinary Institute of Behavioral Sciences (soon to become the home of the Hazards Center), and I was preparing to experiment—inviting their counsel—with administering a Quaker college in Ohio (Wilmington College). Readers of Tax's Festschrift (Hinshaw 1979) may recall my and the college's anthropologist ombudsman's retrospective assessment of our Wilmington involvements on behalf of a "therapeutic anthropology." Magoroh Maruyama, who contributed the Festschrift article, "Trans-epistemological Understanding: Wisdom beyond Theories" (1979), joined me as a teaching colleague at Wilmington, intrigued with our vision of education at the college level incorporating Tax's holistic perspective for the International Center for the Study of Man. Fred Gearing, of the Fox Project era, and Sol Tax also were present for my Wilmington inaugural festivities in 1971, creatively assisting with the brokering between administration and Black students that amiably ended their appropriately symbolic occupation of the administration building (just in time for the inauguration). The weekend included Tax's address, upon accepting the honorary degree whose citation summarized his action tenets for productive living:

> The simple name of an anthropologist with an uncluttered view of human beings: we are distinguished culturally and individually by the choices we make. In his long career he has integrated goals and means in a tidy fashion: to serve one's fellows, contribute as you can knowledge of the choices available to them; to learn about one's fellows, observe the choices they make. Have the respect not to decide for others what is in their best interests; assume you never will understand them that well. But do have the courage to protect wherever possible the freedom of others to make those decisions for themselves, and even to make mistakes. For oneself, avoid premature choices and action. Assume there always is more knowledge to be brought to bear on any matter than is currently available (Hinshaw 1979:vii).

Regarding my retrospective assessment of Tax's counsel to us all, I believe most helpful to me were his urgings: 1) to be patient—with ourselves and with others—in our discernment and decision-making ... to cross no bridges precipitously nor burn them unnecessarily behind us; 2) to not let others' approval and deference flowing from our expertise in delimited experience thereby suggest that we—in any other respect whatsoever—are comparably wise (that humility thing again!); and 3) in our helping, to learn as early in life as possible (at least before parenting!) the hard lesson that good intentions never are enough.

Tax and Gearing kindly maintained their imaginative advisory roles throughout those five Wilmington years before I returned to anthropological scholarship and teaching at Beloit. It may be useful to elaborate briefly on the outcome of our collaborative dialogue during those Wilmington and Beloit years. Ahead of my Wilmington presidency, the College had extended its offerings—much more broadly "applied" in the sciences than in my and White's prior experience at Haverford College—to a nearby state penitentiary whose inmates were allowed to attend campus classes supplementing introductory courses offered at the prison. In addition to deepening that prison collaboration, during my tenure we further diversified both clientele and offerings through merging curricula and sharing faculty with a public community college newly opened adjacent to the College. And to accommodate these diverse students' needs for similarly flexible graduate study, Tax helped orchestrate a University of Chicago/Wilmington program enabling graduates to matriculate at Chicago under the creative provisions that earlier had permitted attendance of students such as Bob Thomas.

Even more to the point of Tax's influence on our Wilmington experimentation, we endeavored to alter the dynamics of administrator/faculty/student relations by reframing pedagogy as an interactive teaching/learning endeavor for all concerned, including practitioners and potential employers on the town side of the town/gown divide. Subject matter remained packaged in disciplinary departments but—as an alternative to a departmental major—students were encouraged to opt for a problem or career-focused major requiring the student's formation of an advisory committee of on- and off-campus specialists to assist through a thesis and graduation. Trustees as well as administrators and the corpus of alumni and parents participated in the collaborative learning and helping. Quite the experiment!

Even when moving on to more tradition-bound Beloit, where disciplinary majors remained sacrosanct, revised graduation requirements included a full semester of away-from-campus, often out-of-country intern employment or individualized study. With anthropology as the College's largest major, we gave much attention to such placements. For a semester following Guatemala's 1976 earthquake—the strongest in Latin America to that point in the 20th century—18 students from diverse majors and I worked with the subjects of our study (e.g., quake victims and aid providers, tourists and their service providers) assessing impacts of the quake and of tourism across highland Guatemala. In retrospect it was much like the Fox Project at the college level, with some papers published and presented at that year's SfAA anthropology meetings in Merida, Yucatan.

My wife and I also hosted Guatemala consciousness-raising tours for trustees, alumni and parents when at Beloit and Wilmington—then for other colleges and universities where employed. At times utilizing Tax and White's networks of international contacts, we eventually organized over fifty Elderhostel-like tours for socially-concerned adults among largely native peoples across South, Central and North America as well as Scandinavia, Russia, and Southeast Asia. I am confident that Tax regarded all such highly diverse endeavors of his former students as doing or applying anthropology.

Tax's Modus Operandi

I turn now to my thesis that to understand Tax's modus operandi it behooves us to understand White's as well (and vice versa). Most already are familiar with Tax's style of servant-leadership in learning while helping, so it remains for me only to acquaint the reader with White's. And fortunately I am assisted in this by the review article co-authored by two of White's Chicago students, Ian Burton and Bob Kates. I discuss in much more detail his modus operandi in my 2006 biography of White (Hinshaw 2006). Just as Tax benefitted from his long associations with Native Americans—in his predilection to lead "from below"—so White's comparably successful leadership across contentious divides benefitted from long association with Quakers, his choice of religious affiliation commencing when a college student at Chicago and continuing until his death at 95. (White was chairing the national board of the American Friends Service Committee when confronting the University of Chicago trustees over U.S. policy in Vietnam.) Tax also had steadily deepening Quaker involvements throughout his life (beginning with his first anthropology mentor, Ralph Linton), both in his inner-city work in Chicago and during the Fox Project where anthropologists worked with the Iowa office of the American Friends Service Committee (directed in that era by my father) in lobbying successfully for the Fox to maintain their own school and then to provide school instruction in their native language.

The tenets of Action Anthropology mirror some fundamental truths about efficacious learning/knowing and wise deciding/helping shared by native peoples in diverse cultural contexts and by communities of diverse religious traditions (from

Jewish to Quaker and beyond). Tax and White simply pushed the limits of group size and diversity theretofore assumed feasible for such collaborative and empathetic discernment and action. Just as many today are recommending that we distance discussion of the merits of Action Anthropology from the Fox Project, might it be comparably wise to distance Action Anthropology from the name and experience of Sol Tax as well? Are we not dealing with epistemological issues that are best not attributed to any individual or school of thought? Hence Maruyama's paper's imaginative title: "Trans-epistemological Understanding: Wisdom beyond Theories" (1979). Fortunately for White, he resisted all efforts to personalize his modus operandi. Nor, unless pushed, would he attribute his leadership practice to Quaker example. But for present purposes, those roots bear brief description (using the non-theological terminology that White—in his eventual agnosticism—preferred). For White, the essence of Quakerism is the "process of knowing" of constant experiential testing … through collective discernment of the efficacy of our beliefs. Implicit in this is the assumption that our narratives and theories—theological as well as scientific—are not sacrosanct … do not wisely become creedal or "schools of thought" in the interest of their refinement through ongoing testing and illumination. His Quakerism and his science are pragmatic and experientially based through and through. Hereby, we are better positioned to survive any challenges occasioned by scientific findings and disillusionment from crises precipitated by unsustainable population increase and depletion of natural resources.

Beginning with the shared assumptions that any problem or disagreement will have a discernable and wisest course of action ("the sense of the meeting" in Quaker parlance), and that consensus to pursue that action must be strong enough to dissuade any participant from impeding implementation, we have the core of Quaker business practice. Such consensus goes far beyond a general agreement, or the will of a majority following Robert's Rules of Order. But of course many entities follow such practice, and wisely so! White's genius lay in his suasion and patience to experiment with such "clerking" (another Quaker term, analogous to chairing) in ever-larger and more problematic contexts of decision-making and peacekeeping. He finally reached the point of declining invitations to "chair" committees and task forces—even in international arenas—unless he could dispense with Robert's Rules of Order and "clerk" in his inimical style. And Tax did much the same, albeit in a somewhat narrower range of institutional/national and international governmental contexts. Given the distinctiveness (if not uniqueness) of each man's legacy in this regard within his respective discipline, I cannot help but believe that Tax and White were subtly—if not overtly—encouraging each other in epistemological bias and leadership style the latter half of their careers. But in part due to living to age 95 and enjoying the health enabling him to remain professionally active almost that long, White—with the help of more students and associates than surrounded Tax—persevered in making a more clearly reasoned and articulated witness to the tenets as fully embraced by Tax.

I frankly lack knowledge of how much legacy of Tax's influence the Center for the Study of Man may represent. Surely the ongoing success of the journal *Current Anthropology* represents considerably more, as do his myriad involvements on behalf of self-determination and cultural persistence of native peoples. But all these initiatives reflect the same spirit—the same interdisciplinary, cybernetic, problem-focused philosophy underlying White's highly successful Boulder Natural Hazards Center. Similar networking centers for research and data-sharing modeled on the Boulder initiative now operate in many North American universities and around the world. In 1970 Tax envisioned a comparably humanistic, problem-focused and revitalized global anthropology enterprise. But students/admirers have not, until recently, picked up his gauntlet. I look forward to discussing what we might yet deem doable under the rubric of anthropology (or science more generally) in our deeply challenged world.

Intellectual History

I have finally read Adam Kuper's *Culture: The Anthropologists' Account* (2000) documenting the strains of theoretical discourse regarding culture in the North Atlantic community of anthropologists and other social scientists. His chapters on the 1960s and 1970s are especially useful, these being my years of Chicago study and regular involvement with Tax. This reading prompts speculation regarding the impact of that national discourse on Tax's thinking/action, as we endeavor to understand his legacy.

The Fox Project was in its twilight years while I was at Chicago, and of diminishing concern to Tax in his deepening involvement with the campus and community dynamics of conflict and change during those tumultuous 1960s. Probably it was fortuitous that his students' challenge to assist in Fox community dynamics came a decade earlier. Pulling that off in the 1960s would have been even more problematic within the Department. 1960 was a watershed year for anthropology at Chicago (I better understand this now than I did when landing there as a student in 1961). The Parsonian attack of the 1940s and 1950s on the sociologizing of cultural anthropology in North America had to have been a preoccupation among anthropologists at Chicago, given the long tradition at Chicago of wedding anthropology and sociology (commencing with A.

R. Radcliffe-Brown's tenure in the Department, joined early on by Warner, then Robert Redfield). But Redfield died in the late 1950s, leaving Tax a pretty solitary voice for applied anthropology within the Department. Fred Eggan, his colleague in study of U.S. Native Americans, decidedly was not a soul mate in urban study/activism (e.g., Joan Ablon's comment, this volume, regarding Eggan's lack of sympathy for her interest in urban anthropology). And apart from Eggan, I do not recall any other Department colleagues who were particularly sympathetic even to Tax's agenda regarding Native American cultural persistence/assimilation challenges.

Might Tax's choice of the rubric "Action Anthropology" have been a considered response to Parson's "action" agenda as promulgated in his 1951 "The Social System" and same year publication of "Toward a General Theory of Action"? I cannot argue this point ... unaware of whether/why Tax (or one of his students?) coined "Action Anthropology." Thoughts of those in Tax's company during the 1950s are welcomed in this regard. Earlier than at Chicago, anthropologists at both Berkeley (under Kroeber's influence) and Harvard's newly established Department of Social Relations (led by Kluckhohn as well as Parsons) were challenging the students of Boas across the continent. And Parson's influence at Chicago, commencing at the turn of the decade, was injected—not through anthropologists of long standing in the Department—but by Parson's associate Edward Shils, hired to establish a Committee for the Comparative Study of New Nations.

Anthropology's coming on board was accomplished through the simultaneous hiring, in 1960, of Clifford Geertz and David Schneider (both graduates of the Harvard Department of Social Relations) and Lloyd Fallers (who—along with Geertz and Schneider—came more immediately from brief sojourns at Berkeley). Ironically, both Kluckhohn and Kroeber passed away that same summer of 1960, possibly accentuating the visibility nationally of Parsonian influence shifting from the two coasts to Chicago. In my recollection, Tax was pleased with those colleague additions, but how much he (and Eggan) had to do with their hiring—and creation of the Committee for the Comparative Study of New Nations—I do not know. Again, others' information in this regard will be welcomed! My entering classmates and I commenced our study under the tutelage of these "young Turks," who had been charged with revamping the Departmental Masters' level core curriculum. Introductory courses in the traditional four-subfields were revised to accommodate a curriculum of team-taught "Human Career" segments in physical anthropology and archaeology, running parallel over two years with "Systems" segments in culture, social structure, and personality. Linguistics was included, but in which track I do not recall. Given the excitement back then over modeling cultural structuring in assorted domains upon the etics/emics of linguistics, I expect these segments were in "Systems."

It was my impression that Tax was fully supportive of the revised curriculum, despite his having a marginal role in its instruction. Geertz and Schneider dominated the cultural systems instruction quite completely in my memory. Might that revamping, with the sidelining it implied for particularly him and Eggan, have facilitated Tax's shift in focus toward the national and international arenas of the—possibly similarly threatened—four subfields amalgam in anthropology? In any case, his juices continued to flow as much during the 1960s as I understood from him that they had during the 1950s. Perhaps his re-immersion in Guatemala those years of mentoring my work there contributed to his good spirits. His energy was exhilarating.

But more to the present point, during the 1960s Tax surely received little encouragement from any quarter at Chicago to elaborate upon and articulate more clearly his "action" tenets for expanded contexts of anthropological inquiry beyond Native American concerns. And his students and admirers were perhaps thereby less motivated to codify and advocate for those fledgling tenets of helping-while-learning. A failing—mine largely—of the Festschrift (Hinshaw 1979) was not taking time to extract from the remarkably disparate contributions of their authors the lessons learned from such collective experience in applying and expanding Tax's modus operandi. Blanchard, in his contribution (1979), led in this regard where I—as editor—should have followed more assiduously.

So how much focus should we give in the future to a "how to" handbook for specifically anthropologists' leadership in problem identification and solving? Will we endeavor to concentrate on several career domains (such as Darby Stapp's in cultural preservation) or do we envision a primer for social scientists in general? In this regard, I have just read Donella Meadows' posthumously published gem, "Thinking in Systems: A Primer" (2008) (she earlier authoring "Limits to Growth" (1972), and co-editing "Limits to Growth: The 30-Year Update" (Meadows et al. 2004)—books of much personal influence). Whereas in Gilbert White's biography I focused more on his personality/character qualities conducive to effective leadership in collaborative action in getting things done (Hinshaw 2006), Meadows much more succinctly explicates "rules" for effective action within organizations of ever-increasing complexity. Her final summary chapter is worth perusal, wherein she anecdotally illustrates these 15 axioms for service-as-scientist:

- Get the bent of the system
- Expose your mental models to the light of day
- Honor, respect and distribute information
- Use language with care and enrich it with systems concepts
- Pay attention to what is important—not just to what is quantifiable
- Make feedback policies for feedback systems
- Go for the good of the whole
- Listen to the wisdom of the system
- Locate responsibility in the system
- Stay humble and a learner
- Celebrate complexity
- Expand time horizons
- Defy the disciplinary boundaries
- Expand the boundary of caring
- Don't erode the goal of goodness.

I am not clear on how much focus is envisioned on the Meadows' kind of "action handbook for getting things done" vs. the assessment and eulogizing of specifically Tax's legacy in this regard. The latter is important: after all, all experience is individual … our consciousness is personal, and the marriage of individual observation/ reflection/analysis with one's career/life journey of action is the best way of "mattering." Purpose coupled with the inspiration of others are the keys to making a difference through one's life. The more complexity and moral ambiguity we experience with evolving consciousness through deepening scientific literacy and expanding globalization, the more critical it becomes to recognize and promote inspirational modeling of leadership. Ideas/wisdom is important, but when embedded in an individual's action their inspirational utility is greatly enhanced. Hence the importance of Tax's life/career.

Summary

Both Tax and White were exemplary in their leadership (White less restricted to academe than was Tax), but with little priority devoted to analysis and interpretation of their strategies (Tax more diligent in this respect than was White). Hence my focus within the last two chapters of White's biography on such explication (Hinshaw 2006). I wish that I had had Meadows' distilled wisdom at hand in the biography's writing, she admirably explicating how to "dance" through the complexities of organizational structures in pursuit of more humane living (Meadows 2008). Much of the "meaning" to me of both Tax and White is summarized in her book. But her book is instructively different from the biography/memoir endeavor. I continue to marvel that Tax's influence, so vicarious through his students and so long after his passing, seems to tower above the influence of other applied anthropologists in the experience of at least some of us. In no more detail than Tax articulated his action tenets, how can it be that our discipline is so lacking in comparable inspiration from any number of other anthropologists? How much of Tax's mentoring influence derives from his personality—how he lived his life—in contrast to his published ideas? Meadows also addresses this: the dearth of perceived caring among our leaders—the erosion of essential goodness with increasing complexity—at least as reflected in the popular media's coverage of leadership. I was impressed by the account in Rubinstein (1986) of an interviewee's testimony comparing her/his unimpressive classroom instruction under Tax with the life-changing influence of his caring spirit. But if choosing between these legacies, would we all not value most the caring spirit in our mentors? Or am I downplaying the importance, even for inspiration, of disembodied ideas in the history of our scientific literacy? Just one of the issues I am pondering of late in endeavoring to answer the questions: who am I, and how did I become this "me!"

CENTER FOR ADVANCED STUDY IN THE BEHAVIORAL SCIENCES

202 Junipero Serra Boulevard • Stanford, California 94305 Telephone (415) 321-2052

June 18, 1970

Professor Robert E. Hinshaw
Department of Anthropology
The University of Kansas
Lawrence, Kansas 66044

Dear Bob:

I am sorry to be so long answering yours of May 18, with its news of your plans. I have been traveling the past weeks, and am just settling back. Although I have read the appended document, I make too little of it because it assumes much knowledge of Wilmington--its size, location, history, general "set"--that I lack. Add to this handicap a general ignorance on my part of the limitations of a liberal arts college (as opposeed to a University) you will understand my difficulty. If we could first compare notes for a few hours, perhaps I could be of some use. My present concern is establishing an International Center for the Study of Man, which I have briefly described in the following paragraph:

> There would be some 30 interdisciplinary Fellows and graduate student junior Fellows who would come for one, two, or three year terms to work on basic problems in the human sciences, and on the social problems which suggest their importance. A series of conferences would suggest subjects for limited-time task forces; a task force might consist of--say--ten or 12 people who would become Fellows for the periods in which they would be in residence; if a task force took five years, its Fellows would be in residence together for three to six months initially, then do research with their students anywhere, returning together at least for a period near the end, for developing conclusions and a publishable report. I imagine at least one such task force being organized each year, so that several would eventually be working simultaneously. The Fellows in residence at any time would of course be in communication with those who comprise the other task forces.

The international membership of the Center, which in effect is its Board of Directors, consists now of: Dr. Fredrik Barth, Institute of Social Anthropology, Bergen; Dr. Laila Shukry El-Hamamsy, Social Research Center, American University in Cairo; Dr. Claude Lévi-Strauss, Laboratoire d'Anthropologie Sociale, Paris; Dr. J. Clyde Mitchell, University of Manchester; Dr. Chie Nakane, University of Tokyo, Institute of Oriental Culture; Dr. Surajit C. Sinha, Anthropological Survey of India, Indian Museum, Calcutta; Dr. M.N. Srinivas, Dept. of Sociology, Delhi.

Figure 6. Sol Tax 1970 letter to Robert Hinshaw concerning the vision for the International Center for the Study of Man.

Professor Robert Hinshaw -2- June 18, 1970

At a recent meeting in Washington, I was asked to develop nominations at once for the selection of three additional members, from Latin America, South East Asia, and Eastern Europe. We are proceeding slowly to bring together a group of what I imagine will consist of from 15 to 25 such scholars. To test the method, we have moved to set up at once a first experimental task force to study the socio-cultural context of family life and fertility.

We have assumed that the Smithsonian could provide the site and substance for the Center; but the international members (at least) are determined to have the Center and to pursue its goals on any terms.

Last week I spent at a conference at the University of Wisconsin in Milwaukee, on Urban Anthropology; and became the more convinced that anthropology itself must change, or is already changing its focus from the small community (including ethnic enclaves) to the whole of the emerging worldwide society. What this means is not that we do everything over as though others have not been studying innumerable aspects of the whole, but rather that we now begin to add our perspective to whatever else is being done. Rather than go on at length, I shall let your imagination fill in the rest, perhaps better than I could.

The question may arise in your mind whether there is something in this that could relate to your task at Wilmington. Clearly, if the CSM is not attached to the Smithsonian, a place like the University of Chicago (with strong anthropology, etc.) would be a good place to attach it at; but there are so many if's to any possibility, that I would not rule out yours. Again, I let your imagination play.

The NSF has funds for summer programs in teacher training in anthropology. I think that the Office of Education also subsidizes such programs. Library book money would be harder to come by, unless perhaps it is in connection with another program.

A good friend of mine in the U.N. is Emil Sady (husband of Rachel Reese Sady), one of our Chicago PhD's and interested in Secondary-school education. Why not write him about the U.N. Peace Corps. Address is: 40 Euclid Ave. Hastings-on-Hudson, New York, N.Y. 10706.

Perhaps in connection with your new job it would be useful to come here for discussion; and I would be glad to see you.

With best regards,

Sincerely,

Sol

Sol Tax
Fellow

ST:has

Figure 6 (continued). Sol Tax letter to Robert Hinshaw concerning the vision for the International Center for the Study of Man.

References Cited

Blanchard, David
1979 Beyond Empathy: the Emergence of an Action Anthropology in the Life and Career of Sol Tax. In *Current Anthropology: Essays in Honor of Sol Tax*, edited by Robert E. Hinshaw, pp. 419–443. Mouton Publishers, New York.

Foley, Douglas E.
2009 Review of The Meskwaki and Anthropologists: Action Anthropology Reconsidered, by Judith M. Daubenmier. *The Annals of Iowa*, 68:331–33.

Hinshaw, Robert E., editor
1979 *Current Anthropology: Essays in Honor of Sol Tax*. Mouton Publishers, New York.

Hinshaw, Robert E.
2006 *Living with Nature's Extremes: The Life of Gilbert Fowler White*. Johnson Books, Boulder, Colorado.

Kuper, Adam
2000 *Culture: The Anthropologists' Account*. Harvard University Press, Cambridge, Massachusetts.

Linton, Ralph
1936 *The Study of Man*. D. Appleton-Century Co., New York.

Maruyama, Magoroh
1979 Transepistemological Understanding: Wisdom Beyond Theories. In *Current Anthropology: Essays in Honor of Sol Tax*, edited by Robert E. Hinshaw, pp. 371–189. Mouton Publishers, New York.

Meadows, Donella H.
1972 *The Limits to Growth*. Signet Books, New York.
2008 *Thinking in Systems: A Primer*. Chelsea Green Publishing, White River Junction, Vermont.

Meadows, Donella H., Jorgen Randers, and Dennis L. Meadows
2004 *Limits to Growth: The 30-Year Update*. Chelsea Green Publishing, White River Junction, Vermont.

Rubinstein, Robert A.
1986 Reflections on Action Anthropology: Some Developmental Dynamics of an Anthropological Tradition. *Human Organization*, 45(3):270–279.
1991 *Fieldwork: The Correspondence of Robert Redfield and Sol Tax*. Westview Press, Boulder, Colorado.

Smith, Joshua
2010 The Political Thought of Sol Tax: The Principles of Non-Assimilation and Self-Government in Action Anthropology. In *Histories of Anthropology Annual* Volume 6, pp. 129–170. University of Nebraska Press, Lincoln.

Tax, Sol
1970 Letter to Professor Robert E. Hinshaw. 18 June 1970. Center for Advanced Study in the Behavioral Sciences, Stanford, California.

CHAPTER 4

SOL TAX AS FATHER

Marianna Tax Choldin

I'm Marianna, the Russian-scholar daughter. I went into Russian studies because of a passion that developed in my early teens, and into Slavic librarianship by accident, when, in the wake of Sputnik, America realized that the Soviets got into space before we did because we didn't have enough Russian specialists in universities. About the same time I fell in love with things Russian, I realized that two anthropologists in a family of four was probably enough. There were really three: our mother, Gertrude, had majored in German, but she worked closely with our father and, like many wives of her generation, she became much more than an anthropologist-by-marriage (Figure 7). And then the number of family members in anthropology and closely related fields increased when Susan and I married. Les Freeman, Susan's husband, is an archeologist and a professor of anthropology; and I married Harvey Choldin, a sociologist.

It was a losing battle, because I too became some kind of anthropologist, by osmosis, I suppose, and by nature and nurture. Of my father's many passions, two seeped into my pores, or were lurking there already, waiting to burst forth. One was bringing together professional colleagues, both domestically and internationally; the other was Action Anthropology, which brings me here today. I'd like to tell you a few stories about Sol Tax—my father—so you see him as a family man who was always an anthropologist, too. And I'll show you how some of his ideas and passions shaped my own academic life, never far from anthropology.

As a small child I was drawn to archaeology. When I was five or six, in 1947 or 1948, Papa (as I'll call him from now on) brought home an orangutan skull from the office, because he had a hunch I'd be interested. I loved that skull and wanted to take it to school for show-and-tell, so he helped me prepare a little talk for my classmates. I was dismayed when several classmates shrieked and made disgusting noises when I held up the skull, and the teacher had to intervene. She and I were the only people who gave that skull the respectful attention it deserved, but I've always been sorry that I didn't get to deliver my little speech to anyone but Miss Thurston. I became something of an anthropological pest at school; I remember another time, probably at or near the same age, when one of my classmates said something belittling about Australian Aborigines, or perhaps about Pygmies. I reared up and gave him a severe little speech about how the Aborigines (or the Pygmies) had a highly developed social organization.

Figure 7. Gertrude Tax, Sol Tax, Marianna Tax, and Susan Tax (standing), in 1942.

When I was seven or eight, a toy nurse's kit turned me on to medicine, and I told my parents I wanted to be a nurse. "How about being a doctor?" Papa asked. He arranged for me to observe an operation on a rabbit at the University Hospital and bought me a copy of *Gray's Anatomy*. But soon I was back into archaeology. I was 11 in 1953, when the "Piltdown Man" hoax was discovered, and I was terrifically intrigued. With Papa's encouragement I wrote a "novel" about it (many pages in a small notebook or two but, alas, only 17 pages typed—really a short story).

Archaeology seemed exotic to me, but cultural anthropology I took for granted: it was part of everyday life. Our home was filled with objects that had been part of the family households in Panajachel, where Papa, Mama, and Susan lived before I was born, and Mexico City, where I spent the first year of my life. My parents and sister spoke Spanish intermittently with English and Yiddish (for Mama's mother, who lived with us). Friends from Mexico and Guatemala came frequently to visit. We played with dozens of tiny children's toys—mainly from Guatemala, I think, collected in a curio cabinet from Papa's boyhood home in Milwaukee. (Susan's and my daughters played with the collection, and Harvey's and my granddaughters enjoy it today, enhanced by a few of my later additions from Russia.)

We helped Papa collate the galley pages of *Penny Capitalism* on the living-room floor. We took working vacations each summer: to Tama, where we danced with the women and children during powwows; to Fort Berthold, North Dakota, where we were blissfully happy to be living in a big silver trailer and playing with local kids on the reservation while Papa consulted with grownups about Garrison Dam, soon to flood them out; to Berkeley, where Papa worked with colleagues for the summer of 1950; to New York City and the Wenner-Gren Foundation for the summer of 1952; to Mexico City, Oaxaca, and Chiapas in 1957; and on and on.

We grew up with so many stories, some from Papa's trip as a student to Algeria with a Beloit College expedition, from which he brought back a marvelous Bedouin shawl, a piece of sandstone we called "the rose of the Sahara," a photo of himself in Bedouin dress (Figure 8), and a wonderful account of the Passover seders he enjoyed with two Algerian families. Other tales came from Papa's first field season, with Ruth Benedict in New Mexico in 1931, when he hitchhiked home, lost his suitcase with all his field notes in it to a dishonest driver, and was picked up by the driver of a fancy car whose wife somehow sensed Papa's resemblance to a rabbi who had "cured" their baby and turned out to be Papa's grandfather! And on and on.

One of these stories made a deep and lasting impression on me and colored my academic life. When Papa was an undergraduate at the University of Wisconsin in Madison, he was very active politically, and was one of the leaders of the Young Liberals Club. He was horrified when Communists took over the club, using undemocratic tactics. From then on, he had a healthy dislike of any political group that was willing to advance its program that way, and he did not believe that the end justified the means. As I studied the Soviet Union and spent time there, his story stuck with me, and nothing I learned or saw persuaded me to disagree with his conclusion.

Figure 8. Sol Tax in Algeria on a Beloit College archaeological excavation in 1930 while an undergraduate at the University of Wisconsin–Madison.

Susan graduated from the University of Chicago Laboratory School, where we both went, in 1954, and Papa gave the commencement address: "The Freedom to Make Mistakes" (published sometime later). It was a bold and elegant talk, advocating rights for children and everyone else, and I love rereading it. When I think of this talk, though, I'm always reminded of the way Papa handled me when I decided to try smoking. I was five or six, I think. Both parents smoked a pack a day at that time (they stopped later), and I wanted to know what smoking was all about. I sneaked a pack (Camels? Lucky Strikes?) and a book of matches out of Mama's purse and went somewhere nearby to light up. I knew that what I was doing was dangerous, but that didn't stop me.

Of course Mama noticed immediately and told me that Papa would deal with me. Then there was nothing for it but to run away from home. I didn't want to, as I loved our apartment and my family, but as I saw it, I had disgraced myself and had to leave. (I wasn't afraid of physical punishment; that wasn't done in our family.) I trudged down University Avenue, where we lived at the time. I think I had my favorite doll with me. Papa came after me, and we walked together for a while, in silence. Then he said, "I understand you'd like to try smoking, and I think you should. Let's go home and smoke together." We turned around, walked back to our apartment building, and sat on the front steps. He lit two cigarettes and gave me one, instructing me how to hold it and how to inhale. I did, and of course I choked and coughed. While this was going on, he talked to me quietly, explaining why I might want to give up smoking right now, before I got started. I didn't argue.

We had another of our walk-and-talk sessions a few years later, when I was ten or eleven. I had developed an intense fear of death, which woke me up at night and kept me, for a time, in a state of terror. This was huge, and I didn't want to talk about it: too scary. But Papa coaxed it out of me one day as we were walking home from school. He listened intently, then began talking to me about girls my age. Our bodies were changing, he explained, and maybe my intense feelings, common to girls in other cultures too, were related to the changes occurring in my body. I was so relieved to know that I wasn't alone, that other girls might be worried too. We didn't resolve the question of death, of course, but he certainly did make me feel better; my terror subsided and I slept well again.

When *Current Anthropology* was in the works, Papa began traveling all over the world to meet with communities of anthropologists in each country. He sent home letters from every stop, his field notes, written in a tiny hand on both sides of onion-skin hotel stationery. He was meticulous about keeping carbon copies of each letter, and taught us to do the same. (Not with carbon paper anymore, of course!) We wrote back on U.S. air letters. (We have all the letters: our parents never threw anything away.) I was enthralled by all those letters, but especially by the ones from the Soviet Union. Our people, both Papa's and Mama's parents, had come around 1900 from what was then the Russian empire. Mama's mother, who helped raise us, had been born in what is now Ukraine in 1870. When I began studying Russian during my first year of college, when she was in her nineties, she startled me by speaking to me in Russian one day, instead of in her usual Yiddish. "Grandma, you're speaking Russian," I exclaimed. "No, I'm not," she assured me, in Russian.

My attraction to things Russian crystalized in 1956, when I was 14. Papa had invited three Soviet anthropologists to Philadelphia, to the Congress of the International Union of Anthropological and Ethnological Sciences, held in the summer in Philadelphia. I came along for fun—I had amused myself in the weeks before by writing a "scholarly paper" made up entirely of titles of real talks listed in the Congress program—but I wasn't going to any sessions. I planned to sit on a bench on the beautiful Penn campus and read *War and Peace*. I'd bought an abridged paperback translation before leaving Chicago. I have no idea why, as I'd always rejected abridgments; maybe I didn't want to lug around the much-heavier complete work. Anyway, the three Soviet anthropologists found me there, and one of them took me to task very sternly for reading an abridged edition, and in English! "Learn Russian!" he roared—I did and never looked back.

In our house it was always unspoken but understood: Susan and I would get PhDs. In something. Susan majored in anthropology at the University of Chicago and went off to Harvard for her PhD, so she was taken care of. I, nearly four years younger, appeared to be on a steady course for a PhD in Russian studies. I never had the feeling that Papa minded that I wasn't going into anthropology; I think he knew that there was a deep connection between each of his daughters and himself, and understood that somehow or other, I would follow in his path, too.

He did tie me into anthropology in one amazing way, though. Both Susan and I had studied German in school and were very good at it. She spent a summer in Austria, and I spent two summers in Germany. One day, probably in the fall of 1960, as I was beginning my second year in college at the University of Chicago, Papa asked me if I'd like to translate an anthropological book from German into English. I recall looking at him, nonplussed, and saying, "But I'm only 18! I couldn't do that!" "Nonsense," he replied. "Just translate a few paragraphs. I'll send it to the author in Germany without mentioning your name, and we'll see what he says." I was full of misgivings, but did what he suggested, and he sent it off. The author liked my work very much, and, to make a very long story very short, I spent the summer of 1960 in Germany working on the translation, and in 1962 the University of Chicago Press published Adolf E. Jensen's *Myth and Cult among Primitive People,* translated by Marianna Tax Choldin and Wolfgang Weissleder. (I did the literal translation and Wolfgang, an anthropologist and native speaker of German, did the polishing and "anthropologizing.")

I had another huge digression from Russian studies when Harvey and I took off, at the end of 1963, to spend two years in what was then East Pakistan (now Bangladesh). Here's how that came about: Harvey and I got married in August 1962. Papa really wanted us to have a big wedding so he could lay out a room-sized kinship chart that he would devise on the floor; he would then arrange the chairs, and the guests, according to the chart. We foiled him by having a total of 13 at the wedding, and we all stood. (We never knew where he planned to seat non-relatives.) A year later Harvey was hired by the Population Council to be a researcher on a community development project, known as the Comilla Project, based at the Pakistan Academy for Rural Development. We were dubious about going. Papa said, "Go for it!" and we're so glad we did. I learned Bengali and hung around with the women and watched and listened. I went into villages with a woman interviewer and later, back at the office, I helped her to put her notes into English. I translated speeches delivered in Bengali by our charismatic leader, Akhter Hameed Khan, for publication in English. We were doing fieldwork; I felt like an anthropologist, maybe even an Action Anthropologist. Papa came to visit once, on a *Current Anthropology* trip. He brought us salami from home and cheese from Denmark, where he had changed planes, and he became a big fan of Akhter Hameed Khan and the work being done in Comilla.

Back home, I learned how to be a Slavic librarian, first at Michigan State University and then at the University of Illinois in Urbana, where Harvey and I spent 33 years (1969 through 2002). At Illinois I was based in a great library with a magnificent Slavic collection. I soon learned, though, that no matter how large the collection, no one library had everything that an individual scholar needed, and I set out to make the connections that would give all of us access to all relevant collections. Working through the American Association for the Advancement of Slavic Studies, the main interdisciplinary organization in our field, I urged my library colleagues to band together, and they did so, enthusiastically.

In the 1970s, Slavic studies as a program was just beginning to come together internationally. The Cold War was still ice-cold in those days, and we couldn't do much with our colleagues in the Soviet Union and Eastern Europe; but we did begin a series of world congresses that eventually, throughout the course of the 1980s, would open up to include all of us. The librarians and I were right there at all the congresses, along with the social scientists (including anthropologists) and humanists. Needless to say, I was inspired and encouraged by Papa, with whom I discussed my strategies, my triumphs and failures. He and Mama would come out to O'Hare airport to see me between flights, and he would debrief me.

I still hadn't finished my PhD, delayed by the stay in Comilla and the birth of twins, who were supposed to be just one baby but turned out to be two. The baby was supposed to be born in East Pakistan, but I had some difficulty with the pregnancy and was advised to fly home. Papa and Mama were waiting at the airport to whisk me to the doctor. Everyone assured me that the baby, predicted to be an eight-pound boy, would arrive on time.

We were all surprised, to say the least, when two identical little girls, whose combined weight did equal eight pounds, arrived six weeks early. No one was more excited than Papa. He kidded that we should send one baby to be raised on a Chinese commune, as an experiment in nature vs. nurture, but he wouldn't have let either one out of his sight. He dashed home from the university every day to help with the babies. Mama and I tended them all day, and Papa and I did night duty. He and I would pass one another on the stairs at 2 a.m., taking bottles up and down, and we would watch movies in the middle of the night, each with a baby in his or her arms.

I did go back to the University of Chicago to finish the PhD in 1976, when the girls were in sixth grade. I lived with my parents for that academic year, commuting home to Champaign each weekend, and had the joy of discussing my thesis topic—censorship in imperial Russia—with Papa five nights a week over supper. When I received the degree he gave me his doctoral hood (he had others, from honorary degrees) and marched with the faculty at commencement while I marched with the students. I know he was relieved that I had finally done what the Tax girls were supposed to do!

In 1989 something wonderful and unexpected happened to me: I became the Mortenson Distinguished Professor for International Library Programs at Illinois and the founding director of the Mortenson Center on the Urbana campus, which brought librarians together from around the world to learn from one another and then return home to develop their libraries. We also formed partnerships with organizations in several countries or groups of countries—Russia and the former Soviet Union, Haiti, Central America, South Africa—to train librarians on their own turf, in their own way, with help from us as needed. At the same time, I began working with George Soros and his foundations in the newly independent countries of the former Soviet Union and Eastern Europe, through a group Soros set up to help libraries. (I've often thought about Papa's connection with Paul Fejos of the Wenner-Gren Foundation, and my own connection with George Soros: two remarkable Hungarians and two Taxes!)

My activity in Russia blossomed after the fall of the Soviet Union, when I began working with Ekaterina Genieva, an amazing woman and the director of a library that is probably the most open and progressive cultural institution in the entire region. Together we mounted a groundbreaking exhibition on censorship in Russia and the Soviet Union; we traveled the country, helping communities to open their libraries, explore their past, and promote tolerance. (We continue these activities today.)

This all happened close to the end of Papa's life. He was beginning to lose some of his incredible energy, but he never tired of talking to me about what I was doing. It wasn't Action Anthropology, strictly speaking, but I did try to learn what communities wanted to accomplish and then help them as best I could to achieve their goals. And then I wrote about it.

Thanks for convening this session to give further recognition to my father's work; and thanks for inviting me.

CHAPTER 5

ON SOL TAX, SOME NOTES

Susan Tax Freeman

Let me offer a few notes on my father's academic biography. In the pre-session exchanges, there was some mention of my father's "forgotten" ethnography. Given the dates of the research, this is perhaps not much more forgotten than much other ethnography is becoming, as academic generations and fashions pass and the world changes. His ethnography had two major phases: kinship (and general social organization) and micro-economics (and general social organization).

Kinship

Sol Tax loved puzzle-solving as doubtless also did his teacher, Radcliffe-Brown. His thesis on the Fox Indians was unpublished but not unremarked, and some of it was renewed by Alan Coult (and perhaps Floyd Lounsbury). I don't think he ever taught kinship as a subject: Fred Eggan was doing that. Eggan was his fellow graduate student and closest friend on the faculty, along with their senior colleague, Robert Redfield. Tax's work on Fox social structure was a model of clarity (Figure 9) and accessible writing that makes one wish that fate had sent him to Australia to bring the same clarity of vision and writing there!

Micro-Economics

Post-doctoral research in Guatemala, under the Carnegie Institution of Washington, where Redfield was his close associate, brought Sol Tax into micro-economics and the general culture and social organization of Guatemala's Midwestern Highlands. Adam Smith—always on his bookshelf—was an informing source (along with Keynes and Polanyi). He was not guided by Karl Marx (and, contrary to some recent biographic suggestions, he never was a socialist). He did not participate in the eventual world-systems approaches to the study of global capitalism, so his work fell to one side. However, many of his abiding friendships among colleagues were with "cultural economists": Bert Hoselitz, Frank Knight, Earl Hamilton, Theodore Schultz, and his junior, Gunder Frank, whose dependency theory spoke to issues of colonialism. In other disciplines, he was close to Everett Hughes and Louis Worth, in sociology, and Louis Gottschalk in history; also Morton Grodzins and Herman Finer in political science. In the general ethnology of Guatemala, Tax's analysis of the *municipios* of the Midwestern Highlands (Tax 1953) remains a signal analysis for indigenous Meso-America and is an important precursor of a study like G. William Skinner's on Chinese marketing systems and the development of studies in regional anthropology. It is also important for studies of the significance of place identity and of ethnic identity and relations.

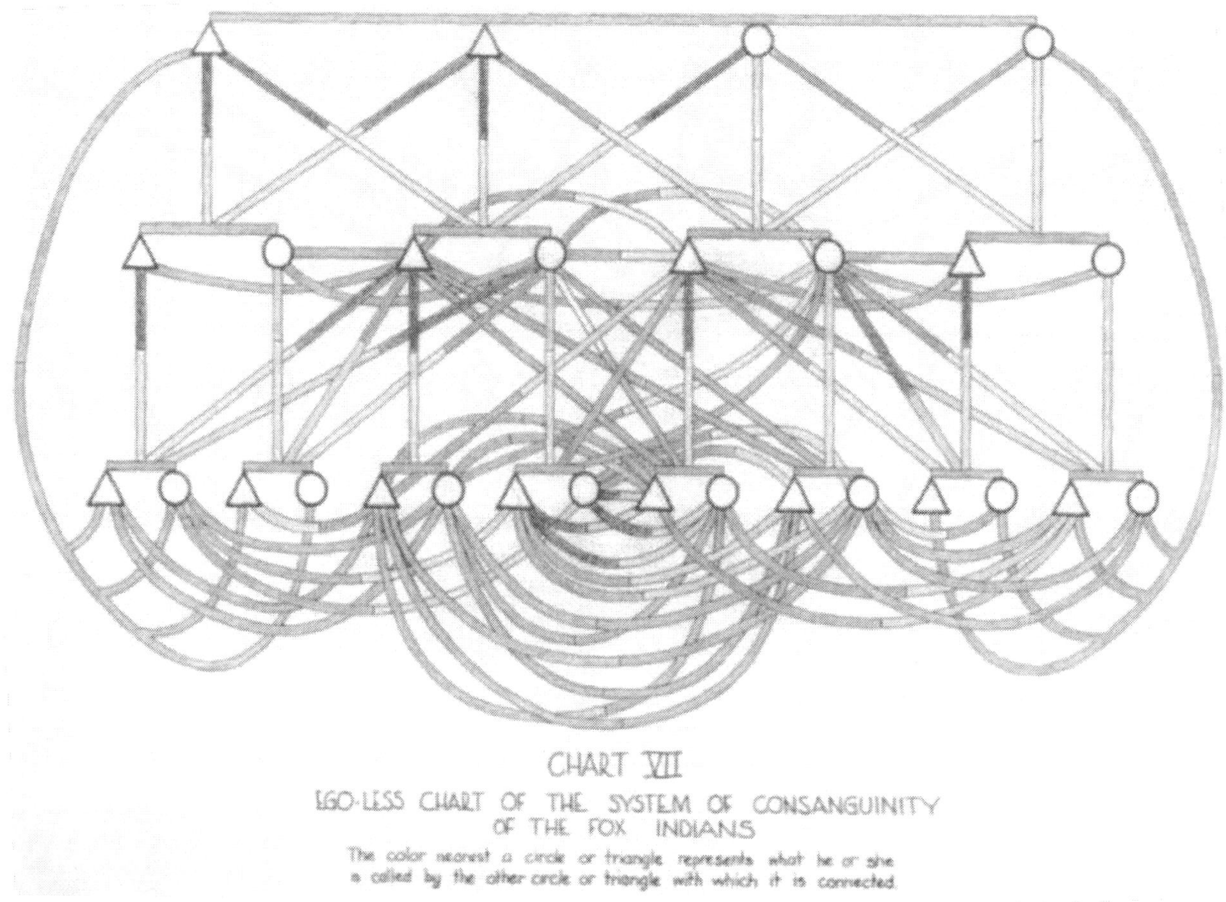

Figure 9. Sol Tax's ego-less kinship chart from his dissertation (Tax 1935).

Post-Fieldwork

Problems raised by colonialism and issues of social justice and cultural freedom governed the post-fieldwork part of my father's career. He had been committed as an undergraduate to economics and politics (I believe purely as an American citizen, not as a cross-cultural scholar) until he met Ralph Linton, whose first student he became, and they had a lifelong friendship. His late undergraduate experience in North Africa, on Beloit College's Logan Museum archeological expedition under Alonzo Pond, and in Europe, under George Grant MacCurdy and the American School of Prehistoric Research, clearly worked, as did Linton, to inspire cross-cultural interests—as well as lifelong interests across anthropology's sub-disciplines. But his abiding interest in being able to work with (but not within) the power system that governed peoples he cared about is part of what I think brought him out of Latin America and back to North American Indians—and the nation of his citizenship—for the rest of his career.

My father never worked outside the Academy—in which I include pure research establishments like the Carnegie Institution; the Wenner-Gren Foundation (which funded *Current Anthropology*); the sector of the Smithsonian which engaged him in part of his later period; and finally, the Center for Advanced Study in the Behavioral Sciences at Palo Alto, where he held a fellowship in 1969–70. After he first joined the University of Chicago, he never left. This life of research and teaching was a great luxury by today's standards. It never brought high salary or participation in any kind of power structure, but it gave the intellectual freedom for the development of Action Anthropology in the late 1940s and onward. At that time, the rubric "applied anthropology" was even sometimes pejorative (as Joan Ablon's commentary suggests) because it was associated with goal-oriented funding emanating from mainstream concerns for "native improvement" by mainstream definitions. As an undergraduate, I audited what may have been the first seminar on Action Anthropology and I remember graduate student Lee Guemple whispering to me, "The slogan for this anthropology is 'Don't just do something; stand there!'" Of course, Lee was being funny: we all knew the Action Anthropologist was supposed to help people do what they wanted for themselves, though Action Anthropologists soon learned that people don't necessarily agree on what they want for themselves. This latter point opens a whole new level of community study. [The syllabus for the first seminar is provided at the end of this chapter.]

Since the world in which anthropologists work is now vastly expanded, the challenge of Action Anthropology to applied anthropologists is to raise consciousness about for whom and toward what they work and to bring these questions to their employers, many of whom these days, fortunately, ask themselves the same questions.

References Cited

Tax , Sol

1935 Primitive Social Organization with Some Descriptions of the Social Organization of the Fox Indians. PhD dissertation, University of Chicago.

1953 *Penny Capitalism: A Guatemalan Indian Economy*. Institute of Social Anthropology, Publication No. 6. Smithsonian Institution Press, Washington, D.C.

SYLLABUS FROM 1958 ACTION ANTHROPOLOGY CLASS

UNIVERSITY OF CHICAGO
Department Of Anthropology

Anthropology 343 - "Action Anthropology"

Winter, 1958
Tu Th 10:00-11:30 a.m.
SS 108

Sol Tax
Leonard Borman

Bibliography, Assignments, and Class Schedule

Bibliography:

Theoretical and case materials on Social and Cultural Change, on problem of method, values, and ethics in Social Science, and on the North American Indians are all relevant in different ways in this course.

A. Two general (mimeographed) bibliographies which can be found in Room 6 (Social Science Building) and two books recently published at Stanford, should be consulted both for reference purposes and to get a range of the subject:

1. Robert Minges, "Induced Culture Change and the Economic Development of Backward Areas." n.d. (in Room 6)

~~2. Ethel Nurge and Richard Patch, "Bibliography on Social Change," 1953(Room 6)~~

3. Keesing, Felix Maxwell, Cultural Change: an Analysis and Bibliography... to 1952. Stanford, 1953 (in Harper Library)

4. Siegal, Bernard, J., ed. Acculturation: Critical Abstracts, North America. Stanford Anthropological Series No. 2,1955 (in Harper Library).

B. A major part of this course will consider the nature of science and especially of applied anthropology as discussed in the variety of literature on the subject. Some of the main sources to be consulted are the following, which are found in Harper Reserve:

Barnett, H.G., Anthropology in Administration. Evanston, Ill: Row, Peterson, and Co. 1956.

*Human Organization (formerly Applied Anthropology) Vol. 1-15, New York: Society for Applied Anthropology.

Keesing, Felix M. et al, Social Anthropology and Industry: Some Exploratory Workpapers, Department of Anthropology,Stanford University, California, 1957.

Mair, Lucy, Studies in Applied Anthropology, New York: Humanities Press, Inc. 1957.

*Paul, Benjamin (ed) Health, Culture, and Community, New York: Russell Sage Foundation, 1955.

Redfield, Robert, The Primitive World and its Transformations, Ithaca: Cornell University Press, 1953.

Russell, Bertrand, The Scientific Outlook, Glencoe, Illinois: Free Press, 1931.

Some Uses of Anthropology: Theoretical and Applied, The Anthropological Society of Washington, D.C., 1956.

*Spicer, Edward H. (ed) Human Problems in Technological Change, New York: Russell Sage Foundation, 1952.

C. Material coming out of the Action programs are contained to two dittoed items, obtainable in Harper Reserve: Summaries of the thinking in the Fox program are contained in two dittoed items, obtainable in Harper Reserve:

Gearing and Peattie, "A Documentary History of the Fox Project," 1955 Symposium on the Fox Project, 1955.

"A Reader in Action Anthropology."

These especially should be read for this course. In addition the following papers, minutes, and reports, available in Harper Reserve, should be read:

Fifth Internation Congress of Anthropological and Ethnological Science: "Minutes of a Discussion on Progress." 1956.

Herekovits, M. "Some Further Comments on Cultural Relativism," 1956.

Lenevski, A. "The Role of the Ethnographer in Soviet Construction in the North," 1929.

Polgar, S. "The Role of Anthropologists in Public Health Programs," 1957.

Tax, S., "The Quality of Peasant Living," 1956.

D. Among general books that should be thought of as "required," though they need not be read equally intensively, are the following:

Brown, G. G. and Hutt A.B.M., Anthropology in Action. London: Oxford University Press, 1935.

Eggan, F. (ed.) Social Organization of North American Indian Tribes. Chicago: University of Chicago Press, 1937.

Emmitt, R. The Last War Trail. Norman: University of Oklahoma Press, 1954.

Economic Development and Cultural Change, Vol. 1-V. Chicago: Research Center in

Economic Development and Cultural Change at the University of Chicago.

Handlin, O. Race and Nationality in American Life. Garden City, N.Y. Doubleday Anchor, 1957.

Herskovits, M., Acculturation: The Study of Cultural Contact, N.Y., J.J. Augustin, 1938.

Kroeber, A.L. (ed), Anthropology Today, Chicago: University of Chicago Press, 1953.

Leighton, A. The Governing of Men, Princeton, N.J., Princeton Univ. Press, 1946.

Linton, R. Acculturation in Seven North American Indian Tribes, New York-London, Appleton Century Co., Inc. 1940.

Landberg, C.A. Can Science Save Us? New York-London, Longmans, Green, & Co., 1947.

Lynd, R. Knowledge for What? Princeton: Princeton University Press, 1939.

Malinowski, B. The Dynamics of Culture Change, New Haven: Yale University Press, 1945.

Mannoni, O. Prospero and Galiban, New York, Fred A. Praeger, 1956.

Social Science Research Council, "Acculturation: An Explanatory Formulation." American Anthropologist, Vol. 56, No. 6, Part 1, Dec. 1954.

Tax, S., et al (eds) Appraisal of Anthropology Today, Chicago: University of Chicago Press, 1953.

Assignments:

Two papers will be required for this course. The first will be due at the end of the fourth week (Jan. 31), the second, at the end of the Quarter (March 21).

The first paper should review the "kinds" of applied anthropology as discussed in the variety of anthropological literature, e.g., the Paul, Spicer, Mair, and Barnett volumes, Human Organization, Anthropology Today, etc. Each of these publications includes further references to other writings in the field of applied anthropology which may be consulted for an overview of the entire field.

The second paper should consider of a critical discussion of one or several topics raised in the readings, lectures, and discussions of the programs, methods, and theories of action anthropology.

Class Schedule:

Session 1 (Jan. 7): Introduction--bibliography and assignments.

Session 2-6 (Jan. 9-23): Lectures on Social and Cultural Change, Acculturation, and Theories, Methods, and Programs of Action Anthropology.

Readings: Above listed material on kinds of applied anthropology in preparation for first paper.

Sessions 7-8 (Jan. 28-30): Discussion and Questions over Preceding Lectures.

Readings: For these discussions and those to follow, read particularly the following:

1. Papers on values and progress listed above, as well as pertinent chapters in Redfield's Primitive World...

2. In the Documentary History of the Fox Project 1948-1959: A Program in Action Anthropology.

CHAPTER 6

BEYOND COLLABORATION: ACTION ANTHROPOLOGY *AS* DECOLONIZATION

Joshua Smith

Sol Tax's political philosophy of cultural persistence and methodology of Action Anthropology is adamantly grounded in his efforts, beginning in the mid-1940s (Tax 1946), to catalyze a shift in anthropology that begins with the problem of colonialism. More importantly, this shift hinged on listening to the ways in which indigenous Nations expressed how the problem of colonialism is experienced and what might be done about it from their point of view. In this sense, Action Anthropology, when understood in the political context of American colonialism, is clearly an early method of decolonized research. It is not merely a foreshadowing of contemporary trends toward what is generally understood to be collaborative research methods, but moves beyond the principles of equality and partnership of collaboration in order to take a more relational and overt stand against, for example, the policies of assimilation as a means to counter the predominant streams of applied anthropological research as it was mobilized on behalf of Native Americans without their input, consent, or, more importantly, their direction, in effect, to further the colonial agenda of assimilation; an aspect of American governmentality that Tax deemed fundamentally undemocratic.

This chapter strives to demonstrate three intersecting points. First, Tax's method of Action Anthropology is aligned with a practice of decolonization. Second, this political alignment distinguishes Action Anthropology from collaborative research. Finally, Action Anthropology holds currency in the context of contemporary Canadian research (where I live and work).

Tax sought to engage in decolonization prior to the discourse(s) of colonialism/post-colonialism that exist today. This is evident in much of his writing, especially in *The Freedom To Make Mistakes* (Tax 1956b), whereby Tax outlines political relations using the discourse of his own time to define a political relationship that is, in a word, colonial. His insistence on listening to how indigenous peoples variously articulated their own positions and understandings of this relationship and making this the basis for a dialogue towards engaging in a practice of decolonization. The word decolonization captures the practical goals of an Action Anthropology method. It is apt given the aims of Action Anthropology projects to contest the myth of assimilation (and their racist assumptions) and helps to understand its immanent relevance to contemporary colonial relations, such as my own in Canada today (see for example, McNeil 2001 and Foster et al. 2007).

Second, in using the word decolonization and ascribing it to Action Anthropology it is vital to explain that the use of this word is both intentional and broad. In asserting that Action Anthropology sustains potential to "decolonize" I am merely pointing to ways our colonial attitudes must be challenged and, ultimately, abandoned. Margaret Kovach argues that:

> the approach to Indigenous epistemology (either in research or pedagogy) is a form of "Indianism" that—as David Newhouse, Don McCaskill, and John Milloy observe—involves an anthropological explication of Indigenous perspectives without the incorporation of Indigenous voices and ideas. This is slowly starting to shift because of a role displacement among non-Indigenous scholars that coincides with an increasing responsibility to be accountable to and conversant with Indigenous knowledges in an anticolonial manner. Non-Indigenous scholars have responded to the uncertainty of living in new territory in a variety of ways, including frustrated backlash or despondency, respectful disengagement, or significant outreach to Indigenous scholars. Non-Indigenous scholars can, however, come to understand Indigenous knowledges and tribal epistemologies by forming community relationships with Aboriginal communities outside the academy. These relationships will demand a more organic, non-institutional approach to knowledge-seeking. If Indigenous knowledges are to flourish, there must be room for story, purpose, place, holism, and protocol, for the ceremonial, relational and spiritual aspects of life, all of which demand a natural, non-institutional learning environment (Kovach 2009:58).

Kovach eloquently describes, in contemporary terms, the scope of what Tax practiced in Action Anthropology, at least, in terms of mobilizing research methods in "an anti-colonial manner" (see especially Tax 1968). Thus, Action Anthropology emerged as a means to move anthropological research to be more relevant in keeping with enormous challenges shaped by the power and politics of colonialism in North America; this differentiates it from, for example, collaborative research.

By collaboration, I only refer to the vast range of methodologies and engaged research that have emerged in the past few decades premised on the notion of partnership. As Luke Lassiter has noted in his editor's introduction to the inaugural issue of *Collaborative Anthropologies:*

> Collaboration—the wide range of theories and practices that relate to the dynamic and processes of navigating joint projects and partnerships—has always been a vital, albeit often implicit, facet of what we do as anthropologists… [and] our still-emergent practices continue to offer formidable challenges to the conventional power differentials between "researchers" and "subjects," and thus are becoming increasingly central to reconceptualizing conventional anthropological theory (Lassiter 2008:vii–viii).

While there is no clear or widely accepted definition of collaborative research, it is a broad category and only understood in general terms and applied in diverse ways. Collaboration, then, might contain the potential for a decolonization in specific Action Anthropology, but the point is that it is not necessarily aligned with decolonization, in the same relational that Kovach articulates or Tax put into practice.

As a historicized subject within the discipline of anthropology, Tax's work in anthropology is grossly misunderstood, *de*-politicized and, to a large extent, ignored. This is ironic, given the enormous growth and interest in various engaged research methods across the sciences, social sciences and humanities today. These are most commonly referred to as community-based-participatory-research (Green 1997; Stringer 1997; Russell and Harshbarger 2002; Stoecker 2002; Ibanez-Carrasco 2004; Brosius et al. 2005; McIntyre 2007; Lutz and Neis 2008; Wilmsen et al. 2008), collaborative-research methods (Harrison 2001; Lassiter 2005, 2008, 2010; Jones and Jenkins 2008), action research (Stringer 1997, 1999; Reason 2007), and decolonized research (Smith 1999; Battiste 2008; Jones and Jenkins 2008; Smith, Denzin et al. 2008).

It is important to point out that Action Anthropology is a theoretical and methodological form of a politically engaged science that is explicitly distinct from other forms of engaged or applied anthropologies (Smith 2010). Contrary to most of the literature within anthropology, Action Anthropology is neither atheoretical social work, nor is it merely characterized by the singular legacy of "The Fox Project" (1948–1959) (Daubenmier 2008; Smith 2010). Action Anthropology is a method driven by Tax's theoretical model of cultural persistence based on his ethnographic fieldwork with both the Meskwaki, near Tama Iowa, and, extensively, with indigenous communities in Guatemala. Problems of social organization (Tax 1935), acculturation (Tax 1942, 1946, 1949, 1951, 1953, 1956a, 1957, 1966, 1975b, 1978), colonialism and imperialism (Tax 1945a, 1951, 1956a, 1956b, 1962, 1968), and democracy and government administration (Tax 1945a, 1945b, 1956b) are all catalysts of Action Anthropology. Through these lenses emerge the two principles of Action Anthropology evident throughout Tax's work: non-assimilation and self-government (Tax 1952, 1962; Polgar 1979; Stanley 1996; Lurie 1999; Smith 2010). These two principles, together with the theory of cultural persistence, mobilized the method of Action Anthropology (Smith 2010), mainly as a catalyst in shifting the discipline toward a praxis of what, in today's vernacular, might be called decolonized research methods.

Several of the projects might be cited as prime examples of Action Anthropology. The Fox Project (1948–1959) emerged out of the University of Chicago field school established by Sol Tax and engaged the Meskwaki in several early Action Anthropology initiatives (Tax 1958; Daubenmier 2008). A 1954 map titled *The North American Indians: 1950 Distribution of Descendants of the Aboriginal Population of Alaska, Canada and the United States* was intended to challenge the U.S. governments own census that tried to assert the myth of assimilation (Levine and Lurie 1968). Beginning in 1957, the Workshop on American Indian Affairs began as a means to educate and train a new generation of Indian leaders (Cobb 2008). In 1961, the American Indian Chicago Conference (AICC) brought together hundreds of American Indians (and delegations of First Nations from Canada) in order to direct U.S. Indian Policy (Hauptman and Campisi 1988; Lurie 1999; Cobb 2008). The Carnegie Cross-Cultural Education Project with the Cherokee supported by the Carnegie Corporation of New York (1963–1967) sought to cross-culturally engage the harms of assimilation through education and advocacy in Oklahoma (Tax and Thomas 1969; Cobb 2007; Wahrhaftig, Chapter 2 in this volume). In 1962, Tax's official role on President Johnson's 'Secret Task Force for Indian Affairs' turned into an activist role as he and Vine Deloria Jr. subversively brought Indian perspectives to bear on the outcome of the Task Force's administrative power (Task Force on Indian Affairs 1962; Cobb 2008).

More importantly, through these projects, Tax and the people he worked with challenged anthropology to *listen* to people and work within a relational framework in an effort to seek solutions to political problems long before the emergence of more recent engaged research methods such as collaborative anthropology. Albert Wahrhaftig, Tax's student-colleague, articulates how Tax reunited anthropology with political philosophy, thus bringing anthropology to the relevance of contemporary relational problems such as colonialism:

> Tax arrived at the heart of the question of persistence. His argument brought Anthropology to a problem which has long occupied political scientists and intellectuals at large: how to comprehend the core of meanings that unites a people and determines its participation in larger political entities (Wahrhaftig 1979:258).

In addition, Raymond Fogelson observes Tax's emphasis on "agency," which was a concept that was fundamental and central to Tax's theoretical and methodological innovations:

> Tax's insistence on listening to Indigenous Peoples' views of their own situation, helping them to articulate their problems, and assisting them in seeking redress for their grievances approach that came to be known as action anthropology whose implications clearly foreshadowed certain contemporary theoretical concerns over agency (Fogelson 1998:107).

Yet, Tax's strides in anthropological innovation went beyond mere breakthroughs and achievements for their own sake. At a 1951 symposium on economic progress, Tax denounced scientific paternalism, imperialism and the compromises of the research in policy or administrative work; namely, the post-war field of applied anthropology. Astutely, he noted how it "assumes that our own values are or ought to be universal and that the practices of other peoples should be changed accordingly. This general view once accompanied the little brown brother variety of imperialism which has so dramatically defeated itself" (Tax 1951:325). This represents a profound critique of the post-war brand of applied anthropology that was used to further colonial and imperial agendas. Tax's statement on this early brand of applied anthropology is clearly a dire warning to those who comply with the business of modernization and progress:

> I am afraid that we shall blunder into other societies and misbehave blissfully on the assumption that our ways must also be their ways, that these undeveloped people must want what is good for them, and will

> surely be grateful to us for supplying it. And our first fatal assumption may well be that economic progress is an absolute good (Tax 1951:320).

Tax never wavered from his position to have never tired of arguing in favor of a praxis that begins, absolutely, with the indigenous position(s), "whatever it is," (Tax 1962:132). In 1971, he argued against the harm of drafting and implementing policies premised on non-indigenous political concepts as opposed to the alternative of actually *listening* to what indigenous peoples and nations were advocating on their own terms:

> It is understandable that when well-meaning non-Indians propose remedies for poverty and disease based on policies supporting individual freedom, equality, and autonomy, they are surprised and disappointed at the reaction of the Indians they hope to benefit. ... Tribal people are hurt more than helped by policies based on values so deceptively similar, if only because they alienate their well wishers. Moreover, they have long since tired of trying vainly to explain, much less defend, what is to them life itself (Tax 1972:xxiv).

In a concise statement regarding the importance of reflexively being aware of our (settlers) history and the methods we implement in our struggles for knowledge, Tax's student-colleagues Wahrhaftig and Thomas remark how "Americans are phenomenologists, more concerned with the things they have created than with the lengthy processes whereby these things have developed, more interested in ends than concerned with means" (Wahrhaftig and Thomas 1972:83). Additionally, Steve Polgar asserts that Action Anthropology's most important theoretical contribution has been in epistemology (Polgar 1979:412); especially, the knowledge that exposed and challenged the truth claims of American mythology.

Altogether, these few comments direct attention to the fundamental and primary distinction between action and collaboration. Action Anthropology begins with a critical awareness that colonialism is an ongoing problem in North America and is premised on facing the challenges of decolonization in North America based on what indigenous peoples themselves articulate. Yet, part of the problem that Tax identified, as Polgar noted above, were the truth claims of American mythology. Part of these claims, Tax noted, had to do predominantly with the mythology of assimilation and "the Little Brown Brother Variety of Imperialism"; a problem in perfect conflict with the democratic principles of free societies. Thus, Tax identified colonialism to be the underlying fabric of the relationship between the many indigenous nations and the United States. As a result, he endeavored to engage in a practice of decolonized research methods that emphasized a relational politics extending far beyond the politics of equality emphasized by collaboration.

In the very first sentences of Tax's seminal position piece, *The Freedom to Make Mistakes* (1956), he explicitly outlined the relationship as one that is colonial:

> This paper addressed a problem that arises when one person or group is in authority over another and has the power to decide what the other one should do *for his own good*. The main concern is with communities who are under some authority, like colonies under the rule of benevolent powers which remain in power to help the colonials prepare themselves for independence. I think especially of American Indian communities who are under the Indian Service, which behaves in a notoriously paternalistic way (Tax 1956:173).

An anti-colonial essay *The Freedom to Make Mistakes* points to the paternalistic logic of U.S. Indian administration, that is, the same logic rooted in the ludicrous mythology of assimilation, but actually tries to implement it. Tax elaborates on the colonial logic, which he exposes as a perfectly illogical, and ineffective way to foster relationships with peoples adept at governing themselves:

> … most administrators in these positions are members of our dominant culture who believe our culture is in fact superior to other cultures, and they assume that the people of the colony are all naturally anxious to become like us. In the United States, our whole policy with respect to the Indians is that they will adopt our ways, and lose their ways; that some of them have made more progress than others, who are more "backward." The fact is that many Indians are not anxious to become like us; they are comfortable in their own culture; and it doesn't help matters at all to call them "backward." The result is a kind of passive resistance and complete breakdown of communication and understanding. The administrator then imagines that the Indians no longer are "reasonable," so he feels justified in using force" (Tax 1956:174–175).

Thus, Tax exposes the U.S. government's absurd tautology that, left to their own powers of decision-making, indigenous peoples will make mistakes because they will not assimilate. In other words, the political agency of indigenous peoples does not fit with Indian policy, thus, whatever they decide will be a "mistake." Tax ends his exposition with a dire warning to the colonial machinations of the state bureaucracy: "And we are now in an era when, in many parts of the world, colonies which are not given the freedom to make their own mistakes, will take that freedom" (Tax 1956:177).

Sol Tax stands as one of the very few non-indigenous intellectuals of the 1950s to articulate the political relationship between Americans and indigenous peoples as one that is colonial. More importantly, his example is a rare instance of someone who reflexively located himself in the colonial relationship and sought to decolonize anthropology as well as his own society by focusing on the problems of governmentality beginning with an unraveling of two major aspects of American colonialism: the myths of assimilation and the fallacious superiority of Euro-American society that animates it.

This aspect of Action Anthropology illustrates a particularly important difference between Action Anthropology and the collaborative research methods of contemporary times. It is the ethico-political stance that Tax thought anthropologists ought to take up in relation to colonialism by 1) building better relationships with indigenous nations, *as* peoples as opposed to subjects (see Asch 2001); 2) making anthropology relevant to *their* problems, as they defined them, if it is desired at all; while 3) decolonizing the self through a practice of understanding the truth of our relationship as opposed to the myth of progress and civilization. This political stance, essential to Action Anthropology, is profoundly clear and distinct from the methods that emphasize a partnership grounded on principles of equality where each participant, partner, co-collaborator or stakeholder gets something out of the contract or "understanding" as opposed to a relationship that begins with the fact of colonialism itself and our (settlers) obligations to deal with it intelligently.

In this sense, Action Anthropology is explicitly premised on a notion akin to what one of Tax's students and participants in Action Anthropology, Michael Asch, has framed as "finding a place to stand" in regards to power and justice (Asch 2001) as well as the unhingeable correlate of decolonizing ones own self in the process. This is why Polgar emphasizes epistemology as the primary focus of Action Anthropology; an intimate knowledge of *how* we come to live on these lands; *what* our relationship is to the peoples on whose lands we now live; and, the stories we invent to console ourselves of our past and deny our contemporary roles in colonial domination (Asch 2002, 2011; Chamberlain 2003).

In Tax's own words:

> Great nations, surely empires, are built on the destruction of peoples and cultures. Those who survive often think this is natural and inevitable, and indeed the survival of the fittest, and so *are able to put aside the unjust and immoral behaviour of their forebears even as they enjoy their profits.* But the peoples and cultures "left for dead" on the wayside have not died; the descendants of those "fittest" whose guilt seemed safely buried with the ashes find that the ashes are embers which burst into flames because the moral values in the culture have never changed. The fittest of earlier days were only at the time the strongest; and our culture never has accepted that might makes right. So *there is no denying the evidence of past wrongs* when the victims rise to show themselves. … Indeed, looking backward, they [*who are we*] seem so to have reveled in guilt as to be driven to collect more and more … The march of industrial and urban "progress" and the need for money rendered untenable the rural life of the hills, the deserts, the plains; the villages and towns; and Indian reservations. Peoples were "flushed out" of their ancestral homes and brought to light, to be seen and heard by the children of those who had taken their better lands and their autonomy … Had they followed the "inevitable" path to disappearance (which Europeans convinced themselves was prescribed by history and justified their occupation of the continent), this story would still have been worth the poignant reading. But we must read it not only because the Indians are still here and growing in numbers and in identification with their tribal forebears, but also because *it is we – 200 million non-Indian Americans in the 1970s – who are behaving still as our forebears did, still taking from them the driblets of land they have left, and living by the same rationalizations* (Tax 1972:xxi–xxii; emphases mine).

This excerpt exemplifies the urgent relevancy of Action Anthropology and provides an insightful critique of the current state of anthropology in general. Written as a foreword to a book entitled *This Country was Ours: A Documentary History of the American Indian* (Vogel 1972), with the "Ours" signifying indigenous peoples. Tax places the responsibility of this history on the shoulders of those of us who continue to *believe* that this land *was* theirs (indigenous peoples) as opposed to the unsettling fact that indigenous peoples are persisting, not only in numbers, but in politically salient ways that remind us, not only of our history, but of our present colonial relationship. Tax implies that the title of the book is erroneous and implicitly reminds the reader that it ought to read: "This land *is* Ours!" Moreover, he asserts: "So much for the hangup of at least the leadership of 200 million non-Indian Americans; and one important effect of this book could be its end. Suppose we now recognize *our* [i.e., settler] irrational block and determine not to let it interfere any longer with intelligent policy—what else would be involved?" (Tax 1972:xxiii; emphasis mine).

What else would be involved? This is the question Tax has left to us to answer. The political philosophy of Action Anthropology sustains immense relevance and stands apart from the general political philosophy of collaboration that does not take colonialism as a meaningful, instrumental fact of our present existence. Yet, there remains a peculiar amnesia in the historiography and popular disciplinary narratives that seek to outline the divergent histories of engaged research methods. Methods in collaborative anthropology are increasingly described as "new" and "innovative" responses to the political problems of the specific communities. However, Action Anthropology is seldom invoked in any of these text-book narratives or associated with contemporary engaged research methods. Most significantly, there is rarely present any self-awareness of being caught up in colonial relations and making this the basis of engaged research.

In their widely used text on fieldwork, for example, Robben and Sluka delimit what they refer to as the "emergence of postmodern perspectives and increasing debate and eclecticism in cultural anthropology" as taking place in the 1970s and 1980s, which is characterized by "a heightened awareness of the relationship between and the construction of knowledge"; "a new concern with reflexivity"; and "new forms of fieldwork relations and ethnographic writing" (Robben and Sluka 2007). Moreover, by identifying the reasons for these changes as "…the theoretical critique of 'neutrality,'" 'objectivity,' 'truth,' and 'reality' in empiricism, and the political critique of the discipline's historical relationship with Western imperialism and colonialism" their revision of the history of fieldwork methods, like others, fails to acknowledge Action Anthropology's political scope in proper context, thus perpetuating and reifying two widely accepted fallacies that persist in the standard historical narrative of anthropology: that anthropology did not engage colonialism before the 1970s and that colonialism does not apply to North America (Asch 2002 and Pinkoski 2008).

Robben and Sluka *do* mention Action Anthropology, but only in an effort to *wrongly* emphasize how the "compassionate turn" is much more politically insightful and empathetic than Action Anthropology. They argue how "[t]his approach carries a political responsibility, which is *not* a return to the Action Anthropology of the 1970s, and only rarely engaged directly in the field" (Robben and Sluka 2007:24; emphasis mine). In their description of collaboration and partnership, they emphasize the key aspects that comprise the methods of collaboration as inclusion, reciprocal learning, and respect for the community. Definitively, they state that "[i]n collaborative research, the participants attempt to work together as equals, and this teamwork includes every aspect of the project—planning, implementation, problem solving, and evaluation" (Robben and Sluka 2007:21–22). With a clear emphasis on "equality," collaboration does not usually succeed in challenging the colonial systemics of the settler state, where, in the context of Canada, for example, indigenous peoples are not equal entities with the Canadian state, but are legally considered to be under the jurisdiction of Canada and do not possess, what Tax referred to as "the freedom to make mistakes." Instead, we continue to treat whole nations as wards of the state who are "protected" from making the "mistake" of turning away from the absurd assimilationist stories we continue to rely upon, such as the notions of "Terra Nullius" or empty land (Asch 2002), "Universal History" (Asch 2011) and "Historical Civilizationalism" (Murphy 2009).

In conclusion, it is vital to point out and underscore the relational dimension to Tax's understanding of colonialism and the means to decolonization that he fused into the spirit of Action Anthropology. Acknowledging the facts of settler colonialism and locating ourselves (settlers) within it infuses us with the power to wholeheartedly enter into relationships with indigenous peoples, if they will welcome us, still. Tax did not maintain the position that settler, or Western cultures, were incommensurable. Indeed, Action Anthropology would be a futile exercise if this were the case. Nor did Tax accept that any single polity was inferior to another due to the "guilt" or "crime" of colonialism. On the contrary, he sincerely promoted the idea that settlers and indigenous peoples could co-exist, but settlers are required to accept responsibility for their actions and enter into non-colonial relations with their host nations.

Asch has further explored this relational question in his groundbreaking works on aboriginal rights and treaty relations in the Canadian context (Asch 1997, 2001, 2007a, 2007b, 2011). Instead, I only allude to the need for us, in Canada, to begin to understand what the relationships are *where each of us lives*, as Tax advocated in the 1950s in the U.S. context, and now Asch continues to argue, and here I especially heed these words: "It is a truth that calls upon us to fully accept that, when it comes to what is fundamental to a people, we may not deny to others what we would never agree that others should deny us. And what could be more fundamental than knowing that the care of your heritage is in your hands?" (Asch 2009:408).

Moreover, *The Free Knowledge Project* of Victoria, B.C., continues to provide community engagement in the form of free educational models that are premised on the principles of Action Anthropology, but are designed and implemented to be relevant to the local context of Victoria, B.C., and the challenges of decolonization in the Coast Salish Territories. Bringing together indigenous and settler communities, Executive Director Marc Pinkoski elaborates on both the relational pedagogy and goals of decolonization that the project, like Action Anthropology, keeps at the core:

> At a minimum, reconciliation and decolonization will require new approaches to conveying information to Indigenous and non-Indigenous communities. In order to foster these new methods, a small group of us has formed the Free Knowledge Project with an eye to offering existing courses and developing and delivering teaching materials about the Canadian state, including representations of Indigenous peoples, law, policy, research and options. It is important to note that the materials are intended to inform Indigenous and non-Indigenous audiences about the actions and attitudes of the Canadian state and its approaches to the issues being raised, not to offer information about Indigenous peoples per se (Pinkoski, http://freeknowledgeproject.wordpress.com/about/, accessed January 9, 2012).

This is one space where Action Anthropology has continued to carry forward the political thought of Tax and engage the public in self-education and decolonization.

In sum, there is a great need for anthropology to reclaim much that has been dismissed and written out of our historiography, beginning with Sol Tax who brought relevance to anthropology in addressing the most urgent and pressing challenge of both his and our times—the challenge of decolonization.

References Cited

Asch, Michael

1997 *Aboriginal and Treaty Rights in Canada: Essays on Law, Equality and Respect for Difference.* University of British Columbia Press, Vancouver.

2001 Indigenous Self-Determination and Applied Anthropology in Canada: Finding a Place to Stand. *Anthropologica,* 43(2):201–207.

2002 From Terra Nullius to Affirmation: Reconciling Aboriginal Rights with the Canadian Constitution. *Canadian Journal of Law and Society*, 17(2):23–39.

2007a Calder and the Representation of Indigenous Society in Canadian Jurisprudence. In *Let Right be Done: Calder, Aboriginal Title, and the Future of Indigenous Rights* Foster, edited by H. Foster, H. Raven, and J. Webber, pp. 101–110. University of British Columbia Press, Vancouver.

2007b Governmentality, State Culture, and Indigenous Rights. *Anthropologica*, 49(2):281–284.

2009 Concluding Thoughts and Fundamental Questions. In *Protection of First Nations Cultural Heritage: Laws Policy, and Reform*, edited by Catherine Bell & Robert K. Patterson, pp. 394–411. University of British Columbia Press, Vancouver.

2011 Canadian Sovereignty and Universal History. In *Storied Communities: Narratives of Contact and Arrival in Constituting Political Community*, edited by Hester Lessard, Rebecca Johnson, and Jeremy Webber, pp. 29–39. University of British Columbia Press, Vancouver.

Battiste, Marie

2008 Research Ethics for Protecting Indigenous Knowledge and Heritage: Institutional and Researcher Responsibilities. In *Handbook of Critical Indigenous Methodology*, edited by N. Denzin, Y. Lincoln and L. T. Smith, pp. 497–510. Sage Publications, Thousand Oaks, California.

Brosius, J. Peter, Anna L. Tsing, and Charles Zerner

2005 *Communities and Conservation: Histories and Politics of Community-Based Natural Resource Management.* AltaMira Press, Walnut Creek, California.

Chamberlain, Edward J.

2003 *If This Is Your Land, Where Are Your Stories? Finding Common Ground.* A.A. Knopf Canada, Toronto.

Cobb, Daniel

2007 Devils in Disguise: The Carnegie Project, the Cherokee Nation, and the 1960s. *The Indian Quarterly*, 3(3):465–490.

2008 *Native Activism in Cold War America: The Struggle for Sovereignty.* University Press of Kansas, Lawrence.

Cobb, Daniel and Loretta Fowler

2007 *Beyond Red Power: American Indian Politics and Activism Since 1900.* School for Advanced Research Press, Santa Fe, New Mexico.

Darnell, Regna

2001 Invisible Genealogies: A History of Americanist Anthropology. University of Nebraska Press, Lincoln.

Darnell, Regna and Frederic Gleach

2005 Editor's Introduction. In *Histories of Anthropology*, V(1):vii–x.

Daubenmier, Judith M.

2008 *The Meskwaki and Anthropologists.* University of Nebraska Press, Lincoln.

De Certeau, Michel

1988 *The Writing of History.* Columbia University Press, New York.

Denzin, Norman, Yvonna Lincoln and Linda T. Smith.

2008 *Handbook of Critical Indigenous Methodology.* Sage, Thousand Oaks, California.

Fogelson, Raymond D.

1998 Bringing Home the Fire: Bob Thomas and Cherokee Studies. In *A Good Cherokee, A Good Anthropologist: Papers in Honor of Robert K. Thomas*, edited by Steve Pavlik, pp. 105–118. Contemporary American Indian Series, 8. American Indian Studies Center, University of California, Los Angeles.

Foster, Hamar, Heather Raven, and Jeremy Webber

2007 *Let Right Be Done: Aboriginal Title, the Calder Case, and the Future of Indigenous Rights.* University of British Columbia Press, Vancouver.

Green, L.W.

1997 Background on Participatory Research. In *Doing Community-Based Research: A Reader*, edited by D. Murphy, M. Scammell, and R. Sclove, pp. 53–66. The Loka Institute, Amherst/The Community Partnership Center, Knoxville, Tennessee.

Harrison, Barbara

2001 *Collaborative Programs in Indigenous Communities, From Fieldwork to Practice.* AltaMira Press, Walnut Creek, California.

Hauptman, M. Laurence and Jack Campisi

1988 The Voice of Easter Indians: The American Indian Chicago Conference of 1961 and the Movement for Federal Recognition. *Proceedings of the American Philosophical Society*, 132(4):316–329.

Ibánez-Carrasco, Francisco

2004 Desire and Betrayal in Community-Based Research. In *Public Acts: Disruptive Readings on Making Curriculum Public*, edited by Francisco Ibánez-Carrasco, Erica Meiners, Suzanne de Castell, pp. 211–236. Taylor & Francis Group, London, England.

Jones, Alison with Kuni Jenkins

2008 Rethinking Collaboration: Working the Indigene-Colonizer Hyphen. In *Handbook of Critical Indigenous Methodology*, edited by N. Denzin, Y. Lincoln and L.T. Smith, pp. 471–486. Sage Publications, Thousand Oaks, California.

Kovach, Margaret

2009 Being Indigenous in the Academy: Creating Space for Indigenous Scholars. In *First Nations First Thoughts: The Impact of Indigenous Thought in Canada.* Edited by Annis May Tisman, pp. 51–78. University of British Columbia Press, Vancouver.

Lassiter, Luke Eric

2005 *The Chicago Guide to Collaborative Ethnography.* University of Chicago Press, Chicago, Illinois.

2008 Moving Past Public Anthropology and Doing Collaborative Research. National Association of Practicing Anthropologists. *Bulletin*, 29:70–86.

2010 [2008] *Collaborative Anthropologies*, volumes 1–2 (editor) and volume 3 (co-editor with Samuel R. Cook). University of Nebraska Press, Lincoln.

Levin, Stuart, and Nancy O. Lurie, editors

1968 *The American Indian Today.* Convention Press, Jacksonville, Florida.

Lurie, Nancy Oestreich

1999 Sol and Tax and Tribal Sovereignty. *Human Organization*, 58(1):108–117.

Lutz, John S. and Barbara Neis (eds.)
2008 *Making and Moving Knowledge: Interdisciplinary and Community-based Research in a World on the Edge.* McGill-Queens University Press, Montreal.

McIntyre, Alice
2007 *Participatory Action Research.* Sage Publications, Thousand Oaks, California.

McNeil, Kent
2001 Emerging Justice? Essays on Indigenous Rights in Canada and Australia. University of Saskatchewan, Native Law Centre, Saskatoon.

Murphy, Michael
2009 Civilization, Self-Determination, and Reconciliation. In *First Nations, First Thoughts: The Impact of Indigenous Thought in Canada*, edited by Annis May Timpson, pp. 251–278. University of British Columbia Press, Vancouver.

Pinkoski, Marc
2008 Julian Steward, American Anthropology, and Colonialism. *Histories of Anthropology Annual*, 4:172–204.

Polgar, Steve
1979 Applied, Action, Radical, and Committed Anthropology. In *Current Anthropology: Essays in Honor of Sol Tax*, edited by Robert Hinshaw, pp. 409–418. Mouton Publishers, New York.

Reason, Peter, and Kate Louise McArdle
2007 Brief Notes on the Theory and Practice of Action Research. In *Understanding Research Methods for Social Policy and Practice*, edited by Saul Becker and Alan Bryman. The Polity Press, Bristol.

Robben, Antonius C.G.M. and Jeffrey A. Sluka
2007 Fieldwork in Cultural Anthropology: An Introduction. In *Ethnographic Fieldwork: An Anthropological Reader*. Blackwell Publishing, Malden, Massachusetts.

Russell, Diane and Camilla Harshbarger
2002 *Groundwork for Community-Based Conservation: Strategies for Social Research.* Rowman & Littlefield, Walnut Creek, California.

Smith, Joshua
2010 The Political Thought of Sol Tax: The Principles of Non-Assimilation and Self-Government in Action Anthropology. In *Histories of Anthropology Annual*, 6:129–170. University of Nebraska Press, Lincoln.

Smith, Linda Tuhiwai
1999 *Decolonizing Methodologies: Research and Indigenous Peoples.* Zed Books, London.

Stanley, Sam
1996 Community, Action, and Continuity: A Narrative Vita of Sol Tax. *Current Anthropology: Supplemental Issue: Anthropology in Public*, 37(1):S131–S137.

Stoecker, Randy
2006 *Research Methods for Community Change: A Project-Based Approach.* Sage Publications, Thousand Oaks, California.

Stringer, Ernest T.
1997 *Community-Based Ethnography: Breaking Traditional Boundaries of Research, Teaching, and Learning.* Lawrence Erlbaum Associates, Mahwah, New Jersey.
1999 *Action Research,* second edition. Sage Publications, Thousand Oaks, California.

Task Force on Indian Affairs
1962 Implementing Change Through Government. *Human Organization,* 21(2):125–136.

Tax, Sol
1935 Primitive Social Organization with Some Description of the Social Organization of the Fox Indians. PhD dissertation, University of Chicago. University Microfilms International, Ann Arbor, Michigan.
1942 Ethnic Relations in Guatemala. *America Indigena,* 2(4):43–47.
1945a Anthropology and Administration. *America Indigena,* 4(1):23–24.
1945b The Problem of Democracy in Middle America. *American Sociological Review,* 10(2):192–199.
1946 The Education of Underprivileged Peoples in Dependent and Independent Territories. *The Journal of Negro Education: The Problem of Education in Dependent Territories,* 15(3):336–345.
1949 Folk Tales in Chichicastenango: An Unsolved Puzzle. *The Journal of American Folklore,* 62(244):125–135.
1951 Selective Culture Change. *The American Economic Review: Papers and Proceedings of the Sixty-third Annual Meeting of the American Economic Association,* 41(2):315–320.
1952 Action Anthropology. *America Indigena,* 12(2):103–109.
1953 *Penny Capitalism: A Guatemalan Indian Economy.* Institute of Social Anthropology, Publication No. 6. Smithsonian Institution Press, Washington, D.C.
1956a Acculturation. In *Men and Cultures: Selected Papers of the Fifth International Congress of Anthropological and Ethnological Sciences,* edited by Anthony F. C. Wallace, pp. 192–196. University of Pennsylvania Press, Philadelphia.
1956b The Freedom to Make Mistakes. *America Indigena,* 16(3):171–177.
1957 Changing Consumption in Indian Guatemala. *Economic Development and Cultural Change,* 5(2):147–158.
1958 The Fox Project. *Human Organization,* 17(1):17–19.
1960 *Issues in Evolution.* The University of Chicago Press, Chicago, Illinois.
1962 Task Force on Indian Affairs: Implementing Change through Government. *Human Organization,* 21(2):125–136.
1966 The Importance of Preserving Indian Culture. *America Indigena,* 26(1):81–86.
1968 Last on the Warpath: A Personalized Account of How an Anthropologist Learned from American Indians. University of Chicago Smithsonian Institution's Center for the Study of Man, Folder 2, Box 273, Series 8, Sol Tax Papers, Special Collections Research Center, Joseph Regenstein Library, University of Chicago, Chicago, Illinois.
1972 Foreword. In *This Land Was Ours.* Virgil J. Vogel, pp. xxi–xxv. Harper and Row, New York.
1975b The Bow and the Hoe: Reflections on Hunters, Villagers, and Anthropologists. *Current Anthropology,* 16(4):507–513.
1978 The Impact of Urbanization on American Indians. *Annals of the American Academy of Political and Social Science,* 436(1):121–136.

Tax, Sol, and Robert K. Thomas
1969 Linguistic-Cultural Differences and American Education. *Florida Reporter,* 7(1):15–19.

Wahrhaftig, Albert L.
1979 We Who Act Right: The Persistent Identity of Cherokee Indians. *In Currents in Anthropology*, edited by Robert Hinshaw, pp. 255–269. Mouton Publishers, New York.

Wahrhaftig, Albert, and Robert Thomas
1972 Renaissance and Repression: The Oklahoma Cherokee. In *Native America Today: Sociological Perspectives*, edited by Howard M. Bahr, Bruce Chadwick, and Robert Day, pp. 80–89. Harper and Row, New York.

Wilmsen, Carl, William Elmendorf, Larry Fisher, and Jacquelyn Ross, editors
2008 Partnerships for Empowerment: Participatory Research for Community-based Natural Resource Management. Earthscan Publications, London.

COMMENTARY FOLLOWING JOSHUA SMITH'S PRESENTATION

Harvey Choldin, Albert L. Wahrhaftig, Kevin Preister,
Sandy Lane, Tim Wallace, Douglas E. Foley, Robert A. Rubinstein

Harvey Choldin: I am Sol's son-in-law. I think Sol would be uncomfortable if somebody told him that he had a coherent political project, because he sort of took things as they came down the pike. He was flexible and responsive. So that term, political project, does not sit right for me from my knowledge of Sol. But I think you are perfectly right that among his principles, self-government and non-assimilation—those are his. You are exactly right there.

Also, I don't know where to put these thoughts, but I would add a couple of things that I understand about Sol's way of thinking. One central principle was that the end never justifies the means. He would come back to that idea over and over again. And another one that he rarely stated was that big national federal projects and probably big corporations—you have to be suspicious of those; the small is preferable to the big.

Albert L. Wahrhaftig: I wanted to bring up something Joshua Smith wrote on December 11, 2010, in the pre-meeting material that was distributed to us.

> One of my personal theories is that Robert Thomas was a huge influence on Tax. Now, I haven't spoken to anyone who was there or who knew any of these people intimately except for Michael Asch, who was an undergraduate student and dedicates much to Tax. I think when Thomas and Tax got together, things really picked up in pace. And when I read what people say about Thomas's and Tax's work, you can easily see how a personality like Tax's might be emboldened by such a personality as Thomas's—thick as thieves. It's a theory.

Yes, I wonder about that. I failed to make a point in my presentation that I certainly wanted to make. Toward the end I said that the tribal attorney who was determined to banish the Carnegie Project from Indian Country turned out to be right in charging that we were subversive. We didn't intend to be subversive. We didn't think we were subversive at the time. But as it turned out, we certainly were subversive. We ended up as dedicated anthropologists looking on in amazement as a social movement took place and ignited new activities in dormant Cherokee communities. The question that is still in my mind is whether Bob Thomas and Sol Tax knew that would be the outcome all along. The proposal to Carnegie was for a formal research project. We stuck to what was proposed, we had a hypothesis, we tested it, we collected data, and so on. Sorry, Joshua. I don't have a better answer for you.

The other thing I want to say briefly: Yes, we did touch off a social movement, however unintentionally, but then it kind of died down and seemed to disappear. I will just take a moment to bring you up to date. Back then, if I had walked into the Cherokee tribal office, they would have just started burning the papers. We were clearly persona non grata, designated the enemy, and in retrospect I think the BIA/tribal government were pretty scared of us. Then, the Principal Chief of the Cherokees was a federal appointee. But in large part as a result of the dissemination of our research and because of new activism in traditional Cherokee communities, the appointed chief and his handpicked government were forced to hold tribal elections and to confront the rapidly changing conditions of America in the 1960s, especially President Johnson's War on Poverty and its community development programs. I think the locally powerful began to realize that you can get your hands on a lot of money if you have Indians in your backyard. Doing things for Indians became big business, and a huge tribal complex and bureaucracy emerged and became the core of a virtual empire that now controls the economy and politics of eastern Oklahoma.

After the Carnegie Project—I never returned to Cherokee Country until 2002—individuals in the Cherokee Nation (as the tribal governmental complex is now called) invited me to visit them. They wanted to see the guy who had written all that stuff 25 years previously, stuff they still considered the best description of Cherokee community life. I walked into an awesomely large multi-building complex with a complex array of programs and industries that covered 14 Oklahoma counties. In short order, however, I discovered that deep inside the Cherokee Nation's bureaucracy there was a cell of very traditional "fullbloods,"—my hosts. Apparently they are tolerated so that they can be shown off when anyone claims that the tribal government ignores the interests of its traditionalists. In these guys, buried in the core of the tribal complex and activity, in contact with local communities, the "new" Cherokee government preserves the seeds from which traditional governance grows. As in the point that I made earlier when I talked about Alex Smith, look deep into the appearance of Cherokee assimilation and you will find a core of people who still place their faith in reconstructing Cherokee life from its foundations in local communities.

Question: What Is the Source of the Action?

Kevin Preister: I have been practicing anthropology for thirty years and even though I have read Tax's writings I still don't quite know what it is or what actually was done on the ground, so I would like elucidation if you can offer it. I am interested in what is the source of the action? Is it the anthropologist or is it the citizen? That is an important distinction for me. Just a little vignette about working with native Hawaiians. The role of the activist is a valued social role in some contexts. When developers and other people impacting the populations are not communicating and really working things out, then it seems that the Kapunas and others give reign to the activists, especially the more militant versions, to espouse their rhetoric in a public setting to get the attention that people want. But the role itself is challenged internally, because it is not aloha, it is not seen as a cultural role. And so I am torn, I would like some clarification about what Action Anthropology is and how you would distinguish it from the activist. In my mind they are a little different, and I want to make sure I understand the Taxian perspective if there is one.

Response A—Robert A. Rubinstein: It is a great question. Of course I was not any part of the original Fox Project, but it strikes me in reading and talking to Sol, that on the question of what is the source of the action, the point of the action is the conversation. It comes relationally from interaction with the community. It is the story of how he shifts from saying no you are a scientist, you have to do science, to respond to Lisa Peattie's letter [1960], about can we do something to help? This opens up the relational question: How do we respond? What do we respond with? What are the values involved. There is not a directional source, there is a dialogic source. As I understand it. I could be totally wrong.

Response B—Sandy Lane: I can answer it specifically for the work we have done in Syracuse for the past decade. We have worked explicitly with activists, but the knowledge that we produce—thinking of Bruno Latour's notion of engaged scholarship being the production of knowledge—the knowledge that we produce on behalf of and at the request of community groups. We try to make our best effort. It is not guided specifically by activism, it is guided by what are the best methods to get at the truest picture of reality, knowing that this is an impossible goal and we have been bludgeoned with that thought for the last decade. The types of things we choose to look at often are from the community, but we try to look at them as much in an unbiased way as possible. And we give our information to any group that needs it. In terms of our community—which is often elected officials, and they may not be the officials I particularly like or have voted for—if they need that information we give it to them.

Response C—Tim Wallace: I have been doing a field school in Guatemala for a number of years. I have been teaching applied anthropology courses for a long time and working in Hungary and Costa Rica and now Guatemala. I always felt like there was something I had to do and there was an expectation on me as applied anthropologist to do something—that I had to do something. That the emphasis was on me—me, me, me. So when I read Sol Tax's work in Action Anthropology, I felt, as Darby said before, Oh, what a relief. It is not up to me to make changes. It is for me to help facilitate in ways that I can. This is something I try to convey to my own students, whether in the field or in the university, that you have to understand what the people you are working with want. You don't want to put yourself in the sense of being the leader as to what they have to do, but there is also an opportunity to be kind of a guardian, in the sense that you may know the other world better than this particular community. For example, in Peru and others, what are some of the consequences of certain groups that might come in? So you can also intercede in a way, say hey, this is what is going on. Maybe your interaction is primarily with the outside group. You have to enter into a dialogue. Dialogue and communication are essential, and that is what the role of the Action Anthropologist is. It is such a relief to be in that role. It is not your responsibility. They can make mistakes just like you are going to make mistakes.

Response D—Douglas E. Foley: The only thing I really know about Tax is what I saw from the Fox Project. You ask how it is activist and different from today. I think you can make a very good case that they were political activists. The way they defended the tribal school and took on the local businessmen to not take over Tama Craft are good examples of their being political activists. I don't think they had any particular ideology other than wanting to collaborate with and form alliances with the Meskwaki. Some of the stuff they did was exactly like what activist anthropologists now try to do: collaborate with groups that have been beaten down by government bureaucrats or beaten down by corporations or exploited in various sorts of ways. And so I think that is the stuff that people in our activist anthropology program at the University of Texas really identify with in terms of what Tax was doing.

Then if you look closely at some of the other projects they did on the settlement, they were less like that. They were projects like the media project and the farming project; they were sort of cooked up and initiated by the Action Anthropologists. They got a few of the Meskwaki to say OK, this looks like an OK project, and then they went along. But once the anthropologist leaves, the project dies, like any applied anthropology project where the outsider produced it.

So my reading of it was that they were very activist in some things and in other things they looked more like the applied anthropologists of old because the project was created. It was their idea; it was initiated and it died because the Meskwaki really didn't think it was that strong. It was a felt need but not as strongly a felt need as the school and protecting their craft production and other sorts of things. Tax definitely was not an ideologist. I think he was a real strong liberal, for social justice. And he kind of did wing it, played it by ear. Sometimes they were real activist and sometimes they were not quite as activist.

I see him as giving root to activist anthropology, which has been forgotten by contemporary activist anthropologists because he had more of an influence among applied anthropologists than he did among those who now identify themselves as activist anthropologists.

Response E—Albert L. Wahrhaftig: I think the various attempts to answer the question reveal that it depends on which part of the elephant you have your hand on. I think I touched a part that nobody else has. I think Action Anthropology, let's say as illustrated by the process that the American Indian Chicago Conference went through—sending all that information out to Indians, seeing what came back and incorporating it and sending it out again, coming back looking different, and so on and so forth—illustrates that Action Anthropology is inherently processual; and therefore as you interact with a community, you are interacting with a living entity. What you are involved in conjointly, with them producing and interpreting, has an emergent quality. So on the one hand this approach really predates the interest of anthropology in moving beyond static description and trying to account for processes that underlie cultural change, while on the other hand it accounts for what Joan commented on, that Robert Reitz and Bob Thomas never published anything. I think at least a partial reason for that is that when you begin thinking in terms of process, writing about behavior that is emergent and systemic is terrifically hard, especially when your audience hasn't learned to think that way. I think this accounts for the paucity of publication from people like Reitz and Thomas (both of whom, by the way, were masters when it came to talking).

Response F—Robert A. Rubinstein: Something Albert just said was actually quite important in my thinking. Sandy Lane and I, and our colleagues and students, have just done an article trying to describe the work we do in Syracuse (see Lane, et al., *Human Organization*, 85(1):224–254). One of the critiques that came back was how is this different from community-based, participatory health research. Part of the response that we have in the paper is exactly along the lines that we are not bounded by a semester: this is organic, processual, and emergent—though we do not use those words in our paper. That is a critical piece. Things grow organically from the dialogue and interaction with the community. That does separate Action Anthropology from other forms of applied work. And of course Sol always denied that Action Anthropology was applied work. So there you go.

CHAPTER 7

A HOMETOWN ETHNOGRAPHER'S VIEW OF THE FOX PROJECT

Douglas E. Foley

It is ironic that I had a small role in making this forum happen. When I contacted Darby Stapp he had been too busy to organize the session. With only a week to get on the program, he went into warp drive and created this very special gathering of folks connected to Sol Tax. I must confess, my reflections on Sol Tax's Fox Project are merely a byproduct of a larger study I was conducting. From 1989 through 1994, I returned to my hometown of Tama, Iowa, to write a book about race relations between whites and Meskwakis. I spent a winter semester and four summers doing fieldwork on the Meskwaki settlement. In addition, I read all of the Fox Project's fieldwork notes in the Smithsonian and some of Tax's papers in the University of Chicago library. I also collected the oral histories of several Meskwaki and had the good fortune of interviewing Sol Tax and Fred Gearing. Much of the material collected went into an ethnography entitled *The Heartland Chronicles* (Foley 1995). I went back a decade later in 2004, and did a follow-up study, and the third printing of *The Heartland Chronicles* also includes an extensive epilog on the Meskwaki casino and how it has affected life on the settlement.

The offshoot from my Tama work was an assessment of the Fox Project, which appeared in *Current Anthropology* (Foley 1999). In that article I gave the Fox Project mixed reviews. I argued that many of the Fox Project programs did not survive after the Action Anthropologists left. Moreover, like many applied anthropology projects of that era, the projects were not always the brainchild of the tribe.

On the other hand, I highlighted the Fox Project's more political activities like saving the tribal school from Bureau of Indian Affairs (BIA) termination. Sol Tax played a huge role in defeating the BIA, which endeared Action Anthropologists to the tribe. A second major contribution was associated with a handicrafts production project run by several Meskwaki artists called Tama Craft (Figure 10). When the Tama Craft project disbanded, due to internal tribal conflict, the white businessmen of Tama were anxious to reorganize it into a handicraft factory. They proposed to Tax that they and Action

Anthropologists convert the old BIA hospital for Native American tuberculosis patients into their factory. It was clear from the letter in the Tax papers that he rejected emphatically the lobbying efforts of local white businessmen. He wanted no part of turning Meskwaki artists into wage laboring factory workers under the local whites.

Figure 10. An image from a Tama Craft tile, made in the 1960s.

The third important Fox Project innovation was a scholarship program, which sent a number of Meskwakis to college. In many ways this project illustrates a basic philosophical difference between Action Anthropology and many applied anthropology projects. Sol Tax wanted Action Anthropology to be very independent and autonomous of government and academic politics. Consequently, he obtained private foundation support to send eighteen Meskwakis to various Iowa colleges. Most of the students who finished their studies worked in social services type jobs off the Meskwaki settlement, but several returned to the settlement, and two in particular became key political activists. I could not verify, however, that Action Anthropologists had a major influence on these Meskwaki "activists." The activists cited the civil rights movement and the American Indian Movement as their main influences. Nevertheless, the scholarship program produced a number of college-educated Meskwakis, and prior to this program, the whole concept of having a white man's education was a bad thing.

The Fox Project disrupted this tribal belief, and in subsequent years many Meskwakis went to college through BIA scholarships or on their own. It is fair to say that Tax's scholarship program surely had an important impact on Meskwaki views of education.

As the three previous examples illustrate, Action Anthropology made a clear break with applied anthropology of the 1950s era. It was more political and in many ways very innovative. Nevertheless, I found Tax's writings on the philosophical foundations of Action Anthropology somewhat underdeveloped. He cites very few of the major philosophy of social science debates of that era. The key idea he articulated was that the social sciences needed a more pragmatic, clinical concept of science. In his view a clinical social scientist consults with the local community leaders and forms a partnership. Once they identified local problems needing solutions, Action Anthropologists helped the community solve its local problems. In this scenario the outsider social scientist is a kind of clinician that "fixes" local problems and accomplishes goals the community sets. This perspective of science and scientists is, of course, very different from the idea of scientific positivism and detached academic studies for the sake of studying things. Tax's perspective has some affinities with a more applied anthropology approach, but it was also trying to be more democratic and better serve community interests. In sharp contrast, too many applied anthropology projects of that era served government and private commercial interests more than community interests. As noted earlier, Action Anthropologists were probably more collaborative than most applied anthropologists of that era, but the Fox field notes suggest that they were not always as collaborative as they imagined themselves to be.

The other thing that Action Anthropology was supposed to do was produce better ethnographic studies. Tax was particularly interested in critiquing assimilation theory and mainstream attitudes that Native Americans were a "vanishing culture." He argued that if anthropologists were more "insiders" and a part of the cultural change and acculturation process, they would be able to produce better ethnographies of cultures in transition. Unlike conventional academic anthropologists, who were "outsiders," Action Anthropologists had greater credibility with local people. Looking back at how anthropology as a field has evolved since the 1950s, Tax was advocating a very innovative concept of ethnographic research. One can make the case that 21st-century American anthropology has evolved in ways that he foretold. Many contemporary writings on reflexivity and "activist" or "public" anthropology have strong affinities with Tax's idea of science and Action Anthropology.

Unfortunately, the ethnography that Action Anthropologists produced about acculturation and cultural change on the Meskwaki settlement does not live up to Tax's theory. The twelve-year Fox Project produced a very revealing, reflexive documentary history of the project (Gearing, McC. Netting, and Peattie 1960), a couple articles, and Fred Gearing's *Face of the Fox* (1970). Gearing's understanding of the Meskwakis is stuck in a 1950s cultural personality view of acculturating indigenous peoples as psychologically and politically dysfunctional. During my fieldwork, I was struck by how much more dynamic and functional Meskwaki culture and their political system were than in Gearing's account. *The Heartland Chronicles* argues that the Meskwakis adopt white cultural practices into their core culture through a creative, selective process of ethnogenesis. There is nothing particularly dysfunctional about the way Meskwakis are creating a hybrid, contemporary culture rooted in ancient religious practices, tribal political communalism, and modern consumer life styles.

The stark difference between my interpretation and Gearing's made me wonder why Action Anthropologists—guided by Tax's innovative idea of collaborative, activist, insider ethnography—produced a negative portrait of Meskwaki culture and politics. One obvious explanation is the considerable ideological divide between pre- and post-1960s anthropology. Our interpretations are shaped by very different historical, ideological contexts. That is certainly part of the story, but I ultimately concluded that Action Anthropology never produced the kind of ethnography that Tax imagined because of local constraints. The Fox Project was, first and foremost, a summer field school for training thirty-six novice anthropologists. The students spent two to three months on the settlement, and very few became deeply involved in settlement life. More importantly, Sol Tax was never there to guide them. The people who actually ran the Fox Project were graduate students. They communicated frequently with Tax, but the documentary history and their field notes convey that the students ended up doing "social work" and "public relations" work instead of in-depth ethnographic fieldwork. The task of navigating tribal politics and creating viable "action projects" simply overwhelmed their attempts to do ethnographic studies.

The theory that Action Anthropology could revitalize academic anthropology is sound, but that never happened during the Fox Project. The conditions for doing this new type of activist ethnography were just not there. This does not discredit the originality of Tax's idea of action-based ethnographic studies. It does, however, call into question his more ardent supporters' claims that Action Anthropology made a big impact on contemporary academic anthropology. Having done a fairly intensive intellectual history of my own subfield, the anthropology of education, I view their claim as wishful thinking. Contemporary "activist anthropologists" and "critical ethnographers" in my field march to very different theoretical drummers than 1950s Action Anthropologists did. Most situate their worldviews in the post-1960s anthropology of feminism, Marxism, critical race, postmodern, and identity theory. They do not acknowledge the early contributions of Tax and Action Anthropology.

I should add that our "activist anthropology" program at the University of Texas does read and acknowledge that Tax's Action Anthropology was an early version of contemporary activist anthropology. My view of Tax is limited to the Fox Project, but I suspect that his influence is much greater in the subfield of applied anthropology than in so-called academic anthropology. Perhaps emerging scholars like Joshua Smith, a participant in this forum, will do the kind of intellectual history needed to demonstrate Tax's overall impact on all types of contemporary American anthropology.

I concluded my article in *Current Anthropology* by saying that, had I been studying anthropology at the University of Chicago in the 1950s, I probably would have been a Tax activist, a Tax groupie, a Tax whatever! Being an activist at heart, I would have embraced Action Anthropology. And after hearing Joan's view of him as a man, I would have loved working with Sol Tax. He was a very intellectually open, ethical person, and most of his students apparently adored him.

One impact Tax made on academic anthropology, which I forgot to mention, was well documented in Robert Rubinstein's fascinating account of his letters from Guatemala to his mentor, Robert Redfield (Rubinstein 1991). Most anthropologists do not make their letters and field notes public. In sharp contrast, Rubinstein's book portrays how profoundly reflexive Tax was about his fieldwork and interpretation. More importantly, Tax put all of the Fox Projects notes in the Smithsonian for future generations to read. This sort of methodological transparency is, of course, the hallmark of good contemporary ethnographic practice. Nevertheless, very few people make public their field notes and letters from the field. Tax practiced intellectual transparency and reflexivity to a higher degree than many contemporary academic anthropologists do.

In conclusion, I must evoke the enormous irony of my hometown connection to Tax and Action Anthropology. When I interviewed Tax, he was quite surprised to meet an anthropologist who grew up in Tama and was digging around in the Fox field notes and his papers. As a teenager in the 1950s, I had no idea a group of anthropologists had a house on the settlement and ferried to town in a station wagon emblazoned with the University of Chicago insignia. I was too busy playing basketball and drinking cokes in the legendary "Tomahawk Sweetshop." Meanwhile, Action Anthropologists toiled away trying to improve life on the settlement, which I viewed as a scary, strange place. Reading the Fox field notes was a real eye-opening experience for me. My doctor, various neighbors, and many Meskwaki classmates appeared like ghosts from my past. They told all manner of stories to these strange anthropologists, who wrote them down dutifully. This treasure trove of historical material helped me makes sense of growing up in a redneck town and my development as an anthropologist. That definitely affected the way I wrote *The Heartland Chronicles*. On one hand, I wanted to "correct" Action Anthropologist's outmoded culture and personality interpretation of Meskwaki cultural and political dysfunction. On the other hand, I admired Sol Tax's innovative way of making anthropological practice more politically engaged, useful, and reflexive. Even though the Fox Project did not always fulfill Tax's visionary concept of "Action Anthropology," it did leave an important legacy for future generations of anthropologists. Thank you for inviting me to share my brief encounter with Sol Tax and the Fox Project.

References Cited

Foley, Douglas E.
1995 *The Heartland Chronicles*. University of Pennsylvania Press, Philadelphia.
1999 The Fox Project: A Reappraisal. *Current Anthropology*, 40(2):171–191.

Gearing, Frederick O.
1970 *Face of the Fox*. Aldine-Atherton, Chicago, Illinois.

Gearing, Fred, Robert McC. Netting, and Lisa Peattie
1960 *Documentary History of the Fox Project*. University of Chicago Department of Anthropology, Chicago, Illinois.

Rubinstein, Robert
1991 *Fieldwork: The Correspondence of Robert Redfield and Sol Tax*. Westview Press, Boulder, Colorado.

COMMENTARY FOLLOWING DOUGLAS E. FOLEY'S PRESENTATION

Joan Ablon, Sarah Anne (Sally) Robinson, Robert A. Rubinstein, and Sandy Lane

April 1, 2011
Sol Tax Symposium

Joan Ablon: I was just thinking about what you were saying about transparency. I think it was in the 1980s—we have gone through so many periods, so little money for fieldwork, then a little more and then less, and so on—when I heard this story, not from Tax but from someone else who had been at a National Institute of Mental Health–sponsored conference. I think it was held perhaps at the Center for Advanced Studies at Stanford. A group of the faculty were discussing the fact that there wasn't money for grants so that students could not go out and do fieldwork. So Sol immediately says, "Look, look around you. All of us have file cabinets full of field notes that we have made on different projects that we haven't written up and will never be able to write up. So why don't we open our file cabinets for selected students who might work with you and are interested in different selected projects and let them do secondary studies." Well, everyone just really hit on him. There was not one person in favor of this. And whoever was telling me this was saying it is very clear that people are jealous of their own field notes. Maybe it is insecurity, maybe they are thinking, "I did such and such wrong and it will be noted," or whatever. This was an example of Tax's openness and his real vision for the field. He cared about students, about the field, and the data that had been collected but not reported on. I think it was a terrific idea, but he was really beat down. Not one person supported him.

Sally Robinson: I didn't write anything at the Fox Project but I was there in 1954, which was kind of a transition period. The university had just bought an old farmhouse adjacent to the settlement. Before I started graduate work I had spent the summer trying to earn myself some money on commission. I never got a single cent because I never sold a single Quonset building. However, when Tax said, "Oh you've been in construction," they gave me $600 to fix up the old farmhouse. That's how I spent my summer, doing very little ethnographic fieldwork, but I really, really, *really* did learn how to drive a bargain, and I can give you a list of all the improvements I made.

I would like to reiterate some of your points and put a slightly different slant on some. This was a training session, primarily a training school. While the idea of doing projects for the Meskwaki was always there, and this was the excuse for being...well, excuse is not the right word...the sort of the *raison d'être.* It was primarily a place for students to get their feet wet and to learn something about fieldwork—not necessarily organized research but how to conduct yourself in a different cultural situation.

Well, not only did I learn about remodeling houses, but I also had an experience of Tax who was very—"I am putting you in charge of this. Get on with it"—and expected you to carry out whatever assignment he had given to you. So he was not around. Meanwhile, one of the Meskwaki came back who was AWOL from the Marine Corps and moved in with us. I was frantic, because my father had been a colonel in the army, and I had visions of the FBI landing on our doorstep. How do you handle such a situation? Tax was busy buying a house in Chicago for his family, so he was not coming out to Tama. Finally, I was so frantic I got on the crank wall-phone party line and really berated him up one side and down the other because he was abandoning us, and how were we going to cope with this?

Well, he came. I was so mad I went off somewhere and finally had to come back to the house to eat. And he said, "Oh Sally, won't you drive me around?" Well, within 10 minutes I was absolutely charmed. All was forgiven. But this was partly his style. I must say that we solved the AWOL problem by persuading Jimmy to turn himself in in Des Moines, and he wouldn't do it unless we went with him. All of us six graduate students went with him and a case of beer, in the university's station wagon with the University of Chicago logo on the doors—you can imagine if the FBI had come. Anyway we made that maneuver. The point I want to make is that Tax gave you a task, expected you to be able to do it, and he was almost always right that you could. But with this sort of sink-or-swim attitude that he had, you learned an enormous amount. This was partly the philosophy behind the Action Anthropology, because you got into a situation, you felt your way around, and instead of coming in as the expert, as the one who knew all, you had to begin to work things out for yourself. Now in doing this you also learned an enormous amount about whoever it was you were working with.

When I subsequently did my own fieldwork here on the Northwest Coast, I spent two years, because that is what the British did, and I discovered that the second year was totally different from the first year. And I began to really feel my way through the situation and to be part of the community, so much so that I was elected secretary and treasurer of the Nanino Indian Social and Athletic Club, and there was no president.

Now, in terms of long-range influences and impact, if you realize that here we are today talking about Sol Tax and his influence in Action Anthropology, this means that he had an enormous impact. Action Anthropology in and of itself was nothing on a theoretical level, but it was very much at a turning point in anthropology historically so it is somewhat unfair to take it out of context and look back and say from a present perspective that this was good, bad, or indifferent. Tax was ahead of his time and at the same time of his time, but the impact has been enormous, which says there was an underlying understanding, if you will, as opposed to theory, and it would be lovely to think of having some kind of quotable theoretical base, but it was an understanding and an attitude and a direction, and those were the primary gifts of Tax and Action Anthropology.

Robert A. Rubinstein: Thanks, Doug, I really appreciate your work and your comments just now. But the thing that strikes me is a more general point about doing the history of our discipline, and trying to understand the names that are attached to the stories that are told about our past. One thing I tried to do in the 1986 article [Rubinstein 1986] and in the introduction to the fieldwork book [Rubinstein 1991] was to begin to parse the stories we tell each other, which become apocryphal, about how we got where we are and about the influences of particular individuals. I agree with Bruno Latour that there is kind of retrospective re-interpretation of what goes on. So I think it's quite fascinating that we might be able to look in places and not find Tax's name at all, but find the resonances of his ideas there. And that, I think, calls for a different kind of historiography, one that ought to make the discipline think about how it organizes itself, about how it moves forward collectively, and would actually make this a more interesting and more complicated history of who we are and where we might be going.

Sandy Lane: I just want to add to what Robert said. I am married to Robert. Joan Ablon fixed us up, so it was an arranged marriage. When I first met Sol he was long retired, and I was on my way to the Middle East. He charged me with the goal of solving the Palestinian-Israeli conflict. I feel that I didn't actually do that. I tried. But, just to reiterate a little bit and take off from what Robert said, in terms of sort of intellectual genealogy, since I am Joan's student, I am Sol's grand student; and I have students who are Sol's great grand students now. And Robert and I and some other colleagues at the University of Syracuse have an ongoing kind of field school at home, which we now have directly said is Action Anthropology. But we were doing it before we had the worldview, which I got from Joan. We had the social justice perspective, which is why I was drawn to Joan, and I had learned a lot about what Joan said because she would talk about Sol all the time. I learned a lot about how you don't tell people what is good for them; you listen to what they want to do and then help them do it. That is ingrained in my mind. In our field school at home, we don't have a good name for it, but we take ideas from community agencies or groups, things they want to know more about and then design research with the community members as part of the research with students involved. The students run the project, which takes a while to do. The students lead every aspect of the project. We do it together. We write it up. We publish it with the community members and students, so it produces knowledge for the community to use. And, it is explicitly pedagogical. Would any of my students be able to say this is Action Anthropology and mention Sol Tax? Frankly, I doubt it—maybe one or two. But they really do benefit from what started with Sol.

CHAPTER 8

FROM ACTIVIST TO ACTION: HOW DR. SOL TAX HELPED ME FIND MY WAY IN ANTHROPOLOGY

Tim Wallace

Like many young undergraduates in the 1960s and 1970s, I came to anthropology with a commitment to working with vulnerable populations outside the United States. Before starting graduate school I had spent a year working and studying in Peru (1967–68). I was profoundly influenced in my career choice by that experience. My studies there led me on a discovery of the plight of colonialized Andean peoples. By the time I left, I believed that in anthropology I would find the skills needed to be able to work with that kind of population.

When I got to Indiana University to begin graduate work in 1969, I was surprised to find that the application of anthropology to practical issues and problems around the world was not one that was well received by the leaders of the field. I was very disappointed to find that in my own graduate program applied perspectives were not popular and that those who held them would not long survive the process of getting a PhD. Though I eventually knuckled down to the rigors of a theoretical and general approach to the study of anthropology, I was not particularly happy about abandoning the focus that had brought me to anthropology in the first place.

When I got my first tenure-track position after completing my graduate studies, I harbored a lingering desire to do applied anthropology, but, knowing the anti-applied tendency of the day, I rarely had the courage to engage in it. Eventually, I had the opportunity to begin teaching a course in applied anthropology. As I prepared for the course, this was the first time that I really ever came to grips with the history of applied anthropology and how it had been practiced in the early and middle part of the 20th century. My preparations led me to discover the idea of Action Anthropology as it had been developed by Dr. Sol Tax.

I would like to say this was a eureka moment for me, but it wasn't. I was not ready to hear what he was saying. Dr. Tax suggests (1975) that no Action Anthropology is possible without being a fieldworker. Action Anthropology, he says, may or may not be a part of applied anthropology. Action Anthropologists are anthropologists and field workers first and change agents second. At the time I wanted to reverse that order. Fortunately, I eventually came to see he was right. He was right also in that for the Action Anthropologist "his problem is less the application of general propositions than the development and classification of goals and the compromising of conflicting ends or values (Tax 1952:104)." This meant for me that I had to think less about what I thought should be solutions to social or economic problems and listen more to what the local people happened to think about their situation and what they wanted to do about it. As I taught the applied course in the beginning, I only saw Action Anthropology as a historical moment in the development of applied anthropology, rather than as a lesson for me in the present. Nevertheless, somehow the idea of Action Anthropology as embodied in the Fox project stayed with me (Tax 1958). Over the years, I was forced again and again to reflect on Action Anthropology as I tried to explain it to students, who, like my early graduate studies self, believed that anthropology had an important role to play in bringing its ideas, concepts and techniques to the solution of practical problems.

Eventually, I did get opportunities to try out my own skills in applied anthropology among vulnerable populations of the sort I had been associated with in my early 20s. I needed to have a set of core beliefs and values to guide me in my work. I was unsure of what they were until I made the connection back to my applied course and the discussions I had had with my students about action and other applied approaches.

In the 1980s, I was hired as a consultant on a USAID project in Ecuador attempting to understand the national potato marketing system; and, in the early 1990s I did the same in Mozambique, but in terms of maize marketing. In neither case did I really apply the principles of Dr. Tax's ideas of Action Anthropology. At the time I was still committed to more of an "applied engineering" approach. However, in the late 1990s when my work as a teacher and applied anthropologist took to me to Hungary and Costa Rica to work on issues of tourism development, I began to realize for the first time the power of what Dr. Tax calls the *Law of Parsimony*, "which tells us [Action Anthropologists] not to settle questions of values unless they concern us" (Tax 1952:105). He further writes, "In the beginning of our Fox program, having decided to interfere for some good purpose, we were beset with value problems… What a marvelously happy moment it was when we realized that this [a value decision] was not a judgment or decision *we* needed to make" (Tax 1952:105).

Today, as a somewhat more mature scholar and applied anthropologist, like Dr. Tax in the 1950s, I find a need to consider the consequences of my work. For whom have I been working? What will be the outcomes of my work? What are the values that local people find most important? How do they feel about change? What will be both the short-term and the long-term consequences of my work? What kind of responsibilities do I have ethically and morally to ensure that the work in which I was engaged was useful, meaningful and sustainable for the populations that would be affected by studies, policies, and activities flowing from my applied work?

As I worked on tourism projects in both Costa Rica and Guatemala, I felt the pressure of these kind of value conflicts and did not know how to resolve both the demands of my role as a consultant/applied anthropologist, and my commitment to responding to specific needs of the local people. (See Wallace and Diamente 2005.) As I searched around for answers, I kept coming back to the notion of the Action Anthropology that had been one of the topics in my applied course. I found relief in Dr. Tax's Action Anthropology the basic idea that value decisions were to be left in the hands of the local people with whom we were working. This simple, yet profound element of applied anthropology would come to shape the handling of my applied work in ways that I think have been both effective without being "engineering from above." I didn't want to make the choices that didn't belong to me. As Dr. Tax writes in his article on Action Anthropology (1952:104), "When it became necessary [during the Fox program] to decide which of the conflicting values to choose, we eventually found ourselves not deciding at all, and finding some way around it. Action anthropologists must avoid making decisions that are clearly not ours to make." I began to work with more and more local residents who assisted me and depended on me and expected that I had some good suggestions for positive outcomes of their livelihoods communities.

I see my own role more as a facilitator for local people who have difficulty achieving what they perceive to be as essential for the achievement of their own goals. Nor am I a "culture broker," someone who tries to mediate between indigenous people and the national or international power structure, though if that is a needed action for local people to attain success, I can take that on. As an Action Anthropologist I may have a professional opinion about the best goals or course of action, but those opinions must never stand in the way of the freedom the people have to choose for themselves and even to make mistakes.

I learned other lessons from Dr. Tax, too. In 2002, I went to Guatemala as a Fulbright professor and once again was asked to teach applied anthropology, but this time the students were Guatemalan university students. Fortuitously, when describing my upcoming sojourn with my closest friend from graduate school, Robert Rubinstein, he reminded me that he had worked with Sol Tax some years before, and had produced a book that compiled a huge packet of letters between Dr. Tax and Robert Redfield during his years in Guatemala (Rubinstein 2002). I devoured that terrific book, discovered that many of the places that he talked about in his letters and later in his book, *Penny Capitalism* (Tax 1953), were still there. As I explored Guatemala, I had vivid reminders of Sol Tax's work, though his work there preceded me by more than 50 years. This is when I really began to incorporate Dr. Tax's wisdom into my fieldwork, both theoretical and applied.

In searching for a location for the first of my ten (and counting) ethnographic field schools there, I visited Lake Atitlán and stumbled onto the locality of Sol Tax's first international field site (Figure 11). Not only was I going to be doing some applied anthropology, but I was also going to be doing it in the backyard of this great man's first major field site!

Figure 11. Motorized transport around Lake Atitlán was less common in Tax's time there, but today most tourists move across the lake in speedy boat taxis such as these on the shore in front of the Santiago dock of Panajachel.

Penny Capitalism and the tremendous amount of very specific data that can be found there impressed me for many reasons, but chief among them was the thoroughness of the work. This enabled a student of his, Robert Hinshaw, to take that data and successfully complete a re-study thirty years later (Hinshaw 1975) to see how the community had changed. Today, most ethnographic monographs seem to devote a lot of space to personal impressions and narratives, which, while valuable, are sometimes less useful to later readers who might be looking for data on how history of lives in a specific locality.

Figure 12. Sol Tax would today still recognize the Maya of Lake Atitlán, including these two people from Santa Catarina Palopó, who have consistently maintained their language, dress and many of their customs in spite of globalization.

The social anthropologists of Dr. Tax's era engaged in data collection strategy that was thorough in a holistic account of the customs of the native peoples he studied in Guatemala (Figure 12). The data collection approach of Dr. Tax's generation (see Ottenberg 1990 and Johnson and Johnson 1990) emphasized collecting data about all aspects of a community or culture. In the last forty years, modern ethnographies have tended increasingly to have a more focused research design on specific aspects of community or cultural behavior. Thus, even though Dr. Tax, like most of the colleagues of his era, had neither tourists nor non-Maya as their central focus, his Atitlán ethnographic work does not exclude observations on both. (For example, contrast Dr.

Tax's Panajachel study with Warren's 1978 study of another Atitlán community, San Andres Semetebaj. See Ottenberg 1990 and Johnson and Johnson 1990.) Dr. Tax understood the importance of putting down on paper everything he saw and heard and making sure it was there for posterity, and although not all of his field notes were converted to publications, he made sure that they would be found in the University of Chicago library, where they could be available for all who needed them (see Foley, Chapter 7 in this volume). Thus, a researcher can come back to his data many decades later and find much historical comparative data, regardless of his theoretical approach. This is the situation for me, as I am very interested in something Dr. Tax was not very interested in—tourism—and learn as much about what was there in the 1930s, and what wasn't there. His meticulous data collection has afforded me many insightful nuggets of data about touristic life in Guatemala in the 1930s and early 1940s.

Like Dr. Tax, I have been returning to Guatemala annually, now going on ten-plus years. I have found that as the database grows from the research done by myself and my apprentice ethnographers, it becomes increasingly important to find ways to bring that data to people who can use it and make sure the data is available for the next generation of ethnographers. Unlike Dr. Tax, I have been interested in the tourism issues of the Lake region, which had only been in its infancy when Dr. Tax was there. He engaged in long-term fieldwork in Guatemala (1934–1943). But, like Dr. Tax, my interests in Lake Atitlán research have been both holistic and focused. Dr. Tax turned his focus on economics aspects of Panajachel life, while mine has been on the touristic elements of Panajachel and other communities of Lake Atitlán. And, like Dr. Tax, who had a great concern with training and bringing local Guatemalans (Mayan and non-Mayan) into his research, wherever he went, I have endeavored to bring local Guatemalans, Mayan and non-Mayan into my research and training programs in Guatemala. My ethnographic field school has been open to Guatemalans from different backgrounds and many of those who went through the program have, both during and after completion of the program, tackled important issues of local, Mayan concern.

Dr. Tax actively searched for local people who were as interested as he in understanding the local lifeways. Ten years before the Fox Project, Dr. Tax was already becoming aware of the importance to listening to local people, training local people and hearing what their goals and dreams were (see Hinshaw, Chapter 9 in this volume). These are themes that come to fruition not only in the Fox program, but also in his working on facilitating communication among Native peoples of North America, and eventually even his work to establish *Current Anthropology* as a means to exchange ideas on a global basis. If he were alive today, I am sure he would be in the forefront of using the Internet as critical technology for doing that. In my own small way I hope I can emulate him, but more on that below.

When I began my applied work in Guatemala, I was glad I had a better understanding of Action Anthropology. In 2002 I was a consultant for a project funded by The Nature Conservancy and USAID, whose goal overall was to encourage local communities around Lake Atitlán to create municipal parks out of communal lands and force local citizens to severely restrict their use of these lands. My role, as a specialist in tourism, was to diagnose ecotourism entrepreneurial opportunities that might provide incentives for locals to change their perception of the forested areas as a place for resource extraction to a site of conservation. As I began my work, it became apparent that The Nature Conservancy was making a flawed assumption, that is, that local citizens were not conservation minded. In fact, this was not the case. Land stewardship was very important, and those who were guilty of excess resource extraction were actually outside commercial developers and well-heeled Guatemalan and international investors who wanted a vacation home on the mountain slopes along the shores of the lake. My concern, then, was to insure that my report indicated such a finding and to see ways in which this idea could be conveyed to members of the community. My report suggested strongly that there should be community conferences to discuss the total report and get people thinking about ways to respond. It was also then that I remembered "Action Anthropology," and how I understood Dr. Tax to use it. When I first came into anthropology as a graduate student I believed I needed to be proactive, to do, to act, to create; however, reading Dr. Tax's work made me realize that my role should rather be to encourage, motivate, and facilitate. Vine DeLoria Jr.'s (1988) critique of anthropologists' role in Native North American groups was not far from my mind. Tax's words, spanning the decades from 1950 to the 2000s helped reassure me that I needed to take on a different role, particularly as facilitator, in my Guatemalan work. My applied work in other settings had left me unsettled, but as I re-read and re-thought what Dr. Tax was saying about Action Anthropology, it was as if Dr. Tax's ideas and his example were "music" to my ears as I came to understand what he meant.

In the years since 2002, I have worked to open dialogue with local Maya to find out what they consider is important about conservation, to better understand their conservation practices, and to work with local Guatemalans to develop their own ideas of conservation and tourism development strategies. I like the indirectness of the approach. Bring people together to discuss what they want, use my expertise to help develop options, and make myself available, if they want me, to help them do what they want done. But, like Dr. Tax, my professional life has been one of continual movement back and forth between a field site and my university home. Here, as Dr. Tax found, there has been little understanding at home about the value of action/applied anthropology. Reading about his life and hearing stories from those who knew him has been another source of inspiration to me. I am speaking here of his service to the discipline (Stanley 1996) and to the application of anthropology, regardless of what colleagues less inclined toward application might say or think. One of Dr. Tax's students, Joan Ablon, recounted to me after the 2011 Seattle SfAA sessions how his Chicago colleagues hoped that one day Tax "would return to anthropology," even though he had been a member of the Chicago anthropology department all along. The reason? They thought that his applied work was not anthropological at all. His applied work was not theoretical, they believed. But Dr. Tax himself addressed this when he said, "In fact, the action anthropologist finds that the proportion of new knowledge which must be developed in the situation is very great in comparison to old knowledge which he can apply. He is and must be a theoretical anthropologist, not only in background, but also in practice" (Tax 1975:516). My own career has similarly been freighted by these kinds of misunderstandings of what applied anthropologists do. So the frustrations I have felt are alleviated a lot by knowing that even as great an anthropologist as Sol Tax had been, he went through something akin to my own university experience.

It is clear that Sol Tax's service to the discipline and to native peoples of North America was a central aspect of his life's work. In addition, he always emphasized the theoretical contributions of his work and maintained that as an action/applied anthropologist he was providing important additions to the corpus of anthropological theory. His model of anthropological fieldwork and service, then, is a beacon to others who find as much satisfaction in organizing, in motivating and in facilitating than in the usual academic pursuits in the world of publish or perish. Contemporary organizations such as the Society for Applied Anthropology (SfAA) and the National Association for the Practice of Anthropology (NAPA), as well as consortia such as COPAA (Consortium of Practicing and Applied Anthropology programs) and committees such as the American Anthropological Association's CoPAPIA (Committee on Practicing, Applied and Public Interest Anthropology) each have made it plain that the application of anthropology in its various forms not only should be rewarded, but also encouraged. As university budgets shrink, fewer tenure track positions are required, and smaller academic departments are the norm, application and practicing anthropology clearly is both the present and the future. Fortunately, there are today many models of successful applied and practicing anthropologists. Sol Tax was one of the great pathfinders who have left their imprint on the field, who is again today relevant for a new generation of Action Anthropologists.

References Cited

Deloria Jr., Vine
1988 *Custer Died for Your Sins: An Indian Manifesto*, third edition. University of Oklahoma Press, Oklahoma City.

Hinshaw, Robert E.
1975 *Panajachel: A Guatemalan Town in Thirty-Five Year Perspective*. University of Pittsburgh Press, Pittsburgh, Pennsylvania.

Johnson, Allan and Orna R. Johnson
1990 Quality into Quantity: On the Measurement Potential of Ethnographic Fieldnotes. In *Fieldnotes: The Makings of Anthropology*, edited by Roger Sanjek, pp. 61–184. Cornell University Press, Ithaca, New York.

Ottenberg, Simon
1990 Thirty Years of Fieldnotes: Changing Relationships to the Text. In *Fieldnotes: The Makings of Anthropology*, edited by Roger Sanjek, pp. 139–160. Cornell University Press, Ithaca, New York.

Rubinstein, Robert A., ed.
2002 *Doing Fieldwork: The Correspondence of Robert Redfield and Sol Tax*. Transaction Publishers, New Brunswick, New Jersey.

Stanley, Sam
1996 Community, Action, and Continuity: A Narrative Vita of Sol Tax. *Current Anthropology*, 37 (Supplement):131–137.

Tax, Sol
1952 Action Anthropology. *America Indígena*, 12:103–109.
1953 *Penny Capitalism: A Guatemalan Indian Economy*. Institute of Social Anthropology, Publication No. 6. Smithsonian Institution Press, Washington, D.C.
1958 The Fox Project. *Human Organization*, 17(1):17–19.
1975 Action Anthropology. *Current Anthropology*, 16(4):514–517.

Wallace, Tim and Daniela Diamente
2005 Keeping the People in the Parks: A Case Study from Guatemala. *NAPA Bulletin*, 23(1):191–216.

Warren Kay
1978 *The Symbolism of Subordination: Indian Identity in a Guatemalan Town*. University of Texas Press, Austin, Texas.

CHAPTER 9

HELPING WHILE STUDYING PEOPLE: GUATEMALA

Robert E. Hinshaw

As a Sol Tax student and admirer with long, ongoing commitment to building on his legacy of helping/learning in Central America, I think it useful for me to point to the distinctive challenge of following Tax's "action" tenets in the rapidly failing state of Guatemala. Note that Guatemala is illustrative of the many more-stagnating-than-developing nations since Tax's firsthand introduction to that neocolonial world 75 years ago. (One hundred and three of the world's current 195 nations have been born—or reborn—since the 1959 Darwin Centennial.)

Tax early on had coined the term "worldview" in his quest to understand and interpret the patterning of Mayan beliefs. Susan Tax Freeman (Chapter 5 in this volume) helpfully has referenced Sol Tax's contribution to Mesoamerican literature in his publication on the *municipios* of the Midwestern highlands of Guatemala (Tax 1953). Left to me is the referencing of his huge corpus of ethnographic data that unfortunately is available only in the microfilmed archives of Tax's career involvements in Mesoamerica. In those archives these data are titled "The Other Side of the Coin," in juxtaposition to *Penny Capitalism.* Gathered throughout the 1933–1941 field seasons in Panajachel, Tax had assembled those data for publication by the University of Chicago Press; one of my early assignments being to internalize and edit that proposed publication. Why Sol then decided to withdraw it from publication, I do not now recall (if, in fact, he did … the Press may have felt uncomfortable with its publication in such encyclopedic format).

In my recollection Sol had envisioned a daughter revisiting those data on belief and behavior patterning in a doctoral dissertation. With Susan moving on to the fertile plains of Spain, and Marianna moving toward Russian studies, the topic subsequently became the subject of my doctoral dissertation. Sol took inordinate interest in the dissertation that, I suspect, was as much his idea as mine. Not that I was in the least disconcerted, were this the case. With no formal undergraduate study in anthropology prior to embarking on graduate study under Sol's tutelage, and a family of three children to support, I was welcoming of all the help available to me in establishing a scholarly career. And with an undergraduate major in philosophy and epistemology, delving into Mayan thought processes and belief patterning was an exhilarating prospect.

Tax, by that point, had not published anything focusing specifically on Mayan cognitive culture, although he had an unpublished paper which he urged me to use as a starting point: "Can World Views Mix?" The deeper he explored the paradox of tribal indigenous peoples of North American having so little in common with Mayas in social/economic organization, the more puzzled he became in reconciling the Mayas' protestant ethic (penny capitalism) with—if anything—an even more animistic worldview than he had encountered among, say, Iowa's Fox Indians.

I accepted his challenge, although—no more satisfactorily than Sol—did I get beyond a literate analytic cataloguing of the precepts of animism. I discussed ad nauseam those precepts with dozens of informants as I dutifully judged and compared informants' awareness of and emotional commitment to a large corpus of beliefs that—for the most part—Tax and Redfield had collected in their collaborative research in towns bordering Lake Atitlán (Figure 13). My focus, because it had been theirs, was on continuity of such belief patterning amidst acculturative influences that were advancing more rapidly in Panajachel than elsewhere around the lake. Panajachel was the best choice of communities for that investigative focus. But such data collection denied to me, as much as it had to Tax and Redfield, understanding the full meaning of such animistic assumptions in terms of Maya experience of their natural/social environment. Sol was intrigued by the staying power of animistic precepts around the margins of urban/literate societies.

Animism's fuller understanding requires less the abstracted analysis by scientists based on interviewing informants than simply participant/observation among the region's least acculturated Mayas and their companion life forms. Only over the course of fifteen years of living half of each year on my own land, in daily association with Mayas, did my wife and I come to share at least a degree of the communion with other life forms sharing habitat with Mayas that is/was the panhuman experience before writing and associated scientific literacy commenced its inevitably alienating process of objectifying all that otherwise in nature—human as well as non-human—is social "event" rather than individuating "view." Animism is based on two-way communication between human and non-human life forms ... on the same communion that we in the scientifically literate world take for granted in human intercourse.

Figure 13. Lake Atitlán, actually a crater lake, is 55 square miles, 1,000 feet deep. About 13 Kaqchikel and Tz'utujil Maya communities dot its banks.

I have come to understand that I owe my resignation as much to a Mayan worldview as to my own upbringing. Although resigned, I do not regard myself as apathetic—far less as depressed. I find myself joyous and energized by the "reality check" afforded by living with neighbors who as recently as fifteen years ago had no running water nor electricity in their community of three thousand Indians. With no land lines, they rely on cell phones. I know of no one who owns a computer, or even a typewriter for that matter. Cable TV is available, but the cost is beyond the means of more than a handful of families. There are no more than a half dozen motor vehicles. We rely on public boats passing by every half hour to get to doctors, a pharmacy, shops and markets, and (in my situation) to internet access and a bank. No newspaper is sold in Tzununa nor even delivered there to my knowledge. There is a school providing six years of training, but with attendance optional and few continuing beyond fourth grade. There is no library, and the overwhelming majority of adults are illiterate. Most men are reasonably fluent in Spanish, whereas fully 75 percent of the women speak only their Mayan language and have not ventured beyond communities bordering Lake Atitlán in the department (state) of Solola.

Most Tzununa families, averaging between eight and nine members per household, grow most of their food and subsist on no more than $2 per capita cash earnings per day. With adult men the only wage earners (there is no craft industry or catering to tourism whatsoever), this means that three wage earners per household bring home the average wage of $6 for an eight-hour day of hard manual labor: $18 for the needs of nine. No one has medical insurance, and very few have employment in the sectors of the economy where employers contribute to retirement benefits. In short, there is none of the safety net that we depend upon so heavily in the United States.

Despite this situation, there is virtually no begging, and I think it fair to say that most do not feel that they are unduly needy. In fact, what questioning I have done suggests that they consider themselves to live more healthily than do most Ladinos (whose diet, heavy in animal protein, they deprecate) and to be materially better off than were their grandparents. This despite longitudinal data on dietary consumption and infant growth rates suggesting that diet/health have been deteriorating among Mayas of the region over the past 75 years. But they define their needs utterly differently than do North Americans: These are limited almost entirely to the subsistence needs of food, clothing, and lodging, almost all of which they grow, make, or build themselves. They are proud of their culture and are not easily convinced that they should be changing their lives in any significant way. After all, they have lived essentially this way in their valley for more than a thousand years. (The nearest archeological excavation—a half dozen miles above the valley—revealed occupation back 2000 years, and there is no oral tradition to suggest other than continuous occupation of the region since then.) Like the hummingbirds of their valley (Tzununa means The Place of Hummingbirds), they keep trucking along with legendary energy at subsistence routines of which they appear never to tire. And they also stop at regular intervals to smell the flowers. The truth of the matter is that—barring climate change that ends atmospheric protection for all humans or produces Central American heat or cold beyond human endurance—Mayas will survive much easier than will the industrialized world any scarcity of electricity and motorized transport accompanying exhaustion of fossil fuels. As a bumper sticker notes, "The Meek Are Getting Ready!"

During my own half-century of Central American involvements, I have become increasingly reluctant to become involved in local politics among Mayas—far less to meddle at the national level. The dilemma is that alluded to in Tax's urging of caution in assessing prematurely the implications of action options (lest consequent inaction rule the day). But it is more complicated even than this, involving the related caution from Tax against unduly trusting anyone's alleged good intentions—especially given Guatemala's downward spiral of government's failure to represent in any accountable way the poorest (largely Maya) half of the citizenry. Bear in mind that there are at least two million more Mayas in Central America and Mexico (most of these in Guatemala) than there are Native peoples in the whole of North America. Perhaps more than in North America, throughout Central America/Mexico native peoples—in comparison with the era of Tax's working there—are less concerned with non-Indian attitudes and government policies regarding their assimilation and cultural identity. Remember that the Peace Accords ending the half-century of civil war last century recognized Mayan languages and religion as never before. Nonetheless, for Mayas to advocate on their behalf as Mayas, rather than as the "poor," is suicidal. Mayas are accepted, and neglected, for whom they are in remarkably different manner than in Tax's experience—when Ubico endeavored to achieve Mayas' assimilation simply by presidential fiat. (The second of my companion novels recalling the Mayas' experience from the 1880s to the 1980s chronicles Mayan responses to Ubico's dictum, including aborted efforts to form exclusively indigenous political parties … something contemporary Mayas would not even contemplate).

Because of Guatemala's proximity to and migratory labor dependence on North America, both U.S. and Canadian citizens have become increasingly aware of—and responsive to—the comparatively unjust impoverishment of most Guatemalans (among Latin Americans). Government at national and local levels accordingly has welcomed and encouraged North American largesse on behalf of whomever in Guatemala foreign providers target for health, education, and welfare assistance. North American Protestant churches already had appeared on this scene when the Taxes resided in Guatemala, but Tax hardly anticipated the extent to which such a solidly Catholic nation would have yielded to the financial enticements of conversion by even my arrival in the early 1960s. By now at least half the population is evangelically Protestant. The result? To query any Maya community regarding needs with which outsider expertise/contacts might appropriately assist, is likely to invite help in getting direct financial assistance from North American networks (or in getting more Mayas safely to North America to work). And hence the concern about trusting the judgments of either donors or recipients of such assistance to supplement (if not replace?) federal tax funding for those basic responsibilities of government. Action Anthropologists, who will not be suffering the consequences of community decisions they may influence, have the responsibility of helping ferret out the implications of all perceived options.

But how deeply must we then "dig" in that discernment process, where acceding to the felt needs of citizens can easily limit pragmatic discussion to accessing foreign resources rather than to addressing the root problem of non-accountability of government? As a Quaker I have observed the experiences of the American Friends Service Committee (AFSC) in rural community development since the advent of their presence in Guatemala about the time I commenced research there. Eventually, the AFSC pulled out of Guatemala from frustration over this issue of subtle cooptation. Like the Peace Corps, Quakers' work in the country required government authorization. This precluded frank public elucidation of these facts of the matter—far less of the deeper roots of poverty—without endangering the program if not the security of personnel.

North American anthropologist Victoria Sanford, recently chairing the AAA committee on human rights, is married to an activist Guatemalan publisher, Raul Figueroa Sarti. In her research and his publishing they have visibly challenged the government on a wide front of human rights issues. Consequently, both have endured informal and legal threats aimed at silencing his press and keeping her outside Guatemala. Tax and I learned this reality of practicing science in Guatemala in the early 1980s when enlisting the support of Secretary of State-elect, George Shultz (Tax's colleague in Economics at Chicago at the time) for studying with State Department endorsement the roots of Guatemala's violence. A request for research proposals on the subject was subsequently circulated among relevant disciplines, with the proposal submitted by myself and Benjamin Paul (another of Tax's former students working in Guatemala) surviving the first cut after peer review. But then a military coup suddenly brought Efrain Rios-Montt to Guatemala's presidency. Within days the Guatemala Desk vetoed State Department involvement in any such study by U.S. scientists, and the endeavor was quashed. Later we learned from Shultz that the Guatemala Desk had been less than enthusiastic from the outset (as also had been a majority of the social scientists invited to submit proposals ... they not understanding the endeavor's history and suspecting State Department cooptation of science).

Do we anthropologists and social scientists in general—which overwhelmingly means the "haves" of globalized society—by our very employment not appear complicit in the trajectory of our consuming scientific/technological enterprise? And the more so if we rationalize what humanitarian counsel we give as contributing to knowledge advancement (and by implication the advancement of our own careers)? Tax's "action" tenets argued rather explicitly for disavowing any authority in our "therapeutic" assistance, this in keeping with our discouragement from academe for undue usurpation of leadership functions assigned to politicians and clergy. After the polite but firm rebuke from both Guatemalan and U.S. officialdom regarding illuminating the roots of Guatemalan violence, I concluded that—if determined to continue residing and helping in Central America—it would wisely be in the domain of mitigating losses from nature's extreme events and assisting their victims. This decision accompanied reduced involvements with anthropology and increased involvements with geography (via association with Tax's geographer associate at Chicago, Gilbert White, and the Natural Hazards Center he subsequently founded at the University of Colorado). In addition to that center's auspices, I have used—for ongoing learning/helping in Central America—the international Guatemala Scholars Network. I suspect that it is only a question of time before a consensus is reached that our applied science resources in time, energy, knowledge and networking for financial assistance to "have-nots" are most efficaciously focused on mitigating disaster losses and assisting victims of natural disasters with survival and relocation. Increasingly this is what foreign philanthropy and NGO expertise end up doing in Guatemala regardless of their initial mandate. (See the 2011 January issue of *Scientific American* wherein the relocation of unacceptably-at-risk populations is highlighted as the most pressing—as well as problematic—of the many human challenges posed by global warming. Mexico and Central America are a featured example in the authors' making this case).

If this will become the consensus within the social and human ecology sciences, in which discipline can we expect that leadership to emerge? To date more initiative has come from geographers. But if—as Tax envisioned—anthropology will be most proactive in plotting the future of our human evolution, how and where does this leadership emerge if not from within the SfAA? Lest the foregoing be interpreted as a turning away from Tax's basic modus operandi, I suggest that Tax has been right all along in how to learn/help most efficaciously. The problem lies in academe's outdated (in theory) subordination to leadership from state and church. In fact, for quite some time the world has been waiting for the only leadership that stands any chance of addressing our dilemma of adjusting to requisite limits: humanitarian scientists the likes of Sol Tax (and my other mentor, Gilbert White) in concert with the stewardship example set largely by native peoples around the world.

A decade after publication of the "Evolution After Darwin" volumes—when he was a visiting Fellow at the Stanford Center for Advanced Study in the Behavioral Sciences Tax was enthusiastically orchestrating (in his collaborative fashion) creation of the Center for the Study of Man. He was assuming that the Smithsonian would be the

Center's feasible home, while cognizant—via his recruitment of the interdisciplinary and international colleagues constituting the Board of Directors—that consensus on such location and foci of study would not come easily. (The trial task force topic for the fledgling center was "the socio-cultural context of family life and fertility"). The relevant paragraph in that letter for our present purpose reads as follows:

> Last week I spent at a conference at the University of Wisconsin on Urban Anthropology, and became the more convinced that anthropology itself must change, or is already changing its focus from the small community (including ethnic enclaves) to the whole of the emerging worldwide society. What this means is NOT that we do everything over as though others have not been studying innumerable aspects of the whole, but rather that we now begin to add our perspective to whatever else is being done. Rather than go on at length, I shall let your imagination fill in the rest, perhaps better than can I (Tax 1970; see Figure 6 in this volume).

Fortuitously, our 2010–2011 efforts provide opportunity forty years later to do just that: unfetter our imagination in collective discernment of what role anthropology might play in addressing a critical impasse that we understand much better than could Tax. Agriculture/civilization/science and technology have brought us to the edge of an abyss: depletion of the fossil energy that accompanied the globalization to which Tax referred—including unsustainable numbers and inequitable wealth sharing—as well as acceleration of global warming producing increased risks to ecological balance and species' survival from extremes of nature and resultant migration pressures. Even as humans largely understand the role of science/technology in these changes, there is no comparable consensus regarding limits to growth (imminent or already surpassed).

Science is largely responsible for our faith in technology's capacity to address any challenge. Accordingly, only leadership from science stands a chance of adjusting such expectations. If still among us, I can imagine that Tax would be querying whether—as Action Anthropologists—we might have distinctive challenge among the disciplines in alerting humanity to the danger of continuing along our present path. After all, Tax clearly articulated late in life that North American anthropologists have a distinctive role in helping Native Americans advocate for opting out of the progress-without-limits ideology of mainstream society. Is it not obvious that "Everyman" now needs such advocacy? If anthropology is not sensitized to this need enough to provide requisite advocacy, who else within the academy of sciences will?

References Cited

Tax, Sol

1953 *Penny Capitalism: A Guatemalan Indian Economy*. Institute of Social Anthropology, Publication No. 6. Smithsonian Institution Press, Washington, D.C.

1970 Letter to Robert Hinshaw, June 18, 1970. Center for Advanced Study of the Behavioral Sciences. Stanford, California.

VIGNETTE: MY LAKE AT THE CENTER OF THE WORLD

Robert Hinshaw

Having alluded to my recently published companion historical novels,[1] I want to comment on their genesis: these perhaps to become my most influential contribution to Tax's Mesoamerican legacy. Both are based on Maya oral histories, with the interviews of Tax some 70 years ago informing the first novel, *My Lake at the Center of the World*. The most extensive memories were those of Santiago Yach, published in the Festschrift. My 1968–1969 acquaintance with the first generation of university-educated, professionally engaged Mayas (while a visiting professor at the public Universidad de San Carlos) inspired the sequel novel, *The Rape of Hope*. One student's memories of that era—suggesting the protagonist's character—were shared at length during subsequent interviewing in Colorado two decades thereafter as he made his way to political asylum in Canada. They are quite different, stand-alone novels, with the first endeavoring to do justice to the preliterate oral tradition before public schooling was available to Mayas, and the sequel tackling the acculturative influences of public schooling and medical care, Protestant and NGO interventions, and the civil war. As the Spanish editions circulate throughout Central America and Mexico, the influence of Tax and his colleagues/students—Maya and non-Maya—will ripple throughout Latin America for decades to come. The first novel, in particular, helps address an important domain of Tax's (and Redfield's) research that was largely overlooked in the correspondence prior to the Seattle forum and during the forum: Maya preliterate worldview in the Midwestern highlands of Guatemala.

1. In the United States the novels in English are least expensively available through me, by check to Look Back Books for $25 (both novels) or $15 (either one), this including mailing cost. Mail payment to Robert Hinshaw, 12500 Summit St., Kansas City, MO 64145.

CHAPTER 10

IMPRESSIONS AND REFLECTIONS: A WEEK IN THE CHEROKEE NATION, 2002

Albert L. Wahrhaftig

Author's Note: With amazement one day over ten years ago—in 2002—I opened an email from a "Richard Allen." I had no idea who he might be, but soon learned that he was a Policy Analyst at the Cherokee Nation in Tahlequah, Oklahoma. His email was an invitation to come to Tahlequah. He and some of his colleagues in the governmental offices wanted to get to know the person whose 40-year-old writings about Cherokee communities they had been reading and regarded as still the best description and analysis of traditional Cherokee life (see Chapter 2 in this volume).

Really? Tribal employees reading and enthusiastic about my writing? Given the state of war that existed between the Cherokee government and the Carnegie Project when I had done my fieldwork in the Cherokee Nation in the 1960s, this was news indeed. Back then, I wrote up a summary of my research in a bilingual Cherokee–English booklet distributed for free in traditional Cherokee communities (Wahrhaftig 1966), submitted a dissertation to the University of Chicago, and published the usual array of essays in academic journals. But given the limited English literacy of the Cherokees I had known, I never imagined that they, or for that matter anyone other than a few anthropological researchers, ever read what I wrote.

Finding out what was going on appeared to me an opportunity to update my 40-year-old Cherokee perspective. I accepted the invitation, travelled to Tahlequah, and discovered that within the labyrinth of the vastly expanded Cherokee governmental bureaucracy there existed a "cell" of very traditional modern Cherokee speakers ensuring that at least some tribal resources were diverted to traditional communities. They were a fascinating bunch.

Mindful of Robert Redfield and Sol Tax's advice many years ago to always record one's first impressions of the field, I recorded my new first impressions and shared them with my hosts. What I wrote then is reported below.

MY WEEK IN THE CHEROKEE NATION, SEPTEMBER 6-12, 2002

The Cherokee Language and Cherokee Literacy

At first glance, you might think that use of the Cherokee language and especially of its written form in Sequoyah's syllabary is in the midst of a strong revival. Sequoyan appears in great golden characters on the various offices of the Cherokee Nation where identifications in Cherokee are both bigger and above the corresponding legends in English. At the Cherokee Nation complex, traffic signs are in English, Sequoyan, and Cherokee transliterated with English orthography and some street signs in Tahlequah are bilingual. Sequoyan characters appear on publications such as the National Park Service's map and brochure about the Trail of Tears and on the covers of the Cherokee Children's Choir CDs. What is now the Bank of America in Tahlequah still bears the signs hand painted in its windows by the Carnegie Project some forty years ago. In an interview with me, Chief Chad Smith emphasized the high priority which he attaches to supporting a renaissance of Cherokee language and literacy. Cherokee literacy materials are being reproduced and Cherokee classes are taught here and there. The children's choir sings in Cherokee, and some, perhaps all, of the young people in the groups I met with can sound out text in Sequoyan.

All of this, however, is superficial, symbolic at best, and tainted with a combination of paternalism and snobbery. Nowhere did I see written Cherokee in use as a *living* language, as a functional and modern means of communication. There is no use of syllabary in the *Report to the Cherokee People 2002*, nor does it appear in the Summer 2002 issue of the *Cherokee Phoenix.* Signs in syllabary appear only in the touristed sections of Tahlequah. There are none in Stilwell with its greater concentration of Cherokee population. Have any of the documents which the Cherokee Nation uses in its programs with rural Cherokee communities, such as contracts for "Indian houses," been translated and published in syllabary? I saw none. Some of the young people who can sound out texts in syllabary do not speak or understand Cherokee and therefore don't know what they are "saying," and this is evidently the case with the children's choir who sound as though they are singing lyrics learned syllable by syllable without having learned the semantically crucial differences of tone which give Cherokee its unique characteristics and which are the respect in which it differs most radically from the family of languages to which English belongs. Although a favorable case might be made for the existence of a Cherokee-language radio program, it is not aired in prime time, nor is it presented in the times conventionally slotted for news. It is heard in the ghetto reserved for religious specialties at 9:30 on Sunday morning.

If there is something positive to be said about this, it at least seems that this elite sanctioning of the use of Cherokee has legitimized the use of the language in public. Perhaps the eastern Oklahoma public is now less disposed to think that Cherokee-speaking is a sign of backward ness. Indeed, in some circles, it seems to be something of a status symbol. Perhaps, too, Cherokees are now less disposed to feel ashamed of their language and less stigmatized by it.

For generations, non-Cherokees have insisted that the language is dying out. I am extremely reluctant to be a part of that chorus. Nevertheless, in my limited visiting among "community Cherokees."[1] I found in virtually all cases that children and young adults, though some may understand Cherokee, do not and probably cannot speak it. I hope that I am in error about this and I strongly suggest that here some solid sociolinguistic research should be a high priority.

So what does the increased visibility of written Cherokee signify? Although there are clearly some individuals who have learned Sequoyan in the old and customary way, my impression is that they are few. The acquisition of Cherokee literacy appears to be an investment in elite status, and the use of the syllabary appears as a reminder of Cherokee history and tradition and seldom if ever is a tool employed in the vigorous present and future of a tribal community contending with the contemporary world through its own brand of literacy. This is disempowering and makes me sad.

Conversation, Intelligence, and Originality

My whole first day was spent in conversation, first in his office with Richard Allen who had handled the email arrangements for my visit, then at lunch with Richard and John Ross, then with several other people I met briefly around the Cherokee Nation offices, then with Marvin Jones, and finally with a larger group of people at a potluck supper at Wilma Mankiller and Charlie Soap's house.

Although I met many other people during the week, it was with Richard, John, and Marvin that I spent the most time, and I think a few remarks about them might be valuable. They strike me as representing three persistent archetypes of Cherokee personality: the (red organization) War Captain, the (white organization) Beloved Man, and the maverick (Sequoyah).

Richard Allen is articulate, lively, full of tales, and likes to joke. He is clearly a competent researcher with a thorough knowledge of Cherokee history, but it looks to me as though he is the tribe's flack catcher. When I first met him, he was talking calmly with a verbose and rather nutty lady from Utah who was expressing her disillusion with the Trail of Tears Drama and "authentic" Cherokee village at the Cherokee Heritage Center, and it was evident that one of his duties has been dealing with those who have complaints about the use of Indians and Indian symbols as mascots for athletic teams. Richard enjoys confrontation and many of his tales involve his crossing swords with members of the Cherokee Nation Tribal Council and other elements of bureaucracy. He is a Vietnam veteran and heavily involved in veterans' affairs. At the close of the meeting with Cherokee youth which I attended, Richard seized the opportunity to tell the youngsters about the two Cherokees whose portraits were prominent on the wall and for whom the American Legion Hall had been named. With a quick mind and a ready tongue, it strikes me that Richard is a specialist in operating on boundaries, between Indian and non-Indian, between the young and the old, between business-oriented and community-oriented elements of the tribal government. His intelligence, personality, and behavior are reminiscent of that of Cherokee warriors throughout the deep span of Cherokee history.

John Ross is a quiet man. His voice is gentle, his face is reposed, there is a stillness in his slender body. He is a man of tradition—especially when one considers that tradition consists not only in what one *retains* but also in what one *transmits.* John speaks the most melodic Cherokee I have ever heard, and I suppose the most correct too, for I frequently heard other Cherokees turn to him to settle some issue having to do with proper Cherokee usage or pronunciation. In informal gatherings, whenever conversation turned to "what the old people did," John always had details to add, doing so in a way that did not push himself forward but simply represented a contribution toward the completeness of discussion. Introducing me to the youth groups with which I met and inconspicuously guiding me in my interactions with them, John manifested an impressive ability to weave me, an alien element, into a seamless social fabric. As is well known, except when not at war, Cherokee villages were coordinated by a "white organization," a council of "Beloved Men" whose knowledge of tradition and magic qualified them for the Cherokees' special form of leadership-through-consensus.[2] In John, I felt that I saw the modern embodiment of that role and personality.

Marvin Jones is a real surprise. I have to admit that when I first encountered him with his odd haircut and super slow drawl, standing in the doorway of his office, I took him for some bumpkin client on his way out and headed home: I was looking past him for the "real" Mr. Jones. Showing through that exterior, however, is an enormous intelligence and one of the most original minds I have met in a long, long time. Of all the people I met, I considered Marvin to have the deepest understanding of the strength and power of Cherokee communities and of how to connect with them. While Richard glories in the stories he tells about his battles with bureaucracies, and rightly so, the stories about Marvin's battles are told *about* him, not by him. Like the tricksters in myth, he wins not by confrontation but by quietly and casually leading others through the steps of their own arguments until they are so entangled in their own position that all that is left is to agree with him. I am reminded of the stories of Payne's visit to the famed Sequoyah. As they sat in his presence that night, Payne's interpreters put off all his requests to translate, saying that what Sequoyah was telling them and the quality of his elocution was far too beautiful to interrupt, and when he asked for a translation the next morning they told him that what Sequoyah had said was too integrated, too subtle, too wise, to distort by pushing it through the coarse grid of the English language. Marvin's like that. A complete out-of-the box thinker. A Sequoyah.

The above may seem excessively idealized and romanticized. Perhaps so. Yet I was fascinated to watch these three characteristic Cherokee personality types effectively at work within the confines of a tribal bureaucracy.[3]

During my fieldwork in the 1960s, I lived in a Cherokee-speaking world and it was painful to do so. I know what Payne went through, for I had my own difficulties with reluctant interpreters and, without them most of the time, spent countless hours sitting in Cherokee churches, meetings, and households without a clue as to what was being said. Now that Cherokees are essentially an English-speaking population, and I can understand and participate in what is going on, for the first time I not only have a sense of what I was missing, but beyond that an appreciation and a fascination with the quality of Cherokee conversation.

I suppose that more often than not Cherokees "clam up" in the presence of whites. I certainly got that impression from several remarks I heard during my visit. But if white people could have the experience I had of Cherokees relaxed, at ease with one another, drifting through the winding paths of a conversation, exploring the kinship of the characters involved, tracing their residence, their origin, their home communities, commenting on their history through the generations, interjecting funny stories and, at times, absurd puns, all this salted often with a sense of irony, there is no way they could sustain the stereotype that Cherokees are taciturn, dull, even intellectually unevolved. Among the middleclass white people with whom I associate, conversation is (pardon the cliché) a lost art, and even when it does become intense, it tends to escalate onto a highly abstract level which leaves behind the richness of personality and place. Among Cherokees, conversation is "grounded" in the inarguable essentials of kinship, place, and personal and particular events from whence it reaches upward not toward abstractions but toward generalizations. Here I am writing of conversations among professional and educated persons like Richard, John, Marvin, Wilma and Charlie, but also of conversations among "country Cherokees" in their homes, and casual conversations with other Cherokees at restaurants, and around town. I don't know how to make the point in a more definite and "scientific" language, but this aspect of Cherokee culture deserves to be highlighted and respected. Again, we have here a very rich area for sociolinguistic study.

The Integrity of Kinship and Community

On the first evening of this visit, Wilma Mankiller urged me to revisit some of the Cherokee communities I once knew well and share my impressions: "I just want to know whether it is crazy of us to think that they are still coherent entities and viable units for community development." Maybe the words aren't exact, but that is the gist of her request.

The disclaimers I must make are obvious: tiny sample and brief time. Given that limitation, my answer is that the communities I looked at are in great shape sociologically and psychologically, though economically no better off than they were in the 1960s.

When in an interview with Chief Chad Smith I made this statement, he expressed doubt and mentioned incidences of familial violence, drug dependency, child abandonment, alcoholism, and so forth. If nothing else, this proves that for an optimist the glass is half full, for a pessimist it is half empty.

With tongue out of cheek now, let's review the discrepancy. In my original report to the Cherokee people (Wahrhaftig 1966:18–20; see also Wahrhaftig 1968), I distinguished three categories of Cherokee communities in northeastern Oklahoma: communities which are stable (staying the same size or growing slowly), communities which were getting very small (and would probably disintegrate), and communities which are new and growing. The communities I observed during this visit were clear-cut examples of the communities I had classed as "stable or growing." All of the observations and impressions which follow are based on communities of this type. I have no doubt, however, that some of the communities so classed may have eroded and that there may be a considerable "displaced" population of Cherokees who have moved into Tahlequah, Stilwell, or small towns, of Cherokee returnees from urban relocation, of Cherokees whose communities have been flooded by new lakes and dams, and in mixed resettlement in crowded housing projects within "stable" Cherokee communities (such as the cluster near Cherry Tree church in Adair County). These situations, lacking the interpersonal social controls that operate within stable Cherokee communities, may well be scenes of dysfunctionality.

As I have described in a companion essay (Wahrhaftig n.d.), it was actually the strength of the bonds within these communities, that resulted in limiting my observations. My initial plan had been to pay brief visits in Cherry Tree (Adair County), Bull Hollow (Delaware County), Blackgum Mountain (Sequoyah County) and Briggs (Cherokee County), but my first visit to Cherokee Tree produced virtually obligatory invitations to visit several households of one kin group spread over two communities (Cherry Tree and Piney), which consumed the whole of the time available. That web of kin-connections, however, is what a community *is*, so the time spent in exploring its current strength and configuration was valuable.

During the week, people continually asked me about the changes I was seeing. Outside the sprawling development of Tahlequah, and beyond the expansion of the Cherokee Nation government's bureaucracies and their activities, I saw little change.

In Cherry Tree and Piney, one generation has simply displaced another. The children of people I knew in the 1960s now live in the houses formerly occupied by their deceased parents (or in new "Indian houses" on the same sites). From conversations (some admittedly brief) with residents from Briggs, Marble City, and Flute Springs, I gather that the situation in their communities has been similar.

Further, I was sometimes amazed by the continuity of some of the cultural patterns I observed. Recently I wrote an essay on "Literacy as a 'Gift': Some Observation about Cherokee Literacy and the Sacred" based on my research in the 1960s. On this trip G.D., 45 years old, proudly showed me how he uses his recently acquired ability to read and write in the Sequoyan syllabary. When I asked him when and how he became literate, his description was point for point identical to the process I had described from my 40-year-old data. This same person comes on as something of a tough guy, proud of his handcrafted knives, chatty about the frequency with which he hunts, full of good ol' boy bluster and tales of dope heroics. The white graduate student who accompanied me on this, his first visit to a Cherokee community, found him a little eerie and then was surprised by the contrast when we visited G.D.'s father, as sedate a Cherokee Baptist deacon as ever you will find. What amazed him most was my remark that Deacon D. in his youth had been very much like his son, G.D. The process of socialization which gentles down headstrong young Cherokee men and converts them into community-oriented elders (see Wahrhaftig 1975) seems quite intact and operative.

There is a dark side to my observations. G.D. works nights at a Stilwell food processing plant. By days, he may work for an electrician in Sallisaw, a landlord with many rental apartments in Fayetteville, or a plumber in Vian, under the table and whenever they call on him. In addition, although his children live with his two ex-wives, he is called upon with some frequency to care for them. His is a patchwork "make do" subsistence. In most of the other Adair County households I visited, males were working nights for similar low-wage enterprises. In several cases, husbands worked nights while their wives worked days. It looks like it is as hard as ever to keep your head above water. Add to that the presence of a large Spanish-speaking population which has appeared since the time of my research. The Cherokees I asked whether they were losing jobs to these newcomers hesitated (the "harmony ethic" again, I think) to say so outright, but they made it clear that Spanish speakers now are recruited for the most menial tasks in local nurseries, canneries, and food processing plants. One nursery employee told me his bosses wanted him to learn Spanish so he can supervise Spanish-speaking workers. I can only suppose that competition from this immigrant group serves to keep the wages available to Cherokee workers very low, as usual. I certainly think careful study of the economic situation of rural Cherokee communities with special attention to the possibility of inter-ethnic competition and tension should be given a high priority.

The Prophecies

So back to Chad Smith's remarks and my own. In the dark days of the Dawes Commission, Enrollment, and pressure for the dissolution of the Cherokee Nation, the head medicine people of the seven clans gathered to divine the future of the Cherokee people. What they learned is known in detail by many Cherokees who quite likely still await the enactment of the events that were foretold, but the essence of their revelation is contained in a little story. During the night, someone accidentally kicked over the bucket of drinking water. In the morning, when they gathered up their paraphernalia to leave, they found the bucket upright and full again. This is the prophesied future of the Cherokees. They will dwindle down, just as the water ran out of the bucket, until all that remain are a trickle of true-hearted Cherokees. And from that minitude, the Cherokees will be restored to their proper power and prosperity. Chad is right. There no doubt are confused, lost, deracinated Cherokees, possibly in increasing numbers. Even so, I have no doubt that there remains in communities like those I visited a core from which the Cherokees can again arise.

That is a matter, of course, that the Cherokee administration under W.W. Keeler could never tolerate. The slightest hint of any effort toward local community autonomy and development was invariably seen as threatening the tribal government's absolute hegemony and was immediately co-opted or stamped out. Prospects for a healthy communal life depend greatly on the present tribal government's willingness to abide by *real* local planning and decision making. The movement toward construction of community buildings in eight local communities is an encouraging first step. Providing an inter-community computer network which would enable local communities to share plans and information *in private* would be a logical next step.

The local communities of which I write are eclipsed by the Cherokee Nation government with its multitude of programs and responsibilities which extend over 14 counties to tens of thousands of assorted technically-Cherokee persons. It is well to remember, however, that throughout by far the largest part of their history, the Cherokee people have organized themselves as a loose assembly of semi-autonomous communities ("towns" in the literature). Centralization has been something that Cherokees tolerated only when necessary to ward off the encroachment of white institutions and white hunger for Cherokee wealth. It is not their "natural condition."

Overheard

Two women discussing the difficulty of getting a parent to sign up for a youth group activity:
"She didn't want to have to sign a paper. 'Are you going to take my land?' she asked."
"'Only half,' I said."

In a conversation in an Adair County household:
"The UKB [United Keetoowah Band] is our tribe."

In a conversation about the Wilma Mankiller clinic in Stilwell:
"They give white people preference."
"Yeah, there are people in the Cherokee Nation [office] who will sell them ID cards."

Another conversation:
"They said he died of diabetes, but I think it was AIDS."
"A lot of what they say is diabetes around here is AIDS."

Another Reflection

I was enormously pleased by the invitation to come to Oklahoma and talk about my work and publications. By email we quickly agreed on a week-long visit. My friends and associates asked me what the Cherokees wanted me to do. I said I didn't know; no doubt they would tell me when I got there.

The first day, Richard told me that there would be a potluck at Wilma's that evening and at lunch, John told me that the youth group would meet at 6 p.m. the next day at the American

Legion Hall on Allen St. Late that first evening, Wilma made her quiet suggestion that I might visit some communities and write her a few informal words later. I went to bed wondering what I was expected to do all the next day.

That day and the next were similar. I kept wondering when they were going to tell me what to do.

Late that day, I came to my senses. "Shit, Albert, they ain't going to tell me what to do. Cherokees don't do that. They expect that you will know what you should be doing."

It's nice to know that hasn't changed, even among people who staff the tribal bureaucracies and direct programs.

I don't even mind discovering that I am as slow to catch on as ever.

Notes

1. During this visit I frequently heard the term "community Cherokees" used in conversations in the tribal offices. The terms seems to equate to "tribal Cherokees" as used in my various publications. I prefer this newer term.
2. For further information, see Gearing 1962.
3. Once again I have to confess ignorance as regards to Cherokee women. Ethnography focused on Cherokee women, their roles, and their personalities, is long overdue. Note the very active female role described in Wahrhaftig n.d.

References Cited

Gearing, Fred O.
1962 Priests and Warriors: Social Structures for Cherokee Politics in the 18th Century. American Anthropological Association Memoir 93. *American Anthropologist*, 65(5):2.

Wahrhaftig, Albert L.
1966 *The Cherokee People Today.* The Carnegie Cross-Cultural Education Project of the University of Chicago, Tahlequah.
1968 The Tribal Cherokee Population in Eastern Oklahoma. *Current Anthropology*, 9(5):510–518.
1975 More than Mere Work. *Appalachian Journal*, 2(4):327–331.
n.d. Cherokee Kinship in Action. Unpublished manuscript.

CHAPTER 11

THE 2011 AMERICAN INDIAN SEATTLE TRADITIONAL FOOD SUMMIT

Darby C. Stapp

The 2011 Traditional Food Summit held in Seattle, Washington, was an organized gathering of 300 people interested in expanding the use of traditional foods by indigenous peoples, primarily in the Pacific Northwest of North America. The multidisciplinary gathering of tribal groups, government agencies, and applied scientists was held in conjunction with the Society for Applied Anthropology (SfAA) 71st Annual Meeting. The summit, designed in the spirit of Sol Tax's Action Anthropology, serves as a collaborative anthropology model for future annual meetings of applied social and natural resource scientists.

Background

American Indian tribes and many indigenous populations around the world are working to maintain and increase the use of their traditional foods. Adoption of western foods is seen as one important factor among many in the decline of health in indigenous peoples. Traditional foods are generally healthy, serve an important role in the perpetuation of indigenous cultures, and are increasingly seen as critical for reversing the decline in the health of many indigenous populations. Unfortunately, supplies of traditional foods continue to decline as worldwide development accelerates. The problem is complex, and solutions will require collaboration among many scientific disciplines as well as a concerted effort by indigenous groups, governments, and the scientific community.

An example of the problem can be found in the Pacific Northwest, where regional development has led to dramatic losses in the availability of traditional foods for coastal and interior indigenous communities. Even where aquatic and terrestrial resources still exist, access to them by indigenous peoples is often restricted by government policies (e.g., no gathering allowed in national parks). Many landscape-restoration efforts are under way, but restoring a traditional food base is no easy matter; little research has been conducted to inform tribal and agency program staff. Efforts are needed to address these problems so that traditional foods will be available for indigenous groups in the future.

The opportunity to make an anthropological contribution to the problems associated with traditional foods can be traced to February 2010, when the SfAA asked me to be program chair for its 2011 annual meeting, to be held in Seattle, Washington. As one who has long admired Dr. Sol Tax and his accomplishments, I have always been interested in the Action Anthropology model to hold problem-oriented gatherings with indigenous groups and applied scientists; the model is best exemplified by the 1961 American Indian Chicago Conference (Ablon 1962, 1979; Lurie 1999). In the Chicago example, Dr. Tax and his staff—which included Joan Ablon, Nancy Lurie, Al Wahrhaftig, Bob Thomas, and others—recognized a need (American Indian sovereignty at risk), went to tribal leaders to present the idea (through the National Congress of American Indians), assisted in creating a forum (the American Indian Chicago Conference), and worked in the background to assist the tribal representatives in accomplishing their goals (e.g., produce a statement of Indian purpose). I wanted to do something similar.

Tom May, SfAA executive director, early on supported my proposal for a focused gathering that would bring applied anthropology and other applied social sciences to a contemporary problem. SfAA regularly encourages other groups to meet with SfAA at its annual meeting, so there was a long precedent for such a collaboration. There is always a desire among the SfAA membership wherever the annual meeting is held to involve local indigenous groups. This idea was slightly different from previous efforts in that we would bring together a diverse group to focus on a particular issue. Especially appealing to me was the fact that all of the Grand Hyatt conference rooms would be available on Tuesday, essentially for no additional cost, because the SfAA reserved the hotel, but most sessions and events typically did not begin until Wednesdays.

The next step was finding a contemporary issue to address. Natural-resources management was an early candidate, given the many SfAA members working in this area, the strong environmental presence in the Pacific Northwest, and the contemporary conflicts associated with indigenous uses. The idea of holding a natural resources–oriented gathering gained momentum in July 2010, when SfAA member Eric Jones responded to an email I sent to regional colleagues offering space to organizations and groups interested in participating in the Seattle meeting. He indicated that the Institute for Culture and Ecology (IFCAE), a nonprofit multidisciplinary group of natural-resource professionals in the Northwest (www.ifcae.org), was interested. This would bring a regional group of environmental and social scientists to the Seattle meeting and would complement the interests of many SfAA applied scientists working on similar issues. Dr. Melissa Poe, an IFCAE and SfAA member, agreed to serve on the Seattle planning committee and help with planning.

I then approached Teara Farrow Ferman, a manager in the Natural Resources Department of the Confederated Tribes of the Umatilla Indian Reservation (CTUIR), an Oregon tribe I have worked with for 20 years. I described the opportunity to participate in the SfAA meeting, described the 1,500 applied social scientists who would be participating, and mentioned the availability of conference rooms at no cost. I asked if they would be interested in participating in a focused gathering, perhaps building on their "First Foods" management approach. She presented the idea to her manager, Eric Quaempts, and they soon proposed a two-day "summit" meeting format that would address issues surrounding the protection and use of traditional native foods and involve professionals, agencies, and tribal groups. To broaden interest, the name Traditional Food Summit was suggested.

The next challenge was to get other tribes involved, especially those from the coastal regions as well as First Nations from Canada. A major breakthrough occurred when Melissa Poe (IFCAE/SfAA) provided IFCAE intern Joyce LeCompte-Mastenbrook to help. As an anthropology graduate student at the University of Washington, LeCompte-Mastenbrook was pursuing research on traditional foods and was connected with various coastal tribal programs working with traditional-food issues.

Next I contacted SfAA members Neil and Carson Henderson (University of Oklahoma American Indian Diabetes Center), with whom I had worked previously as part of the SfAA American Indian Issues Committee. They agreed to help and to bring their perspective on nutrition and health based on their professional work with Oklahoma tribes.

By July 2010, it was clear that a traditional food summit was a viable idea and one that would attract much interest. A project plan was developed and additional people found to serve on the planning group, which would oversee the design and implementation. The planning group included representatives from Northwest Indian College, other tribes, SfAA members, and state agencies (Table 1), including two additional anthropologists, Maurice Major of the Washington State Department of Natural Resources and Dennis Lewarch from the Suquamish Tribe.

Table 1. The Traditional Food Summit Planning Group

Name	Professional Affiliation
Julia Bennett-Gladstone	Suquamish Tribe
Heidi Bohan	Snoqualmie Tribe
Larry Campbell	Swinomish Tribe
Rodney Cawston	Washington Department of Natural Resources
Vanessa Cooper	Northwest Indian College
Teara Farrow Ferman	Confederated Tribes of the Umatilla Indian Reservation
Rhonda Foster	Squaxin Island Tribe
Neil Henderson	University of Oklahoma
Warren King George	Muckleshoot Tribe
Elise Krohn	Northwest Indian College
Joyce LeCompte-Mastenbrook	University of Washington
Dennis Lewarch	Suquamish Tribe
Maurice Major	Washington Department of Natural Resources
Libby Halpin Nelson	Tulalip Tribes
Melissa Poe	Institute for Culture and Ecology
Eric Quaempts	Confederated Tribes of the Umatilla Indian Reservation
Valerie Segrest	Northwest Indian College
Darby Stapp	Northwest Anthropology LLC

Design

The planning group met via phone and email several times from May 2010 through January 2011. The group identified the following objectives for the summit:

- Review traditional food resource concepts.
- Share current approaches being pursued by tribes and agencies for increasing use and protection.
- Identify roadblocks for using and protecting traditional food resources.
- Identify potential policy and research needs and actions.

Key goals were to highlight innovative approaches, foster dialogue, share experiences, and build collaborative networks. There also emerged a general desire to focus on indigenous content presented by indigenous groups and professionals working collaboratively. While formal professional presentations were of interest, the planning group really wanted a venue where people would have time to talk together and share experiences in a more interactive format than the professional 20-minute presentation usually provides.

The contribution by the SfAA business office was critical and cannot be overstated. In addition to the meeting rooms, the SfAA agreed to provide virtually all administrative support, handle the preregistration, develop a flyer, send out announcements and letters, print the program, and manage the onsite registration. Further, the business office created a special cost structure to facilitate tribal involvement. Anyone could attend the two-day summit for $60, a phenomenal rate; anyone registered for the summit could also have a display table free of charge; and anyone registered for the full SfAA conference ($120) could attend the summit for no additional cost. Finally, the SfAA business office would extend the deadline for submission of abstracts by a month, which allowed more time to develop a program that would meet the objectives. My time and that of the planning group would all be donated.

The design of the project drew upon basic principles of Action Anthropology and collaborative anthropology. The primary goal was to bring applied knowledge to address a community issue. Following the Sol Tax model, the anthropologists on the planning group would serve as facilitators, providing options for the planning group to consider. The results would need to be disseminated to indigenous communities as well as the professional applied science communities, so that each could benefit. Anthropological concepts at work included self-determination, cultural perpetuation, community collaboration, informed decision making, multidisciplinary research, mutual understanding and respect, traditional ecological knowledge, the importance of language, the importance of place, and various health-related topics.

The Summit Program and Registration

Efforts commenced in August 2010 to attract attendees and participants. Messages went out on a variety of internet lists made available by the steering committee members. These included tribal networks, agency networks, anthropology networks, and traditional food networks. The summit was also advertised to the SfAA membership though direct-mail, letters, and the *SfAA Newsletter.* Abstracts were due November 15, 2010, for the professional presentations, with reservations for the displays and roundtables extended to February 1, 2011. By December 2010, the following preliminary agenda was set:

- *Day 1, Morning:* CTUIR First Foods Initiative. The summit would begin with members of CTUIR describing their successes and challenges to date in applying first-foods concepts to managing the natural resource base.
- *Day 1, Afternoon:* Displays. Interactive traditional food displays would give participants the time to hold in-depth discussions with the display presenters.
- *Day 1, Afternoon:* Roundtables. Plans called for twelve two-hour roundtables in which small groups would be able to pursue topics such as contamination and traditional foods, water, strategies to protect cultural resources, restoration, establishing traditional gardens, urban issues, and agency policies.
- *Day 2:* Professional Tracks. In concert with the start of the main SfAA meeting, the summit would have professional-type sessions and papers. Northwest Indian College agreed to organize one day-long track.
- *Day 2:* Summit Closeout. Time would be set aside at the end of the day to allow participants to discuss the summit and develop recommendations for next steps.

The Traditional Food Summit Planning Group continued to meet, and progress reports were submitted regularly. Details that had to be worked out included a tribal welcome and funding for refreshments. The chairman of the Suquamish Tribe, Leonard Forsman, a practicing applied anthropologist, agreed to give the tribal welcome. Peter Goldmark, the elected Washington director of state lands who had grown up on the Colville Indian Reservation, offered to give an opening welcome. Funds were raised for refreshments.

Registration numbers were an important concern and difficult to predict because we had not instituted a preregistration date or a final registration date. One method to encourage people to register was signups for the roundtables, which was sent out in February 2011. The registration numbers grew as the summit approached: January, 43; February, 68; March 4, 96; March 15, 138. Reservations for the roundtables and displays followed in a similar fashion, with 123 reserving space at the 10 roundtables and 21 reserving display tables.

A major problem arose two weeks prior to the summit date, when I was notified by the SfAA business office that the larger conference rooms promised (and in fact already printed in the main program) were not available for the summit on Day 1 (Tuesday). Tom May took full responsibility for the contractual mishap, and we worked to explore options. The rooms scheduled for Day 2 were available. The best option for Day 1, given the number of registrants at the time, was to take a series of rooms on the seventh floor. It would be tight, but at least everyone would be together. Unexpectedly, registrations continued to increase every day, and an additional 50 people arrived on Day 1, who had not preregistered.

The Traditional Food Summit

The Traditional Food Summit took place on March 29–30, 2011, on the seventh floor of the Seattle Grand Hyatt (Figures 14, 15, and 16). Registration totals indicate that 258 people registered for the two-day summit. We estimate 50 to 75 SfAA members also attended; SfAA meeting registrants had been told they could attend the Traditional Food Summit for no additional cost. When registration, travel, hotel, and wages are considered, over $600,000 was spent collectively by all the registrants to attend the summit.

Figure 14. Traditional Food Summit Program. Society for Applied Anthropology, 71st Annual Meeting.

We did our best to accommodate everyone, but the overcrowding heavily affected the effectiveness of the first day. We arranged for the opening-session speakers to give their presentations twice; we turned the original roundtables into group sessions; and the interactive displays opened up several hours early to provide something else for people to do. Still, it was hectic. Day 2, fortunately, went flawlessly. Below are some of the highlights of the summit.

Display-table topics included the following:

- Bringing Back the Wapato
- Columbia River Inter-Tribal Fish Commission Project & Information Display
- NW Indian College Traditional Plants & Foods Program, Spring Edible Foods
- Coastal Louisiana Communities
- Douglas Indian Association Elders and Youth Program
- Diabetes Education for Tribal Schools
- Helping Ourselves to Health Program
- Edible Marine Limu (Seaweed) in Hawaii
- Suquamish Traditional Foods Program
- Healthy Traditions
- Traditional Amerindian Foods of the Rio Negro (Brazilian Amazon)
- First Foods from Washington State Lands
- Physical Activity Kit Developed by Indian Health Services that Draws on Traditional Native Games

Roundtable topics were:

- Traditional Foods and Nutrition
- First Foods on Washington State Lands
- Traditional Foods and Contamination: Aquatic Resources
- Honoring Traditions from Rural to Urban Living
- Food, Cultural Places, and Historic Properties: Using the National Historic Preservation Act to Protect Traditional Food Sources
- Impacts to Traditional Foods are not Restricted by International Boundaries
- Traditional Foods and Water
- Wy-Kan-Ush-Mi Wa-Kish-Wit or "Spirit of the Salmon": An Update to the Columbia River Tribal Salmon Restoration Plan
- Restoring Traditional Food Systems through Contemporary Restoration and Cultivation Practices

Session presentations included:

- Nisqually Indian Tribe's Work on Traditional Foods
- Tanoak Dreamtime: Safeguarding a Native Nut Tree
- Wapato in the World
- What's in a Name? How USDA's Definition of a "Farmer or Rancher" Fails to Support Traditional Alaska Native Methods of Food Procurement such as Hunting, Gathering, Fishing, and Subsistence Gardening
- 49th Parallel: Inhibitor to the Natural World Experience of the Syilx
- Revitalizing Food Choice
- Sustainable Cultivation of Camas as Food: Learning from Ethnography and Ecology
- Remember the Treaty: Sustaining Treaty-Reserved Gathering Opportunities on National Forests through Government-to-Government Agreements
- A Recipe for Success: Preserving Our Heritage, a Native Foods Bank and Restoration Project
- Tacoma Indian Center: Positive Change through Nutrition and Wellness Classes
- Rebalancing Land, Restoring Foodways: Numic Pine Nut Harvest on Southern Nevada Federal Lands

Figure 15. Eric Quaempts, Confederated Tribes of the Umatilla Indian Reservation, giving the keynote presentation on first-foods management.

Figure 16. Example of one of the displays at the Traditional Food Summit.

Assessment

An online survey using *SurveyMonkey* was conducted following the summit. The feedback indicated that people were energized by the gathering. Over 80 percent of the respondents said they were inspired to action. The large crowd and the diversity of attendees demonstrated the importance and multidisciplinary interest in traditional foods to agencies and scientists—and to the indigenous participants themselves. While there had been traditional-food gatherings held before among various tribal and professional groups, this was the largest and most multidisciplinary one that most had attended. The summit was unique in its holism and in the combination of applied social scientists and agency people working with tribal members and tribal staff.

Another benefit of the gathering was that participants were exposed to a wide variety of ongoing programs from which they learned and made contacts. Collaborations have started, people are excited, and cross-fertilization is occurring. There is much talk for follow-on summits. For example, the CTUIR decided to host the 2012 Northwest Anthropology Conference (the first time it has been hosted by a tribe) and Haskell Indian Nations University sponsored a food summit drawing from our lessons learned. To facilitate similar efforts and disseminate the information produced at the Traditional Food Summit, a summary report—including the *SurveyMonkey* results, roundtable summaries, and presentations—has been prepared and is available electronically (Stapp 2011).

From my perspective as summit organizer, its greatest benefit was the demonstration of the value of multidisciplinary approaches to solving human problems. At the Traditional Food Summit, it wasn't anthropologists talking to anthropologists, or tribal members talking to tribal members, or natural-resources people talking to natural-resources people. Here we had tribal elders, tribal professional staff, educators, nutritionists, diabetes specialists, archaeologists, resource managers, bureaucrats, university professors, ethnographers, biologists, and so on all working together on one topic: finding ways to enhance traditional foods for indigenous peoples. For two days, we knocked down the cultural, organizational, and disciplinary walls, and it felt great!

The 2011 Traditional Food Summit provides a good model for future SfAA meetings to build upon. Bringing together cultural groups and professionals from diverse backgrounds to focus on a particular contemporary issue is a compelling concept.

Applied social scientists have much to offer, and the annual meeting becomes an economical way to fund a project such as this. Not only do we use our knowledge to help solve a problem, we learn much about a problem and our discipline.

Summary

This was not the first time anthropologists had met with American Indians in the Pacific Northwest at a professional meeting. In fact, Sol Tax organized a special session on Indian rights in 1968 as part of the American Anthropological Association held that year in Seattle. Sol Tax, with the assistance of anthropologist Deward E. Walker Jr., brought tribal participants, attorneys, and natural resource scientists together to discuss the emerging Indian fishing crisis and other issues surrounding hunting and general protection of Indian places. A transcription of the speaker presentations and audience comments was then published in the regional journal *Northwest Anthropological Research Notes* by Walker (Tax 1968). A summary of the 1968 session appeared in the *Anthropology Newsletter* (Stanley 1968), which is reprinted following this chapter. David G. Rice, who attended both the 1968 and 2011 Seattle sessions, reflects on the impact that the 1968 session had on his professional development in a vignette included following the Stanley reprint.

Looking forward, the 2011 Seattle Traditional Food Summit provides a glimpse of the role that anthropology can play in helping solve regional problems in the future. The summit brought together a diverse set of specialists to focus on a specific problem. Archaeologists, anthropologists, natural-resource professionals, educators, biologists, nutritionists, and others all came to pursue ways to increase the availability and consumption of traditional indigenous foods. To accomplish these goals, all parts of the food system were represented: the users, tribal families and elders who maintain traditional diets; tribal managers interacting with those in control to represent tribal interests, concerns, and expectations; health specialists informing about medical conditions, especially those that are diet and abuse related; educators helping perpetuate traditional culture through the classroom or involved in nutrition education and trying to effect changes toward healthier diets; natural-resource managers taking ecosystem approaches and helping agencies implement sustainable practices while protecting traditional resources; cultural-resource managers protecting traditional-use areas where the resources exist; and archaeologists providing ecological information from earlier eras. The inclusive and holistic nature of the Traditional Food Summit was a reflection of the influences from Action Anthropology. Action Anthropologists are good organizers and facilitators and, more importantly, have the drive and commitment to make things happen. The Action Anthropology process of involving and listening to those with the problem ensures that the right problems will be addressed, and that solutions will be appropriate and realistic. Organizing a professional gathering may not be the typical anthropology project, but from my perspective, this effort will probably have a larger impact on the quality of life for Indian people in the future than any other project I have been involved in during my 35-year career. Thank you, Sol Tax, for the inspiration!

References Cited

Ablon, Joan

1962 The American Indian Chicago Conference. *Journal of American Education*, 1:17–23.

1979 The Indian Chicago Conference. In *Current Anthropology: Essays in Honor of Sol Tax*, edited by Robert E. Hinshaw, pp. 445–456. Mouton Publishers, New York.

Lurie, Nancy O.

1999 Sol Tax and Tribal Sovereignty. *Human Organization*, 58(1):108–117.

Stanley, Sam

1968 Legal Session is New Departure. *Anthropology Newsletter*. December, pp. 3–4. American Anthropological Association.

Stapp, Darby C.

2011 Expanding the Influence of Applied Social Science: Traditional Food Summit Documentation Package. Journal of Northwest Anthropology, Summer 2011, Electronic Edition. http://www.northwestanthropology.com/volumes.php.

Tax, Sol

1968 American Anthropological Association Symposium on American Indian Fishing and Hunting Rights. *Northwest Anthropological Research Notes*, 2 (2):1–43.

THE 1968 SEATTLE SESSION ON INDIAN HUNTING AND FISHING RIGHTS, AMERICAN ANTHROPOLOGICAL ASSOCIATION ANNUAL MEETING

Sam Stanley

Editor's Note: This summary of the 1968 Indian hunting and fishing rights session coordinated by Sol Tax at the 1968 Annual Meeting of the American Anthropological Association in Seattle, Washington, first appeared in the *Anthropology Newsletter* (Stanley 1968). The three-hour session involved a diverse group of anthropologists, attorneys, tribal members, and Indian rights advocates. A transcript of the session was published in *Northwest Anthropological Research Notes* (Tax 1968).

Legal Session Is New Departure

Sam Stanley contributes the following account of the Amerind Hunting and Fishing Rights session held Friday evening, Nov. 22.

One feature of the recent meeting in Seattle was an experimental session on Indian hunting and fishing rights, suggested and organized by Sol Tax, assisted by Sam Stanley, Smithsonian Institution, and Joe Muskrat, a young Cherokee Indian lawyer and Visiting Fellow of the Adlai Stevenson Institute of International Affairs. The major objective of the "experimental session" was to openly examine an important public issue and discover what anthropology might contribute to its clarification.

As originally conceived the session was to be conducted in a moot court format; with opposing lawyers, witnesses and a judge or judges. Briefs were to be prepared and presented and at the end of the "trial" a verdict would be handed down. As planning proceeded it became clear that the format would have to be changed. All the lawyers objected to a "trial" in which they might face unknown witnesses as well as the prospect of losing even a "moot" case. Judges who preside over "moot" cases as emotionally laden as these may be disqualifying themselves from future "real" cases. The new format, which proved more acceptable, was a panel discussion with Tax as moderator and each member of the panel having an opportunity to make a short presentation.

It was obvious from the beginning that any exploration of this complex and emotionally charged issue could not rely on anthropology alone. As a result the panel consisted largely of a number of "experts" who were able to present knowledge from outside the field of anthropology. There were statements given by: lawyers associated with the State of Washington's position, with the federal government's position, with the Indians position; a conservationist; a resource management economist; and a fish biologist. Nancy Lurie, University of Wisconsin-Milwaukee, and Deward Walker, University of Idaho, read statements on traditional and modern Indian fishing, hunting and gathering practices. As soon as the experts had finished their presentations, the American Indians began to state their positions from the floor. The result was some of the most stirring oratory that has ever graced an AAA annual meeting.

The three-hour session ended at 10:30 p.m. with at least two obvious accomplishments. It crystallized some views on Indian fishing rights which were formerly somewhat amorphous. Hence it would appear that Indians are entitled to a "fair share" of the fish which they have traditionally depended upon for subsistence. Whatever rights a state may have to regulate Indian fishing, it must not continue to force the Indian to bear all of the brunt of conservation. There has to be recognition of what lawyers call an Indian's "superior right" in this important resource. Ultimately these issues will be decided in the courts and it is obvious that anthropologists must contribute what they know to help clarify them. Another important accomplishment of this session was that it provided a forum for confrontation between contending parties. For the Indians who were present, this was an opportunity to face the representatives of the state who have been prosecuting them for violations of the fishing laws. They were able to talk directly to them and that dialogue was most instructive to everyone who attended the session.

The session was very well attended with over four hundred persons present and many unable to even get into the meeting room. Most who did attend would favor sessions like this at every national meeting. Perhaps someone should plan to discuss the issue of non-recognition of the Houma at the meetings in New Orleans next year. It might even be more worthwhile to reexamine the issue of white racism.

Whatever is done in the future should profit from the Seattle "fishing rights" session. The most conspicuous failure was lack of publicity. The program was taped, but it should have been videotaped. There should also have been representatives from all the media, whereas there was really very little coverage.

References Cited

Stanley, Sam

1968 Legal Session is New Departure. *Anthropology Newsletter,* December, pp. 3–4. American Anthropological Association.

Tax, Sol

1968 American Anthropological Association Symposium on American Indian Fishing and Hunting Rights. *Northwest Anthropological Research Notes,* 2 (2):1–43.

VIGNETTE: THE IMPACT OF SOL TAX ON THE DEVELOPMENT OF MY PROFESSIONAL CAREER

David G. Rice

My initial acquaintance with Dr. Tax stems from a 1949 Viking Fund Seminar on the status of Mesoamerican anthropology which he edited into the book entitled *Heritage of Conquest* (1952), a text used in one of my 1960s undergraduate classes at the University of Washington. This work, and his famous *Penny Capitalism* (1953) monograph, laid out formative elements of his approach to the principles of applied anthropology, and impressed me with the possibilities for anthropology in the course of social and economic change.

In response to National Congress of American Indians efforts to promote Indian self-determination, the U.S. government reversed its Indian policy from assimilation. With the Indian Self Determination Acts of 1964 and 1965, the U.S. government set a new course for Indian policy, embracing elements of self governance, cultural survival and identity, and control of financial affairs. This reflects some changes induced by Action Anthropology in support of tribal identity and self government. As tribes began organizing to take control of their own political and economic destinies there were continuing problems. In the area of treaty rights, tribes ran into continuing legal and jurisdictional difficulties regarding their traditional hunting and fishing practices with some state and federal agencies.

In view of tribal difficulties in the northwestern United States, Deward E. Walker Jr. requested Sol Tax to conduct a symposium on Indian treaty fishing and hunting rights for a forthcoming American Anthropological Association annual meeting. So, it was in 1968 at the AAA annual meeting in Seattle, Washington, where I finally met Dr. Tax. True to his principles, Dr. Tax invited representatives of the aggrieved tribes to attend as panelists so that they could tell their own stories at the symposium. Then, after their presentations and ensuing dialogue, he searched for ways that would empower the tribes to address these issues. He pointed out that anthropologists and their students could work collaboratively in many ways with individual tribes to achieve change, but he emphasized that self-governing tribes need to speak for themselves. Indeed, I had provided support to Yakama Nation in helping to document Columbia River fishing rights two years earlier, so I had a special interest. Although it took years before Federal Court decisions heard the tribes (such as the Boldt Decision in 1974), the immediate call for action to anthropologists was made at the end of the 1968 symposium session.

The challenge given by Dr. Tax at the 1968 symposium was fresh in my mind as I took classes in the organizational phases of social movements, and visited students in Washington State University Department of Sociology's new Urban Indian Studies program office in Seattle in 1969. This program contributed to Bahr, Chadwick, and Day (1972), *Native Americans Today:*

Sociological Perspectives. That work was especially important in describing the conditions that prevailed at that time both in Indian Country and urban settings. This would become an "existing condition" database of potential initiatives for *Action Anthropology*.

Later in 1969, I attended the Alaska Science Conference at Fairbanks, Alaska, to participate in open sessions on "Social Change and Native People," "Strategies for Social Change," and "Man and the Environment" (Viereck 1970). Of course, it was the discovery of oil on the North Slope in Alaska that was driving this impromptu, international conference. What would happen to develop oil resources? What would be the environmental consequences for natural resources on the land? And what would be the impacts and changes that Native Alaskans would have to endure? These were the questions of the day. The conference featured organizational meetings of the Alaska Federation of Natives (AFN)—the foundation of a social movement that would lead to the unique Alaska Native Claims and Settlement Act (ANCSA) in 1971. AFN was composed of 12 Alaska Native self-governing associations. At the conference I met with AFN leaders of the incipient associations, particularly from the North Slope. Secretary of the Interior Watts was on hand to discuss land title issues, and federal policies that would have to be addressed for expedited petroleum development to occur. The processes for change were nearly instantaneous, particularly a governmental mechanism for consultation with individual native groups, since *aboriginal title* to most Alaskan lands at that time was still in effect, and needed to be settled for drilling permits to be issued. This later became known as the "d-2" (Federal interest lands) provision of the 1971 ANCSA legislation. This was the first governmental fast-track program in my experience that embraced so many elements of what we call *Action Anthropology* today. I did not realize at the time that this experience and Dr. Tax's 1968 challenge to students in Seattle would provide a template for a number of my future professional undertakings.

In the Alaska experience, I also caught a glimpse of an early example of a broader "pan-Indian" movement element. Owing to my incipient relationship with the Yakama Indian Nation, I learned from Tribal Council members that they had voted to provide a financial loan to the AFN in Alaska to help achieve the objective of Alaska Natives and self-governance there. When ANCSA was passed in 1971, this loan was repaid. This common interest mutualism later became an international trend among some Indian tribes as part of their outreach. For example, many years later, in the 1990s, the Yakama Nation provided support to the Lacandon Maya in Chiapas, Mexico, regarding public policy issues of habitat protection and cultural preservation and survival there.

In 1972 I began teaching an anthropology class in "Contemporary American Indians" at the University of Idaho, which I inherited from Deward Walker Jr. when he moved on to the University of Colorado. My course included regional tribal students as well as regular upper division college students. The purpose was to review federal legislative history affecting U.S. Indian tribes, the changes wrought by each piece of legislation, the effect of federal legislation and presidential executive orders, the unique tribal treaty status, and to consider their futures. A highlight of this experience was a 1972 guest lecture by Vine Deloria Jr., who at that time was assisting in the formation of special tribal student organizations for Indians on U.S. college campuses. This course was one of few offered in the West in the 1970s that examined present-day Native Americans in terms of their present economic and political condition, unique federal status, and their problems and prospects for cultural survival in the emerging era of economic and political self-determination.

In the 1980s Indian tribes were left out of the huge expansion in archaeological fieldwork generated by the Archaeological and Historic Preservation Act of 1974 (P.L. 93-291), and there was no effective communication between archaeologists and Indian tribes. The situation festered, leading to many misconceptions and misunderstandings regarding actions by archaeologists, but also about the interest and status of tribes. The work of illegal amateur relic collectors and grave robbers was attributed to professional archaeologists, complicating the matter, and scientifically trained university archaeologists were often insensitive to the cultural and religious significance of archaeological finds to tribes. At that time federal agency archaeologists were relatively few, and they were more concerned with problems of managing and protecting historic and cultural sites on their lands. But they also recognized the trust responsibilities of the federal government to treaty tribes, so they represented a middle ground in the dialogue. In this role, they were outcasts, like the tribes, respected by neither tribes nor academic archaeologists.

Between 1986 and 1988, the Affiliated Tribes of Northwest Indians (ATNI) sponsored Indian conferences on cultural preservation to close an apparent gap in trust and communication between Indians and archaeologists. A primary objective was to open communication to achieve common understanding. The first conference in 1986, sponsored by the Oregon Governor's Office for Indian Affairs, was held in Salem, Oregon. Professional archaeologists who attended were mostly university and museum practitioners. Communication between the professional archaeologists and tribal representatives broke down and the objectives of the conference were not met. Stereotype labeling, lack of trust, and accusations of atrocities like plundering ancestral graves, polarized the dialogue between the two groups. Many archaeologists who participated stated later that they would not attend future Indian conferences of this kind. There was no communication. No common ground.

The conference in 1987 was hosted by the Warm Springs Tribe, attended by about 250 elders and representatives of 40 ATNI tribes from four states. Tribal cultural staff identified a few professionals to present perspectives about archaeology to tribal elders. I was one of three anthropologists invited to present at the meeting, and I chose the topic of "Indian Consultation: What Does It Mean," followed by "Native American Cultural Resources." Randall Schalk, an archaeologist from Seattle, spoke about the use of archaeology in Indian claims cases; and Philip Walker, physical anthropologist from University of California, Davis (who later served on the NAGPRA Committee), spoke about information from human osteology that could contribute information about Indian diet and health. These varied subjects were intended to speak about the benefits for tribes of scientific archaeology. Non-Indian attendees were few: federal attendees included Dave Corliss and Mary Keith from the U.S. Forest Service Whitman National Forest; Kevin Clarke from the Department of Energy, Richland Operations; David Rice from Seattle District Corps of Engineers; and Paul Shroy, an attorney from NW Division Army Corps of Engineers in Portland, Oregon.

Details of these meetings and proceedings are important to describe here because they are not documented by the individual tribes or federal agencies that supported them, nor by academic anthropologists, many of whom were not interested in working relationships with tribes in the 1980s. It also illustrates how change occurs within government agency cultures. Only the memory of those who lived the experience now remains. Yet it is this segment of university-trained archaeologists working for or within federal agencies who became the Action Anthropology adherents (Rice 1997). These persons were the leaders that made a difference in improving the relationship between Indians tribes and archaeologists over the next 25 years. On the basis of building non-exploitative mutual respect, they are the professionals who achieved common ground for the mutual benefits and collaborative partnerships that now exist on a routine basis. More recently, university Indian programs supporting these common interests have also emerged, and now have their champions for tribal outreach.

Although I regard myself as a passionate champion of these causes, I do not claim personal credit for all of these accomplishments. However, I definitely registered an impression and had a catalyst effect among those present to make needed changes. Personally, I endured countless internal bureaucratic battles to achieve small changes in agency attitudes and practices on a project-by-project basis, tribe by tribe. In my mind, I am inclined to attribute my unacknowledged successes to the ripple effect of Dr. Sol Tax and his approach to the 1968 American Anthropological Association symposium on Indian Hunting and Fishing Rights in the Pacific Northwest (Tax 1968).

Two milestone moments came late in my federal professional career. The first came about 1992–93 when the interagency environmental impact statement (EIS) study for operation of the Federal Columbia River Power System (FCRPS) was initiated by the Army Corps of Engineers, Bonneville Power Administration, and Bureau of Reclamation (1994). The driving force was the Endangered Species Act listing of Columbia River salmon. As a federal participant I had responsibilities for cultural resource impact assessment and National Environmental Policy Act compliance. When the agency heads initiated the study, I met with the three agency program managers and insisted that existing laws required direct involvement and participation of the treaty tribes along the Columbia River, especially since fishery impacts would be a major focus of study. They agreed. I proposed that I attend regional ATNI meetings and make informational presentations to affected tribal leaders and staff. I was sent to ATNI meetings in

Port Angeles, Washington, and Portland, Oregon. In addition, I contacted tribal governments, soliciting their attendance at agency study meetings in Portland. In a matter of months, enclaves of tribal government representatives arrived at the governmental study sessions in Portland. Initially, lower river treaty tribes came, including the Yakama Nation, Warm Springs, and Umatilla tribes, but soon upriver tribal groups were represented, including Colville, Spokane, Coeur d'Alene, Nez Perce, and Confederated Salish and Kootenai tribes. As a result of their direct meeting with agency heads, and concerns about treaty fishing, arrangements were made to provide funding to all affected tribes in Washington, Idaho, Oregon, and Montana during the study and EIS phases.

The outcome for tribes in the EIS Records of Decision brought about major changes in the way NW agencies communicate with regional Indian tribes. Tribes were organized into federally sponsored cooperating groups for fish, wildlife, and cultural resources in each federal reservoir within the FCRPS. All agency undertakings within FCRPS since the late 1990s have routinely involved the affected federally recognized Indian tribes. Contracts were also initiated with Indian tribes to conduct studies that would help to mitigate the adverse effects of reservoir operations. I do not claim to have made all of these things happen, but they might not have happened as quickly or systematically if I had not been involved. It helped to initiate the action coherently and with a plan sustained by legal and treaty authorities. I also was an effective champion for contracting with tribes. This would not have happened if I had not first been well informed, and had an understanding of social movements, pertinent legal authorities, and Indian treaty rights.

My second milestone achievement came in 1994–95 when the Assistant Secretary of the Army (Civil Works) Dr. John Zirschky made a request to HQ, USACE, to organize a workshop for Indian tribes. This was in response to President Clinton's Executive Memorandum of April 29, 1994, entitled "Government-to-Government Relations with Native American Tribal Governments." The request to Corps HQ was sent to Corps field offices, and an internal agency search was carried out for knowledgeable staff to respond to the assistant secretary. I was one of 18 persons selected and was instructed to attend a planning meeting at Fort Belvoir, Virginia.

Native American Coordinators at North Pacific (now Northwestern) Division of the Corps in Portland, Oregon, met with the division commander, Major General Ernest J. Harrell, to discuss the request and how to respond. Independently, and concurrently, I prepared a position paper that recommended against a single workshop in Washington, D.C., and out of respect for tribal sovereignty, and consideration of different environmental issues, histories of contact, and cultural traditions, I instead recommended multiple workshops to be conducted in each Corps Division nationwide. General Harrell decided to send me to Fort Belvoir as the North Pacific Division representative, and to bring back planning details and recommended roles for the Division.

Meanwhile, Major General Stanley Genega, director of Civil Works at Corps HQ, responded to Dr. Zirschky by forming the *Native American Intergovernmental Relations Task Force*. There were 18 active members of the Task Force, including a Project Manager, 11 Corps Division representatives, five HQ representatives, and management oversight by the Director of the Institute of Water Resources at Fort Belvoir.

At Fort Belvoir I was able to convince other members of the Task Force that there should be multiple workshops spread across the country and hosted by the Corps Divisions. Also, that the workshop sessions should be primarily *listening sessions*, so that tribal leaders would have individual opportunities to speak. A further objective would be to assess tribal comments regarding particular Corps programs during the workshops to provide better and more consistent communication between the Corps and tribal governments. Part of this assessment was to document and provide feedback from the tribes to the Corps regarding successful relations and particular issues that needed to be addressed. These tribal comments would describe to Corps administrative leaders where (under what programs) the tribes meet the Corps, what was working, what was not. When Dr. Zirschky came to Fort Belvoir to meet the Task Force members he was amazed that we were able to make so much progress with a challenging task. On that occasion I was selected to present preliminary Task Force recommendations, explaining the rationale behind hosting multiple workshops in different regions of the country. Dr. Zirschky agreed, and it was decided that 11 Division workshops would be planned for April 1995, and one to be held in Alaska later that year.

When I returned to the North Pacific Division, I briefed General Harrell and worked with the Native American coordinators in the Division to establish a Division planning committee to host our regional tribal workshop in the northwest. Tribal members were selected to participate on the planning committee. Then three district engineers in the Division were invited to a planning meeting in Portland to discuss financial costs to cover the tribal workshop. At the right hand of General Harrell, I presented the estimated funding costs for this project, and made the funding requests to each District commander. On this occasion, they could not say "no." General Harrell also decided that Seattle District would host the event, and I was instructed to work with the Seattle District commander to establish a committee there to procure and manage the funding and logistical services needed to host the event. A financial manager was designated, and duties assigned to about 50 Seattle staff in public affairs, technical services, contracting, security, and motor pool, to support a two-day tribal meeting. My next task was to prepare the written invitations to each of 43 tribal governments located in Oregon, Montana, Idaho, and Washington, requesting their attendance for a two-day event, and arranging for invitational travel orders to tribal chairs to cover their travel expenses and lodging in Seattle.

Next was the problem of where in Seattle the Indian workshop should be held. I visited an Indian-owned facility at Daybreak Star Indian Center, operated by United Indians of All Tribes Foundation, located on a former military base in Seattle, and managed by Bernie White Bear, a well-known Native American Army war veteran. When I asked about use of the facility for an Indian meeting, Mr. White Bear graciously offered to provide the facility to the government at no cost.

When April 11, 1995, arrived the Seattle District Tribal Relations Workshop event began. Twenty-two tribal leaders and additional attended staff attended, along with three Corps District commanders, General Harrell, Division commander and his Deputy, Corps tribal coordinators, and about 25 Corps program staff members were present to listen and answer questions. The workshop began with a blessing by Louie Dick Jr., a Umatilla religious leader. The deputy division commander opened the meeting, then described the Corps of Engineers mission and authorities as they apply to Indian tribes. The luncheon speaker was Dr. Catherine Vandemoer from the Office of the Assistant Secretary for Indian Affairs. Tribal leaders from Colville (Eddie Palmanteer), Yakama (Fred Ike Sr.), Warm Springs (Louie Pitt), Nez Perce (Allen Slickpoo) and Umatilla (Louie Dick Jr.) spoke, followed by round-table discussions by tribal leaders, facilitated by Ron Eggers, Assistant Bureau of Indian Affairs (BIA) Area Director for Programs, Portland, Oregon.

On April 12, 1995, the meetings were opened with a blessing by Lionel Boyer, a Shoshone religious leader. This was followed by individual tribal meetings held with individual Corps District commanders. Concurrently, there was a general session concerning "Communication with Tribes." BIA and tribal councilmen discussed treaties and tribal sovereignty, the Federal Trust relationship, tribal government structures, and authority. Following a salmon feast luncheon hosted by United Indians of All Tribes Foundation, a closing session was opened by General Harrell with a panel of Corps District Commanders and Corps tribal coordinators, and BIA Area Assistant Director Eggers. Each presented a meeting summary, their own synthesis, and discussions to be continued with individual tribes. Colonel Donald Wynn, Seattle District commander and workshop host, provided a closing statement explaining that the Corps of Engineers now had an Indian policy and that the door was always open for future discussions and partnerships. Fred Ike Sr., a Yakama religious leader, gave a parting prayer.

The difference between a governmental meeting with Indian tribes, and an academic conference by anthropologists about Indian tribes, is in the results. This requires effective communication and recognition of the underlying federal trust responsibility. In this case, Corps of Engineers tribal assistance programs and authorities became a pipeline to millions of dollars in funding for on-the-ground assistance, training, and resource protection for Northwest tribes over the next decade (1995–2005). It was also the basis for future partnerships with Indian tribes through expanded Corps authorities and initiatives, such as the Native American Lands Environmental Mitigation Program. Most of this positive change in the relationship with Northwest tribes was due to the communication lines opened by this particular governmental meeting. And this was only *one* of 12 similar meetings of the same design held in Corps Divisions across the country in 1995, as determined by Task Force members at Fort Belvoir, VA.

The 12 after-action reports for Corps Native American workshops are contained in Institute of Water Resources Report 96-R-6a (U.S. Army Corps of Engineers 1996).

For many years I worked as a consultant to federal agencies and private companies. I always pushed program managers and clients to consider tribal treaty rights and direct involvement of tribes through consultation. However, my recommendations were not always adopted by management, so in some cases, gaps in project coordination occurred where there should have been tribal involvement. In later years, I was sometimes blamed by tribes for not securing their participation, but those authorities were not yet in place, and that was beyond my control. But I always tried. I learned that you have to "take flack" in Action Anthropology for all of *the undone things* during the "action" moments, when you have to keep focus for the bigger picture and larger gain. Never mind narrow time frames for action, limited budget, regulatory constraints, or tight administrative control by superiors. The guiding impulse is that if you have a vision, then you have to seize the best moment of opportunity when it comes, and make amends later. It is timing and circumstance that mark our opportunities for success.

References Cited

Bahr, H.M., B.A. Chadwick, and R.C. Day, editors
1972 *Native Americans Today: Sociological Perspectives*. Harper & Row, New York.

Rice, David G.
1997 The Seeds of Common Ground: Experimentations in Indian Consultation. In *Native Americans and Archaeologists: Stepping Stones to Common Ground*, Nina Swidler, editor, pp. 217–226. Society for American Archaeology. AltaMira Press, Walnut Creek, California.

Tax, Sol
1952 *Heritage of Conquest: The Ethnology of Middle America*. Free Press, Glencoe, Illinois.
1953 *Penny Capitalism: A Guatemalan Indian Economy*. Institute of Social Anthropology, Publication No. 6. Smithsonian Institution Press, Washington, D.C.
1968 American Anthropological Association Symposium on American Indian Fishing and Hunting Rights. *Northwest Anthropological Research Notes*, 2 (2):1–43.

U.S. Army Corps of Engineers, Bonneville Power Administration, Bureau of Reclamation
1994 *Columbia River System Operation Review* Interagency DEIS (July 1994), Portland, Oregon.

U.S. Army Corps of Engineers
1996 *Assessment of Corps/Tribal Intergovernmental Relations*, Interim Report, 2 Volumes. Institute of Water Resources Report 96-R-6. Alexandria, Virginia.

Viereck, Eleanor, editor
1970 Science in Alaska, 1969. *Proceedings of the 20th Alaska Science Conference, College, Alaska, August 24–27, 1969*. Alaska Division, American Association for the Advancement of Science.

CHAPTER 12

SOL TAX'S GLOBAL FUTURIST MODEL AND SMALL-NATION SOLUTIONS

John H. Bodley

My first indirect connection with Sol Tax was in 1960 when I passed through the *Municipio* of Panajachel on the shore of Lake Atitlán in Guatemala where Tax had conducted field research from 1935 to 1941 as part of Robert Redfield's Maya Project for the Carnegie Institution of Washington. Guatemala's rich cultural diversity has inspired many anthropologists, and my brief early experience in Guatemala helped nudge me into an anthropological career that drew on Tax's intellectual support at crucial points, and eventually led me through a pathway focused on scale and power theory to adopt a variation of Tax's visionary solution to the central global problem of concentrated social power. Tax's Guatemalan experience and many of his related beliefs about culture and the role of anthropology in helping to solve global problems are clearly reflected in his remarkable 1977 futuristic model of a two-level world based on 10,000 "Localities" coordinated by a global level public communication system (Tax 1977). I take my contribution to this tribute volume as an opportunity to re-examine the continuing relevance of Tax's creative and far-sighted work in relation to contemporary human problems of poverty and conflict.

Tax's work with Indian communities in the Guatemalan highlands resulted in several important publications, but is especially represented in his ethnographic monograph, *Penny Capitalism,* which appeared in 1953 (Tax 1953). *Penny Capitalism* is a remarkably detailed description of Panajachel, a single community embedded in a thriving multi-cultural regional market economy. It occurs to me now that Tax's experience in Guatemala may have been a major inspiration for his later concept of "Localities" that formed the basis of his provocative "model for the future." He outlined this model tantalizingly briefly in his Malinowski Award address to the Society for Applied Anthropology in 1977 (Tax 1977).

Tax's Model of a Future World

Tax thought that a two-level world system with small self-sufficient localities at the base could respond to the threat created by a global economy in a world dominated by heavily armed and competing nation states. Tax's futurist model was a thought experiment imagining a world of five billion people in which multinational corporations succeeded in abolishing nation states as we know them, and replaced them with 10,000 relatively self-sufficient, politically independent local territories averaging 500,000 people. He called these small territories "Localities," and imagined that their interactions would be coordinated by a global public communication system remarkably like what the Internet had become by the 1990s. In this paper I discuss Tax's futurist model in relation to my Small-Nation Solution to global problems based on scale and power theory. My "Small Nations" are roughly equivalent to Tax's "Localities," but there are important conceptual differences, and they envision a somewhat different global system than suggested by Tax's model. The two approaches are complementary and their similarities may reflect our similar experiences grappling with the meaning of small-scale cultures and cultural differences in general in relation to global problems. The points of difference may be due to my use of a somewhat different theoretical approach, and they may also reflect new realities of the contemporary world. The still accelerating pace of change and the volatility of the global system have brought about events and possibilities that Tax could have only imagined lay far in the future.

The importance that Tax attributed to global problems is indicated by his specific inclusion of his "localities solution" in his 1988 autobiographical retrospective on his previous 60 years in anthropology (Tax 1988). In this retrospective he was quite unapologetic for bypassing purely theoretical problems during his career in favor of problems that most people actually care about. He referred to his 1977 futurist model as an example of the "intellectual problems and practical topics to which anthropology could be applied," noting that such practical pursuits had occupied his professional activities for decades (Tax 1988). This time he offered some further elaborations to his futurist model, and shrunk the average size of his localities, speaking of his "... idea of substituting for powerful nation-states powerless 'localities' of 250,000 people under a democratic constitution ensuring open information and movement but not the possibility of forming alliances" (Tax 1988:5). This careful qualification of the model may have been a response to the pejorative label "balkanization" often invoked as a criticism of political decentralization. The Localities that Tax proposed would be "powerless," in the sense that they would not be hostile to their neighbors, and would not have the capacity for armed intervention in other Localities. He stresses that Localities would be "voluntary communities" produced by a peaceful and legal transformation process that would reverse the process by which local communities lost control over the conditions of their life.

Tax was always flexible on the size of his Localities, suggesting a range of 100,000 to 800,000 people and an average of 500,000 in his original 1977 article. In 1988 he uses an average of 250,000 people, and suggests that federal Congressional Districts in the U.S. could be useful models of Localities, because they are standardized at that size range. They remain within state boundaries, and are covered by census data. However, Congressional Districts would be somewhat problematic as Localities, because in practice their boundaries shift due to the gerrymandering redistricting process. The number of districts has been set at 435 since 1911. This meant that each House Representative represented about 500,000 persons in 1980, but that number had risen to over 700,000 by 2010. Again stressing the helplessness that people feel facing a globalizing economy and the threat of nuclear weapons, Tax declared that anthropologists know that "basically humans want more than anything to control their lives and destinies" (Tax 1988:19). He felt that there were indications that people would decide to use new technologies to form smaller communities. "There are signs that many even in complex urban societies would choose to use our new technologies to form controllable, smaller communities, …thus beginning a new evolution to replace the course subverted in the Neolithic when villages became subject to nation-states" (Tax 1988:20). This reference to Neolithic villages as independent hints at Tax's high regard for tribal peoples, past and present, and his sympathy with contemporary indigenous peoples.

Background

My visit to Guatemala in 1960 was my first exposure to anthropological subjects. At that time I was apprenticing as a very junior field naturalist collecting mammal specimens in southern Mexico and Guatemala with zoologist Ernest S. Booth (1915–1984). We collected specimens in Tzotzil country in Chiapas and throughout southern Guatemala. Our itinerary included visits to the major Maya market centers of Quetzltenango, Sololá, Chichicastenango, and Coban in the Guatemalan highlands. It was February and March and the markets were crowded and ritual activities were intense. At that time I intended to become a field ornithologist and I saw Guatemala as an opportunity to see the Resplendent Quetzal, Guatemala's national bird. However, observing Guatemalan Indians helped me decide to shift my career choice from biology to anthropology, and within twelve years I crossed paths directly with Sol Tax, in his role as editor of *Current Anthropology* and organizer of international conferences.

I was so impressed by the vibrancy of Mayan culture that I selected Guatemalan Indians as the subject of my freshman composition term paper while I was still a biology major. My undergraduate and graduate work at the University of Oregon focused on Latin America and led me to Tax's *Heritage of Conquest* (1958) as well as several of Robert Redfield's works. One of the first anthropology texts that I read at the University of Oregon was Ralph Linton's *The Study of Man*, assigned by David Aberle, who had studied with Linton at Columbia University. Linton, of course, was also one of Tax's important mentors at the University of Wisconsin-Madison. During more zoological fieldwork I was constantly confronted by culturally diverse peoples living self-sufficiently in small-scale societies, often in very remote, biologically rich territories. Shortly after first seeing Guatemalan Indians in 1960, from 1962 to 1964 I successively encountered the Tarahumara in Chihuahua, the Tsáchila people in western Ecuador, and then the Asháninka and Shipibo in the Peruvian Amazon. I returned to the Peruvian Amazon for my MA thesis. My dissertation fieldwork in 1968–1969 examined how the Asháninka were being impacted by outsiders. Many Asháninka were still living independently, but their continued autonomy was threatened by outside intrusion. I immediately saw this as a violation of their basic human rights that was obviously linked to the inability of the developed world to set limits on its own expansion. At that point I decided to make small-scale societies and their survival in the contemporary world the primary focus of my anthropological career.

My first professional anthropological paper was a report published in 1972 on the situation of the Asháninka written for the newly created International Work Group on Indigenous Affairs (IWGIA), arguing that the Peruvian government needed to designate Asháninka territory as permanent Asháninka land and prohibit outside development in order to ensure their survival (Bodley 1972). I was engaged in Tax's "Action Anthropology" and followed up by submitting to *Current Anthropology* an extended argument in favor of what I called "cultural autonomy" as a policy alternative to the ethnocide being forced on tribal peoples worldwide.

My cultural autonomy viewpoint clearly resonated with Tax's perspectives on indigenous people, as represented by his discussion comments at the 1965 Man the Hunter Conference about the place of small-scale (tribal) hunters and gatherers:

> I just want to put one idea in the record, and that is, that we should study the reasons for the persistence of these peoples all over the world in light of all the conditions militating against their persistence. I think that the case of the North American Indians is especially significant. They seem to be waiting for us to go away. I am certain that there is something for us peasant agriculturalists or, if you like, industrialists to learn from the values associated with the tribal life and with the determination of these peoples to preserve this way of life at all costs (Tax 1968:345–346).

After receiving my *Alternatives to Ethnocide* submission, Tax immediately wrote back suggesting that instead of placing it in *Current Anthropology*, my paper needed to be presented at the Ninth International Congress of Anthropological and Ethnological Sciences (ICAES), which was held in Chicago in 1973. My *Alternatives* paper subsequently appeared in two of the multi-volume *World Anthropology* series (Bodley 1977, 1978). I later included a revised version of *Alternatives* in the first edition of *Victims of Progress*, a book which expanded on the cultural autonomy argument with supporting case studies from around the world (Bodley 1975). The link between cultural autonomy as an alternative to ethnocide and Tax's later concept of "Localities" is that both involved the objective of a culturally distinct people living self-sufficiently within their own territories, both required acceptance of cultural relativity principles, and both concepts were offered as solutions to problems created by an expanding global economy.

The Guatemalan Highlands as a 1930s Locality

In the early 1970s I was still uncertain how best to categorize the small-scale societies that I was seeing, calling them variously primitive, tribal, and indigenous, although I was increasingly drawn to Redfield's concept of "folk society" (Redfield 1947). Much earlier, Tax had also struggled with how to characterize, Guatemalan Indians in relation to Redfield's then current folk-urban categories. Guatemalans Indians were Mayan-speaking peoples like the Yucatan Mayan "folk" that Redfield described, and they had similar "primitive" world-views, but Guatemalan Indians had "civilized" social relations. They were firmly commercial, entrepreneurial people operating with money in a "civilized" market economy (Tax 1937, 1939, 1941). Tax characterized their economic system as a pure capitalist, free-market economy, based on private enterprise in the sense envisioned by Adam Smith's *Wealth of Nations*. To the extent that this was an accurate characterization, it would have worked precisely because the system was small-scale and localized, and in the absence of monopoly power. Significantly, the Indians were using preindustrial technology, and this presumably helped to keep their level of production and capital accumulation very low, aside from the reality that Ladinos and foreigners controlled the most productive lands. Tax also provided fine quantitative detail on the operation of the civil-religious hierarchy and related ritual. This was the crucial cultural feature that helped integrate and stabilize each *municipio* and to redistribute social power and consumption, and it set a practical ceiling on capital accumulation.

The region that Tax described in the highlands of southwest Guatemala covered about 5,000 square miles and according to his figures probably contained at least 250,000 people in the 1930s. Only about 10 percent were Ladino, or culturally considered non-Indians. The regional cultural similarities within local diversity made the entire region a small internal nation, but as with tribal societies, there were no single political officials to represent the nation within a federal system of nations. Tax concluded that the Indians recognized the cultural differences between Guatemalan municipalities, which he also called communities. The people themselves viewed these local differences as cultural "specialties," rather than cultural alternatives from which to choose. Their recognition of cultural differences was accompanied by an acceptance of difference, and even an indifference to difference that, according to Tax, helped them maintain their cultural integration. Culture was a "local" phenomenon in Guatemala—and local people recognized in a sophisticated way that their own cultural practices that worked for them, might not work someplace else. In effect, the Indians were an example of the practical "live and let live" application of the very anthropological concept of cultural relativity. Tax later argued that one of the most important roles of anthropologists in preparing people to live in the world of the future is transmitting this concept of applied cultural relativity. This relates directly to the "heterogeneity" principle that contemporary futurist Paul Raskin speaks of as crucial support for "constrained pluralism" in a regionally diversified future "planetary society" (Raskin 2006).

The ideal Locality that Tax described in 1977, which constituted the base level of his two-level future world, had the following features:

> Each of these units, called 'Localities,' produces most of what it uses in both services and products and extras of some things for exchange. People live and work here, organizing and spacing themselves as they find meet,

> and having full local control. Interlocality trade moves in a kind of free market only as far as necessary to satisfy needs (Tax 1977:229).

I suggest that the regional cultural system Tax described for Panajachel and interconnected *municipios* clearly had many of the characteristics of such Localities. Tax's quantitative ethnography documents high levels of economic self-sufficiency for the Indian sector of the highland region at that time. Self-sufficiency of the Indian sector is also demonstrated by cultural geographer Felix McBryde's meticulous mapping of southwest Guatemala's regional crafts and industries, commerce and trade, including house construction, the production and distribution of staple foods, ceramics, *metates*, baskets, mats, textiles, footwear, and miscellaneous household goods. McBryde's diagrams of the highland markets show that Indian people could acquire from within the region virtually everything they needed, from foodstuffs to raw materials and finished goods (McBryde 1947). Markets were shopping centers that supported household consumption, and they were supplied by local and regional Indian entrepreneurs. Unlike today's global supermarkets, Indian market places in the Southwest Guatemala Locality of the 1930s were publicly owned, non-profit enterprises. The Indians operated no large-scale business enterprises. The regional market system supported a presumably sustainable, stationary economy that distributed, rather than concentrated, wealth and income. Only a handful of imported manufactured items such as matches and metal goods originated from outside of the Locality.

All of this ethnography paints a picture that now sounds very much like Guatemalan Indians had achieved many of the goals of the economic re-localization and "post-carbon" social movements currently underway in Europe and North America in response to concerns over global warming, social inequality, the financial crisis, and the economic downturn. The highland *municipios* were already buying local. Most of their currency must have circulated internally. They had community-supported agriculture, farmers' markets, food sovereignty, and negligible carbon footprints. There were also no business corporations, no banks, no factories, no machines, and no credit, but there was money, and commerce. However, even if we can imagine that an idealized highland Guatemala inspired Tax's concept of a futurist Level 1 Locality, it is important not to view it as a perfect small society. Tax repeatedly describes the difficulties of daily life, and poor health conditions, and he details the heavy workloads, the overall low material level, and barely hidden interpersonal conflicts. Tax also did not disregard the historical reality that in the 1930s the Guatemalan central government's policies were aimed at forcing Indians into low wage labor in the plantation export economy. This must have helped to depress wages for Indian labor. Ladino control of the municipal governments, Ladino monopoly over the most productive land, foreign ownership of the coffee and banana plantations, and foreign control of the export market were also part of the larger cultural context (Handy 1994). And of course, a bloody civil war engulfed the region from 1960 to 1996.

Searching For Solutions: Small Nations, and the Scale and Power Perspective

Tax's futurist model appeared one year after the first edition of my wide-ranging *Anthropology and Contemporary Human Problems* (Bodley 1976) and coincided with my closer reading of the 1978 edition of Leopold Kohr's 1957 *Breakdown of Nations* and Schumacher's 1972 *Small is Beautiful* (Schumacher 1973). All of these new works gradually caused me to revise my thinking until by 1983 I was ready to consider *scale itself* as a crucial dimension of any solution to global problems. Even in 1976 I was convinced that our problem was somehow a culture problem. Our industrial civilization was damaging if not destroying the very world and planetary resources on which it depends, but it was still not clear why. I even suggested that the subtitle needed to read: "A Critique of Civilization," but my editor at Cummings had already rejected the "Anthropology and the World Crisis" title that I had originally proposed. At that time I knew there was a cultural crisis, but still didn't have a convincing solution. I specifically disavowed a "capitalist, socialist, Marxist, or communist solution," and instead emphasized the virtues of "primitive culture" and advocated a "Paraprimitive Solution," borrowing the term from British author Gordon Rattray Taylor (1972). Paraprimitive imagined a fuzzy blending of "the best of both worlds," primitive and civilized. I'm sure that many of my readers heard this as a hopelessly romantic "Back to the Stone Age" approach. I knew even then that the term "primitive" was on the way out of the anthropological lexicon. The most promising model I could cite was the 1972 *Blueprint for Survival* produced by a team led by British environmentalist Edward Goldsmith (Goldsmith and Allen 1972). The *Blueprint* called for the adoption of less energy-intensive technology and radical political decentralization of existing nation states based on neighborhoods of 500 people within communities of 5,000, and regions of 500,000 with national representation. The minimum number of 500 was explicitly based on a tribal model, because Goldsmith was also a strong advocate for "primitive people," even helping to found the London-based indigenous people advocacy organization *Survival International.*

In the second edition of *Problems* (Bodley 1983), I dropped "primitive" and added a small-scale/large-scale culture contrast, along with the small-nation concept specifically linked to Tax's Localities and Kohr's argument for political decentralization. I was never comfortable with the term "primitive" because it had so many negative connotations, although I had readily embraced Stanley Diamond's unsuccessful attempt to rehabilitate it (Diamond 1968, 1974). This time I carefully expunged the word and replaced it with "tribal" and the characterization "small scale."

My views on the connection between scale and solutions to global problems began to expand during my brief visit to the small Scandinavian nations of Denmark and Norway to lecture on indigenous people in 1978. This was followed by several-months-long residence in Denmark in 1980, when I worked at the International Work Group for Indigenous Affairs, and a visiting lecture position at the University of Uppsala, Sweden, in 1985, but I lacked a theory for why small nations were better than large. These small nations obviously had striking advantages over much larger nations, and were clearly more focused on the well-being of their citizens. In the second edition of *Problems* (1983), I proposed a "Small-Nation Alternative" in which "tribal states" of a million people or less would implement the "Paraprimitive Solution." I cited Tax's futurist model as an independently derived and "strikingly similar" solution to global problems. In contrast to Tax's model, my Small-Nation Alternative as I imagined it would not replace nation states and would not prevent war. As I elaborated:

> A world of small nations would of course still contain nations, and each nation would presumably still be stratified and hierarchical, but they could in theory be more responsive to the needs of their people. Furthermore, like tribes, they would be dependent on their own resources, and would have an immediate interest in taking care of them. There would be room for great diversity in the kinds of solutions that might be developed to solve problems relating local cultures to local environments. It is not assumed that a small-nation world would be a utopia or totally free from war. There would still be internal conflict and local wars, but

> both would be easier to contain and much less destructive. Nuclear weapons, however, would certainly present a special problem (Bodley 1983:229).

I had not yet discovered a theory to explain why scale was both problem and solution, but by 1981 I had already begun work on a long-term project to produce an anthropology text based specifically on scale principles. This became *Cultural Anthropology: Tribes, States, and the Global System* (Bodley 1994), which was based on a scale framework that sorted cultures into three categories: Small, Large, and Global by population and the organization of social power. Small-scale cultures were tribal, large-scale culture were states, and global-scale culture referred to the present industrial and commercial system. The critical tone of *Problems* carried over to my *Cultural Anthropology* text where I characterized large-scale cultures as representing "The End of Equality." This echoed Tax's comment cited above that many people in contemporary "small communities" now wanted to take back control over their lives thereby changing the previous course of cultural evolution. How this "subversion" might have happened, and how it might be reversed is a scale and power issue. In the last chapter, I again cited Tax's futurist model alongside the Small-Nation Alternative, defined as "A proposal for restoring ecological balances and social equity by returning maximum autonomy and self-reliance to small-scale cultural communities within a framework of regional and global institutions" (Bodley 1994:405).

The Power of Scale, and the Problem of Elite-Directed Growth

From 1996–1998 I carried out a large research project looking for scale effects in the assessed value of individually owned real estate in 27 municipalities in eastern Washington State known regionally as "the Palouse." I used a detailed quantitative ethnographic approach that closely resembled Tax's work in Panajachel, only I was looking at *all* the *municipios*. The total urban population of these Washington municipalities was 243,605, almost exactly the same as the Guatemalan Locality that Tax had studied. My Palouse research involved sorting through many thousands of parcels and owners. Unlike Tax's work, my analysis was computer assisted, and I quickly found that as the absolute size, or scale, of urban places in the region increased, the assessed value of the holdings of the wealthiest property owners in each place also increased, but by orders of magnitude. Average owner values and even the average of the top quintile owners increased only linearly. The absolute number of poor and landless households also increased. The rich were getting richer and the poor were getting poorer, just as people commonly imagine, but in this case I could show that it was the elite-directed growth process itself that was causing this process. Growth in scale seemed to produce a general negative effect on household well-being, even as it disproportionately benefited the wealthiest. The best or most widespread distribution of property ownership was in the smallest places that showed the least growth. These findings were the basis for what I called the "power elite hypothesis": that socioeconomic growth is an elite-directed process that concentrates social power and economic power in a minority and socializes, or disperses the costs to the majority (Bodley 1999).

I expanded this research to look for possible scale effects on household income and business revenues in all 277 municipalities in the state of Washington, and found a similar scale trend that produced more support for the power-elite hypothesis (Bodley 2001). I confirmed my findings by repeating the property ownership and business revenue research in Vermont in 2000. I then spent two years applying the scale and power approach to the entire span of world history and prehistory and found even more examples of scale effects (Bodley 2003). I began to recognize that such scale effects were best understood as examples of the ubiquitous mathematical power law distributions of the sort discovered nearly a century earlier by pioneer Italian civil engineer turned political philosopher Vilfredo Pareto (1971). Such distributions are very common in nature and in human societies, and their significance for understanding the development process has not been widely appreciated. When a power law is operating unimpeded by political intervention, growth in the dimension measured will "naturally" concentrate power in the top size ranks. This helps explain why revenue becomes more concentrated in the largest business corporations, or wealth in the wealthiest households, when economic growth occurs. Concentrated power implies a vicious feed back cycle in which elite directors are rewarded for shaping policies that encourage more growth which, in turn, increases the concentration of power.

These findings immediately suggested that successful small nations, especially if they were not growing rapidly, might be ideal models for how scale principles might be applied to control elite-directed growth and thereby prevent, reduce, or mitigate problems of environmental degradation, poverty, and conflict within particular territories. In order to field test this idea I conducted a comparison of the Hawaiian island county of Kauai and the small Caribbean nation of Dominica, visiting each in 2004 and 2007 respectively (Bodley 2011). The populations and land areas were similar with 62,800 people in Kauai and 72,000 in Dominica, and both had similar histories of colonial conquest and the establishment of plantation economies, followed by a recent shift toward nature tourism. The big difference was that even though its economy was three-fold larger than Dominica's, more than a third of Kauai's residents were "economically needy" and fewer than half were home owners. Ownership of the most productive lands was highly concentrated, and the hotel industry was dominated by giant outside corporations.

About a third of Dominicans were officially income poor, but most people owned their own homes, produced much of their own food, and enjoyed overall good health. Dominica rated number four in the Happy Planet Index based on high life expectancy, high personal satisfaction, and a very low ecological footprint. People were highly engaged in the local market economy, buying and selling local products much like the Penny Capitalists that Tax described in the Guatemalan *municipios* of the 1930s. Most businesses were small and locally owned, including the hotels and restaurants. Unlike on Kauai, there was no Wal-Mart and only one visible American franchise. Dominica had no stock market. There were only four publicly traded corporations operating in the country, and the few large corporate businesses appeared to have revenues of under about $30 million USD. The key difference was that Dominica gained full independence from Britain in 1978, but Kauai is economically still much like an internal colony of the United States. With only 30 members in its national House of Assembly, and five prominent political parties, Dominica can maintain an effective consensus in support of the principles of social justice contained in their Constitution's Preamble:

> … the operation of the economic system should result in so distributing the material resources of the community as to subserve the common good that there should be adequate means of livelihood for all, that labour should not be exploited or forced by economic necessity to operate in inhumane conditions but that there should be opportunity for advancement on the basis of recognition of merit, ability and integrity. …

The Small-Nation Solution

In order to apply the power and scale perspective to my proposed Small-Nation Alternative, I created a scale-ranked sample of 260 independent nation states, and autonomous, or semi-autonomous subnational territories and looked for scale-related patterns. I defined a Small Nation as any territorial jurisdiction with ten million or fewer people, a shared sociocultural system, consensus decision-making, and the power to manage their own internal affairs. Small Nations meeting most of these criteria represented 70 percent of my sample, but there were only 425 million people or barely five percent of global population in these nations. Small nations, because they are small, can be expected to have less concentrated social power than large nations. This would be reflected in a more equitable distribution of wealth and income, with an effective minimum living standard, and a relatively short spread from top to bottom. There would be fewer growth subsidies, which are the social and environmental costs that everyone must pay to have a larger economy, larger business enterprises, larger markets, and bigger government. Small nations will be able to practice democratic decision-making, and to the extent that they must depend on their own natural resources, they will have a stronger incentive to set limits to materially based economic growth.

Many small nations are already solving global problems. They demonstrate that a country does not need a very large economy, or an especially high GDP per capita, or even a growing economy to have high life expectancy, high human development, and a low impact on the environment. These are among the prime measures of sustainable development. For example, I found that seven small nations (Costa Rica, Uruguay, Cape Verde, Saint Lucia, Saint Vincent/Grenadines, Dominica, Turks and Caicos Islands) had already met international carbon emission goals while effectively ending poverty, and achieving life expectancies of over 70 years, and high ratings on the UN Human Development Index (Bodley 2011). All of these countries had small economies, but their GDPs/capita at were or above a $7,500 development threshold, which is thought to allow a country to meet basic subsistence needs and meet Millennium Development Goals.

Many small nations also satisfy Tax's specific concern for ending the threat of dangerous armaments, and they can solve a range of other political and economic problems. There is a direct correlation between size of national economies and military expenditures. High military expenditures can be seen as a growth subsidy, seemingly required to produce or maintain very large corporations and economies. Giant defense corporations are closely tied to highly developed financial sectors in large economies, and to the wealthy individual investors and institutions that own them. In contrast, small nations with small economies are the conspicuous drop outs from the economic growth and military expenditures trend line. Many have no military expenditures, and their total economies are far smaller than the $6 billion construction cost of a single aircraft carrier, and would have no conceivable capacity to long-range missiles or nuclear weapons. Many small nations have no stock markets and are not even in the international market capitalization ranking. Their small markets do not require enormous advertising expenditures. More of their wealth is in tangible rather than financial assets. They are also insulated from the wild gyrations of global financial markets, although there are conspicuous exceptions such as Iceland, where renegade bankers caused enormous financial losses to the country. Small nations, because they are much less likely to have very large corporations, are also less likely to have corporations corrupting the political policies.

Small Nations and Tax's Level 2 System

The promise and proven successes of small nations suggests that people in large nations could solve their own problems now by decentralizing and down-scaling themselves into networks, or federations of small, more functional and more democratic nations, and by adopting some of the small-scale social and cultural structures already developed by small nations. This need not imply a significantly different world model than Tax proposed. The second of his two levels is an Internet-like global public communication system to which everyone has input and access. He suggests that all interests would have representation in "the system," but does not explain how this would actually work, although Tax mentions "discussion" occurring at level 2. "The system" is regulated by an "egalitarian and libertarian" Constitution "designed to limit the growth of power of individual localities, and to prevent arrangements which give localities power through alliances" (Tax 1977:229). This would fit well with a small-nation world in which no individual nations had the capability nor the incentive to maintain costly military systems. Like the Internet, there are "operators" to make Tax's system work, but there are no official level 2 political rulers and no global government. There are "procedures" through which local level individuals and groups can raise constitutional issues and presumably bring about changes in the top system. Tax left out the details of how the level 2 system would work in practice, and he did not speculate on how such a system might be established. Instead, he preferred to focus on the kind of person that would be suited to such a decentralized world of small autonomous localities. In this regard, as in the Guatemalan highlands, it was the anthropological values of cultural relativism that made the system functional, and it was the job of anthropologists to encourage their spread.

Because global problems are problems of scale and social power, as well as values, they cannot be solved by technology alone. Representatives of small nations will need to construct an international system that accepts cultural diversity, and gets decision-making at the right level. A small-nation world would require implementation of some version of the subsidiarity principle, as originally envisioned by political decentralization in the European Union. Subsidiarity means that high-level decision-making is called for only when lower levels are unable to solve a particular problem. It is also clear that some problems, such as global climate change, will need to be dealt with at a global level. The most important obstacle to such transformation is concentrated and globalized financial power, which effectively gives enormous political and economic decision-making power to a few elite directors.

There are many examples of this small-nation integration process already in place. Indigenous people have for example the Inuit Circumpolar Conference (ICC) and the Coordinating Body for the Indigenous Organizations of the Amazon Basin (COICA). In Siberia there is the Russian Association of Indigenous Peoples of the North (RAIPON). Six Celtic nations are united in the Celtic League. Eight nations form the Nordic Council. The Association of Small Island States (AOSIS) is a network of 39 small, mostly Pacific, island nations which is primarily concerned with environmental protection and sustainable development. Existing small-nation international organizations are strikingly different in form and function from intergovernmental organizations dominated by big nations, such as the OECD, the Group of Nine, the World Bank, the IMF, and the World Trade Organization. These big nation organizations largely exist to promote globalization in the interests of the world's wealthiest investors and giant transnational corporations, not the interests of the global majority.

Down-scaled large nations could thrive with small businesses, small governments, and small markets, and could join with already successful small nations to build truly democratic international and planetary-scale institutions that would effectively address world problems in a newly reconstructed global system. This approach would not necessarily abolish the nation state, but it could be founded on subsidiarity-based representative international decision-making hierarchies or networks of various sorts that could well resemble the level 2 system that Tax envisioned.

The Internet certainly has many of the features that Tax attributed to "The System," but as it has evolved it also has come to differ in important respects. I commented on this issue in the final sentence of the 1996 third edition of *Problems* as follows: "The rapidly evolving decentralized global communications and information networks could help to strengthen the autonomy of small-scale cultures and communities, if these technologies can remain noncommercial" (Bodley 1996:214).

Like radio and television, and even to some extent like telephones, the Internet has certainly not remained noncommercial, and it is not entirely public or totally accessible as Tax had hoped. As presently constructed, the Internet itself is embedded within and is totally dependent on the existing global network of giant transnational corporations which in turn is controlled by decision-makers in the financial sector of the global economy. The digital devices, cables, transmitters and receivers that comprise the infrastructure of the system are commercial products, and Internet service providers are typically, but not always commercial businesses. Although individual ownership of the diverse infrastructural components of the Internet is widely dispersed, the Internet as a whole is contained and operated within a global corporate ownership network of commercial entities. Significantly, recent research by a team of network theorists shows that ownership of 40 percent of the economic value of the world's 43,000 largest publicly traded transnational corporations is controlled by a "super-entity" of just 147 mostly financial corporations (Vitali, Glattfelder, and Battiston 2011). The top ten super-entity companies, which include Barclays, Capital Group Companies, FMR, AXA, State Street, JP Morgan, and Merrill Lynch, are all financials, and together they control nearly 20 percent of the entire corporate ownership network. This gives enormous power to a handful of corporate directors. The principal beneficiaries of this commercial system that contains the Internet are the 11 million high net worth individuals (HNWIs), defined here as those with at least $1 million and often much more in investible financial assets (Capgemini 2011). These HNWI individuals, who include the directors of the super-entity companies, constitute one tenth of a percent of the world's 7 billion people, but they are the elite directors of the commercial world as presently organized. Their decisions ultimately determine much of the information content flowing through the Internet along with corporate revenues.

In spite of all the concentrated power in the control of the financial super-entity and the world's HNWIs, the organizational structure of the Internet is an ideal model of a decentralized overlapping network, much as Tax envisioned in 1977. ICANN, the Internet Corporation for Assigned Names and Numbers, is a non-profit corporation. W3C, the World Wide Web Consortium, which is the primary advisory organization guiding Internet policy and procedures, is an unincorporated organization. Furthermore, recent events in the Middle East and Russia in the mobilization of the Occupy movement in the United States show the Internet's enormous potential for effecting large-scale cultural change. Significantly, the Occupy movement's concept of the 99 percent clearly grasps the central problem of power and scale. In the final analysis, the most critical problem is how to reduce elite power over the cultural symbols that allows them to shape majority beliefs and behavior in their own interests. The non-elite majority needs to use its political and economic power to reorder the dominant cultural processes so that human well-being comes ahead of the needs of government and commerce. The best way to maintain majority control will be in a world of small, autonomous nations, or localities much as Sol Tax envisioned.

References Cited

Bodley, John H.
1972 *Tribal Survival in the Amazon: The Campa Case.* IWGIA (International Work Group for Indigenous Affairs) Document No. 5. Copenhagen.
1975 *Victim of Progress.* Cummings Publishing Co., Menlo Park California.
1976 *Anthropology and Contemporary Human Problems.* Cummings Publishing Co., Menlo Park, California.
1977 Alternatives to Ethnocide: Human Zoos, Living Museums, and Real People. In *Western Expansion and Indigenous Peoples,* edited by Elias Sevilla-Casas, pp. 31–50. Mouton Publishers, New York.
1978 Alternative to Ethnocide: Human Zoos, Living Museum, and Real People, in *The World as a Company Town,* edited by Ahmed Idris-Soven, Elizabeth Idris-Soven, and M. D. Vaughn, pp. 189–207. Mouton Publishers, New York.
1983 *Anthropology and Contemporary Human Problems,* second edition. Mayfield Publishers, Palo Alto, California.
1994 *Cultural Anthropology: Tribes, States, and the Global System.* Mayfield Publishing Co, Mountain View, California.
1996 *Anthropology and Contemporary Human Problems,* third edition. Mayfield Publishing, Mountain View, California.
1999 Socio-Economic Growth, Culture Scale, and Household Well-Being: A Test of the Power-Elite Hypothesis. *Current Anthropology,* 40(5):595–620.
2001 Growth, Scale, and Power in Washington State. *Human Organization,* 60(4):367–379.
2003 *The Power of Scale: A Global History Approach.* M. E. Sharpe, Armonk, New York.
2011 *Cultural Anthropology: Tribe, State, and the Global System,* fifth edition. AltaMira Press. Rowman & Littlefield Publishers, Lanham, Maryland.

Capgemini
2011 *World Wealth Report 2011.* www.capgemini.com.

Diamond, Stanley
1968 The Search for the Primitive in *The Concept of the Primitive.* Edited by Ashley Montagu, pp. 96–147. Free Press, New York.
1974 *In Search of the* Primitive. Transaction, New Brunswick, New Jersey.

Goldsmith, Edward and Robert Allen
1972 *Blueprint for Survival.* Houghton Mifflin, Boston, Massachusetts.

Handy, Jim
1994 *Revolution in the Countryside: Rural Conflict and Agrarian Reform in Guatemala, 1944–1954.* The University of North Carolina Press, Chapel Hill.

Kohr, Leopold
1978 *The Breakdown of Nations.* Dutton, New York. Originally published in 1957.

McBryde, Felix Webster
1947 Cultural and Historical Geography of Southwest Guatemala. *Institute of Social Anthropology Publication,* No. 4. Smithsonian Institution, Government Printing Office, Washington, D.C.

Pareto, Vilfredo
1971 *Manual of Political Economy.* Translated by Ann S. Schwier and Alfred N. Page. A. M. Kelley, New York.

Raskin, Paul D
2006 *The Great Transition Today: A Report from the Future.* GTI Paper Series 2, Frontiers of a Great Transition. Tellus Institute, Boston, Massachusetts.

Redfield, Robert
1947 The Folk Society. *American Journal of Sociology,* 52(4):293–308.

Schumacher, E.F
1973 *Small Is Beautiful: Economics As If People Mattered.* Harper & Row, New York.

Tax, Sol
1937 Municipios of the Midwestern Highlands Guatemala. *American Anthropologist,* 39(3): Part 1, 423–444.
1939 Culture and Civilization in Guatemalan Societies. *The Scientific Monthly,* 48(5):463–467.
1941 World View and Social Relations in Guatemala. *American Anthropologist,* 43(1):27–42.
1953 *Penny Capitalism: A Guatemalan Indian Economy.* Institute of Social Anthropology, Publication No. 6. Smithsonian Institution Press, Washington, D.C.
1968 Discussion. In *Man the Hunter,* edited by Richard B. Lee and Irven DeVore, pp. 345–346. Aldine, Chicago, Illinois.
1977 Anthropology for the World of the Future: Thirteen Professions and Three Proposals. *Human Organization,* 36(3):225–234.
1988 Pride and Puzzlement: A Retro-introspective Record of 60 Years of Anthropology. *Annual Reviews of Anthropology,* 17:1–21.

Taylor, Gordon Rattray
1972 *Rethink: A Paraprimitive Solution.* Secker and Warburg, London.

Vitali, Stefania, James B. Glattfelder, and Stefano Battiston
2011 The Network of Global Corporate Control. *PLoS ONE,* 6(10):e25995. doi:10.1371/journal.pone.0025995

CHAPTER 13

ACTION ANTHROPOLOGY: ITS PAST, PRESENT, AND FUTURE

Solomon H. Katz

This chapter presents a combination of my personal connections with Sol Tax and how the principles of Action Anthropology intersected with and came to influence my work. In order to create this overview, I have developed five vignettes from my personal experience within the field of what I used to think of as "anthropology" but have come to realize in recent years is really "applied anthropology" with a heavy dose of "Action Anthropology." Although as a scientist I am used to writing empirically, I have taken off this hat and replaced it with a historian's hat to develop these memoir-like vignettes that explore the past and present, and suggest a future of Action Anthropology for this concluding chapter of the book.

The Anthropological Background to Action Anthropology

Under the leadership of Franz Boas, there was a serious attempt to shift anthropology from an armchair exercise largely begun in the turn-of-the-19th-century British school, where data collected anecdotally by travelers, explorers, missionaries and others was used to formulate theories about the origins and evolution of humankind, to an active, empirically based science that derives from first-hand insights collected systematically by trained anthropologists living in societies using commonly accepted methodologies. This became known as the basis for the American school of anthropology and was additionally fueled by a "new" methodology that we now call participant observation. This methodology traditionally developed through the recruitment and establishment of a trusted relationship with one or more local members of a social group who "inform" the anthropologist/ethnographer as he/she observes and participates in the social life of a group through an extended time period (usually not less than a year and often for much longer periods) to learn about their culture.

Together with some theoretical ideas about how societies work and what their general constraints were, the anthropologists could begin to put together a picture of the society. Ideally, a series of coherent images based on the empirically observed data would be the basis for establishing a perspective on how a particular culture operated. Ultimately, a general scientific framework would emerge about human nature from putting together compendia of knowledge and/or testing specific hypotheses about human nature using the cumulative knowledge from the vast numbers of studies completed.[1]

A part of the scientific tradition that developed required a very serious attempt by the ethnographer to participate and observe without upsetting the natural order that existed before they arrived. This was to address the question about the impact of being observed by another human being on the nature of the society without the people being observed instituting sociocultural change to respond to the presence of an outsider asking questions and studying them. This was an important concern, because so many of the societies anthropologists studied were remote but were already undergoing rapid change with early 20th-century contact and industrialization of the world. Thus not changing the society was scientifically the best an anthropologist could do in developing generalizations and insights about the origin and sources of the traditions and social institutions he or she was studying.

Many anthropologists who came into a foreign or unfamiliar society with a compassionate sense of responsibility encountered instances in the everyday life of a society and in working with trusted informants in which they would have liked to provide some kind of help. This help might have been out of place within the traditional knowledge base of the society; but within the experience and understanding of the anthropologist, an outsider's knowledge could have been very helpful in a particular situation. For example, an anthropologist might have an antibiotic to treat a festering wound of one of the members of the community. However, for the anthropologist to act on his/her outsider knowledge could have changed the society and introduced a completely new factor in their traditional sense of their identity and worldview. Since the scientist was to be an observer and not an agent of change, anthropology's primary method of participant observation as practiced in the field had built into its framework what many would see in retrospect as an ethical dilemma. This sense of dilemma increased as the societies with whom the anthropologists were working over the last century became more sophisticated and worldly. The dilemma deepened when, as was sometimes the case, the insider member of society knew that the outsider may have been able to help.

After World War II, when cultural contact dramatically increased, the worldliness of the insiders of the kinds of societies that anthropologists and ethnographers studied made the relationship between the anthropologist as scientist and participant observer more difficult to reconcile. What does the anthropologist do when he or she is confronted with what might be a life-or-death problem and the anthropologist knows the solution from his outsider experience? Does he or she do the "right thing" and help solve the problem? Or does he or she let the society carry out its traditional response in order to understand what the social outcomes are and how it all works within a traditional society? On the face of it, helping seems like a simple choice. However, in so doing, a cascade of other factors could be set in motion to institute change, and those changes could be more costly to the lives of other people in the society than the advantage of doing the "right act" for saving an individual. Of course, not all issues have to be defined in extreme life-or-death ways, but the related questions have confronted many anthropologists over the years.

During World War II and after in the reconstruction periods, many anthropologists were recruited by the U.S. government and other agencies to gather much-needed information about societies with whom they had had limited contact but for which they needed to develop policies that fit with the needs and wishes of the society as a whole. A classic example of this kind of applied anthropology was the remarkably significant book by Ruth Benedict, *The Chrysanthemum and the Sword,* which influenced the U.S. occupation of post-WWII Japan. However, there were many other cases during and after that time that created ethical dilemmas. Perhaps one of the most egregious occurred during the Vietnam War, when U.S. anthropologists were accused of being spies for the CIA. There was no systematic response from the field to the question about how an anthropologist should behave when invited to provide assistance to or about a society.

Action Anthropology as developed by Sol Tax lays out this problem and provides the first set of comprehensive answers based on his collective experiences and discussions with many of his students and colleagues. As the reader can see by examining the key issues of Action Anthropology, there is a set of roles that, if followed, should help the anthropologist negotiate the ethical questions. They provided a new paradigm for how to overcome the increasingly obvious problems that surfaced when anthropologists were asked to help. On the one hand, their scientific participant observation methodology worked well. However, on the other hand, the way in which the knowledge was collected from traditional peoples could also be construed as a continuation of 19th-century colonialism and paternalism, since the anthropologists came from the traditions of a rich technologically developed society with power and privilege to "study" poor underdeveloped societies. It could be further concluded that the anthropologist brought little to the society except some friendship and solace, while returning to their own society to write books about "them" ("the other") to enjoy successful and comfortable careers as those they "studied" continued to live often in poverty and sometimes in ill health and even hunger. Did this mean that the anthropologist's dispassionate scientific mode of observation of "primitive" people was an offshoot of the 19th-century perspective of the social place of "the other"? Was the anthropologist's choice of whom to study merely an extension of the past colonial paternalism that helped indirectly to continue—if not the political, the socioeconomic—subjugation of the "primitive and/or native" society?

Historically, it is perfectly clear that Sol Tax attempted to avoid these pitfalls. Action Anthropology was born out of his concerns for working with American native Indian peoples. These peoples were living in tribal enclaves created mostly during the 19th century against their wills, and were now living post–World War II in the mid-20th century after having, in many cases, helped the U.S. government and people win the War. They experienced many problems under the "bureaucratic care" of the Bureau of Indian affairs, which carried many syncretic vestiges of 19th-century paternalism and antagonism from the legacy of Western expansionist policies of previous U.S. governments.[2] This is where Sol Tax came to the fore. Basically, as described in this book and elsewhere,[3] he completed a PhD dissertation based on field work near Tama, Iowa, with the Fox (Mesquakie) Indian tribes in 1935; after returning to Chicago following WWII, he began the Fox Project that led to the formation of Action Anthropology starting in the late 1940s. This was a time when it was no longer conceivable that American Indians should be looked at as some kind of primitive indigenous population when, in fact, poverty and lack of opportunity were the greatest factors influencing the life of every American native living on a reservation. Therefore, it is perfectly logical that a rejection of the old paternalism would emerge in the post–World War II social logic, where all aspects of human equality were undergoing a revolutionary change. Furthermore, with Sol Tax's background favoring social action and a value system that was tuned by the anti-Semitism he personally experienced early in his life, it is not surprising that he would revolt against the accepted and partially ill-defined ethical underpinnings of applied anthropology and develop a very clear vision and, ultimately, the tenets for how anthropologists should work to avoid the ethical pitfalls that could trap applied anthropologists in a regrettable morass that could lead to the undoing of the future of the field.

Thus Action Anthropology provided a new and meaningful way to negotiate the process of working with (and conducting research with) American Indian populations. By directly responding to these ethical issues, Action Anthropology opened up a new paradigm for how applied anthropology could take hold and grow into a very large enterprise around the world. However, Action Anthropology does not stop here. When Sol Tax first laid out these tenets in the early 1960s, the field was still small and the scope of the problems that anthropologists worked on was still limited, compared to what it is now and is likely to be in the future. Since the early 1960s, the number of anthropologists in the world has grown exponentially and number in the tens of thousands. Moreover, many are no longer academics, as was the case in Tax's time, and this trend is continuing so that the number of nonacademic applied anthropologists may quickly outnumber those in the theoretical areas. Further, the nature of the problems applied anthropology is working on has widened. The "primitive" is no longer the only place anthropologists do fieldwork, and the agencies they work with may not exhibit the old paternalism of the agencies that Tax encountered. In order to do justice to these issues, I have taken the liberty of tracking my personal connections with both Sol Tax and with Action Anthropology, both before I knew him and after. I present this as an intellectual journey of someone who was close, but far enough removed to see the advantages and disadvantages of his approach, and who has been active in a period of about forty years after Tax reached the peak of his leadership in the early 1970s. From this personal perspective, I hope to track out a rich perspective on how we proceed from here.

Vignette 1: Issues of Race, Biology, and the U.S. Supreme Court: The Anti-Miscegenation Laws

In late 1966 and early 1967, while still a graduate student at the University of Pennsylvania, I was invited by a young attorney friend, Don Kramer, to be the principal anthropological consultant to the Japanese American Association's U.S. Supreme Court *amicus curiae* brief in *Loving vs. The Commonwealth of Virginia,* the case that tested the validity of the racial anti-miscegenation laws that were on the books in 16 states (three states quietly dropped them before the case was heard). My job was to present to the senior attorney, William M. Marutani, Esq., who was petitioning the court (headed by Chief Justice Earl Warren) on behalf of the Association, what was known about the biological basis of race and its potentials for justifying the applicability of these laws. (See http://caselaw.lp.findlaw.com/scripts/getcase.pl?court=us&vol=388&invol=1). I was advised by two senior anthropologists, Paul Baker and Bill Politzer, to be circumspect about my role in this case so as not to "end my career before it began," because race was such a hot-button topic at the time in the American Association of Physical Anthropologists.[4] Thus, in keeping with a tradition that I later learned about in the related work of Sol Tax, I carefully downplayed my apparent role into a simple footnote in the brief. (I remember that, after the submission of the brief, I was warned by Anthony F.C. Wallace that I had better get back to writing my doctoral dissertation if I expected to graduate that May—I listened and fortunately I did!)

I was rather surprised to be invited to attend the oral argument at the U.S. Supreme Court in early April 1967 to hear Mr. Marutani's and the other lawyers' presentations and to have a choice seat next to U.S. Senator Daniel K. Inouye from Hawaii and closely behind the imposing figure of the Lyndon Johnson–appointed U.S. solicitor general, Thurgood Marshall, who argued against these laws on behalf of the federal government. However, when it came time for Mr. Marutani to testify, I was truly shocked and somewhat overwhelmed to discover (he had not told me in advance) that his argument to the Supreme Court was based almost entirely on the materials about the physical anthropology of race that I had developed for the brief! And this was not all. Nearly every member of the court asked serious and knowing questions about these anthropological issues, indicating that they not only had read the brief carefully, but more importantly from my perspective, had understood it in its entirety. The rest is history: the court held that the laws were unconstitutional on the last day of the court in June (a few weeks after receiving my PhD in May!).

I went on to other things thinking I was through with an interesting chapter of my life. However, I never dreamed that over 25 years later I would chair the rewrite of the very UNESCO statement on race that I nearly learned by heart in working on the *Loving* case).[5] But the lessons learned from this episode also became deeply ingrained in my ethical worldview. I gained the insight very early in my career that knowledge accurately applied to the problems confronting society could provide a powerful tool to help bridge the gap between what we knew in the sciences and what our society needed to know at the level of public understanding, policy and law. I believed then, and still do believe almost 50 years later, that there is a social responsibility to use and engage this knowledge wisely and constructively in trying to advance a greater understanding, even when it is risky. As a professional, it is not always sufficient to wait for knowledge to disseminate to the general public. Sometimes it is not enough to wait for someone else to translate scientific findings into more general or popular arenas of knowledge, especially when the need is great. So in the tradition of Sol Tax, I felt and feel comfortable with attempting to translate key research topics in which I had expertise into the realm of potential public benefit.[6]

Vignette 2: The Norton Sound Health Corporation: A Classic Example of the Tenets of Action Anthropology

In 1969, a couple of years after the Supreme Court work, I visited the Arctic as a part of a project being conducted in collaboration with Anthony F.C. Wallace and Edward Foulks, both in the anthropology department at the University of Pennsylvania, studying a carefully developed hypothesis on the role of calcium metabolic abnormalities in the expression of Arctic hysterias. Soon after my arrival, it became clear that Barrow, Alaska—then the largest native community in Alaska, numbering about 2,000 people—was a poor Inuit village that followed a tradition of hunting and gathering. This community was located very close to the Naval Arctic Research Laboratory complex that supported the Strategic Air Command Dew Line, which patrolled the Arctic defenses to prevent incursion by the Soviet Union and was a hotbed of activity. It also sat on what was, at the time, the largest known petroleum reserve in Alaska (Pet 4). Needless to say, Barrow was not just a small community of "American Eskimo Natives"; it was also the outer limit of U.S. defenses at a time when it was a first priority. Hence, the Indian Health Service division of the U.S. Public Health Service (US-PHS) located one of its major hospitals in Barrow. Their work in the delivery of health services was defined on the basis of medicine as practiced in the rest of the PHS hospital system in the lower 48 states, but was complicated by poverty and considerable alcoholism-associated social, behavioral, and health disorders and by an isolated arctic environment in which there was a very high accident rate associated with the early adoption of snowmobile use. There were also inadequate housing, heavy sewage pollution problems, and a very high level of infectious childhood diseases, which were complicated by various degrees of iron deficiency anemia and other forms of infant malnutrition.

So there I was studying calcium metabolism but also observing an enormous number of social health problems that were complicated by the nature of the social interactions and the previous policies of the U.S. and state governments that ended up causing such significant social dislocation that it was difficult for the locals to survive under those circumstances. After a great deal of reflection, I decided that the best contribution I could make to this community and to the plight of indigenous people in the Arctic, would be to better understand the multiple determinants that underlay the health problems of the region. Thus, I began to look at the epidemiology of the various major diseases that were present at that time. I conducted this research to develop an ecosystems approach to health in the Arctic and to work it out for Barrow in the early 1970s, which was just before the land-claim settlement with the Alaska natives and before the development of the oil wells and oil exploration in Prudhoe Bay. I did this work before I knew anything about Sol Tax's work formulating Action Anthropology.

Although I thought, perhaps naively, that the native peoples would embrace a holistic concept like this to provide additional help to them, I was quite wrong in that I was unable to convince anyone in the state, the federal government, or the community to support such a notion. Nevertheless, I developed a scientific paper on my approach and presented it as a participant in a Circumpolar Health Research Program Conference in Finland in 1971, one of a series of meetings beginning in 1966 that convened in different locations each year or two. The idea behind this program was that the problems encountered in the unique environment of the Arctic could be better solved with the cross-fertilization of public-health experts working in the circumpolar area that came from meeting around the world to discuss them every few years. When I presented this ecosystems model for the delivery of health services in Barrow, which I co-authored with Ed Foulks at the meetings in Finland, I never expected anyone but public-health officials to respond about the theory of my work.

Basically, a couple of key representatives of a group of Inuit people from the Norton Sound area of Alaska attended the Circumpolar Health Conference in Oulu, Finland, to see what was going on that might help them with their work. At that lecture, I presented an ecosystems model of health in the Arctic that was based on my experiences conducting research on health in Barrow. At the end of the lecture I was surprised to be greeted and asked questions by an Alaska native, Caleb Pungowiyi, who came from the Norton Sound area, along with a young nonnative, Bill Dann. (Caleb Pungowiyi was just starting out at 28 years of age and was from St. Lawrence Island, the largest island in the Bering Straits region. He ultimately became one of the greatest Inuit leaders in Alaskan history.)[7] They had just received "anti-poverty" funding from the federal government to form a native-run health corporation and wanted to use my "ecosystems model for health delivery in the Arctic" as the primary resource for structuring how they were going to deliver health services in their region. Needless to say, I was delighted and overwhelmed by their enthusiastic interest in my model (which was going nowhere in Barrow), and developed an approach that would subsequently be implemented as an alternate indigenous health system that became a working model of native-centered and native-developed health-care priorities and services.

This was the first of this kind of health service in Alaska (and maybe anywhere in the U.S.), and I encouraged Jim Hahn, one of the graduate students studying with me at the time, to go to Alaska to determine the extent to which he could conduct his research for his dissertation and also help implement this new model of health delivery. The model was designed to take into account the important interests of the community in implementing various health policies that would guide the spending of the money that Dann and Pungowiyi received on the grant to the Norton Sound Health Corporation (NSHC). In addition, they would build into the model all aspects of the ecosystem that were required to improve the health of the people. Soon after the work began, I traveled to the NSHC located in Nome, Alaska, and provided on-the-spot suggestions and guidance to implement the model. I recommended the formation of a trained staff for local delivery of services, helping them with prioritizing the restoration of dental health as one of their first major projects, and also starting an "all about health" newspaper that would be authored, edited, and illustrated by the various native people of the region as a way of improving their identity with the prioritized health needs being recommended.

What began as a way to communicate with and inform people about their own issues (before this newspaper the other information sheets they received were put to "good use" by burning them in their stoves to produce heat) became over the next several years a true "collectible" at the time and thereafter. In order to supply the newspaper with illustrations, they created original high-quality drawings that were specially printed, resulting in a number of works of art that then became "collectibles." These woodblock-type prints became heavily sought after, creating an unexpected market that turned into an additional source of income, pride, and identity for those who owned the papers.

It also became a source of added jobs for those creating the illustrations. This example is, of course, one of many that transpired as the native people in the 16 villages in the region became more and more involved in the directions of their Health Corporation. It finally reached the point that the Health Corporation was routinely selected as the most trusted organization in the community when compared with other agencies, both federal and local. Remarkably, NSHC has survived and prospered now for about 40 years and is not only the oldest of its kind that still exists but has had a profoundly important positive impact on the health and welfare of the people in the region.

Perhaps most of all, this example illustrates Sol Tax's point in Action Anthropology about encouraging the local people to make their own decisions and even their own mistakes in the process, which in the case of NSHC were very few. I think it is important to note that my connection with the corporation only lasted about four to five more years before the people with whom I was connected moved on and others took their places. Furthermore, I would add that this work at Norton Sound helped some basic anthropology research get started in the region through my involvement with Michael Crawford in setting up the Trans-Alaskan Siberian genetic studies that began in the mid-1970s. This NSHC work also exemplifies what can develop after helping to establish a set of foundational principles, then letting go to allow those principles to take hold and evolve in different directions as the local people may desire on their own without necessarily involving any more anthropological input.

If we were to convert the Action Anthropology tenets to a checklist (and I did this as a trial), it is clear that the "fit" of the NSHC project with the list was 100 percent. There is no doubt in my mind that this is not a coincidence and that the tenets of Action Anthropology work and can work extraordinarily well under such circumstances. Hence the question is not whether the tenets work outside of the Fox example but rather how they can continue to help us structure our work elsewhere, and to what extent the Action Anthropology tenets will work universally.

Vignette 3: "Take It *and* Leave It"

My meeting in Oulu, Finland, was in June 1972. By November of that year, I had not yet met Sol Tax, but I did know of his work and realized there was a significant connection between what he was doing and what I was proposing to do for the fall 1972 meeting of the American Anthropological Association in Toronto. As a result of the work I was doing in Alaska with native health problems, I came to realize that every project done in the field needed to be examined as a balanced exchange between what I wanted to get done scientifically and the needs of the people with whom I was working. I reasoned that it was not ethically appropriate to "take" my data out without leaving something behind that was helpful to the people. I had already reasoned that it was not appropriate for me to be working in areas of great poverty without leaving a substantial proportion of my financial earnings with the communities in which I was working. This was accomplished not by any outright gifts but rather by buying local arts and crafts, which helped support the growth of these nascent industries. (This is the first time that I have written about this practice, but it has been consistent from the beginning of my work as an anthropologist.) However, this was not enough. There had to be a way of leaving resources that were more closely related to my/our expertise in order to balance what I might be taking out professionally to benefit my career. Physical anthropology was also different from cultural anthropology in that it was more likely to involve biological measurements and less likely to require as long a period of contact as the cultural anthropologists. The physical anthropologist was also trained differently and was much more likely to be dealing with problems of human biology that could overlap with the health of the people in the community.

At the time I learned generally about Sol Tax's work, and I had already decided that people in my field of physical anthropology in human biology (as it was termed in those days) should begin to develop an ethic for the kinds of fieldwork that we were doing. I decided to create a symposium proposal for the American Anthropological Association meetings that were going to take place in Toronto, Canada, later in 1972. The title of the symposium session still summarizes its intent: "Take It *and* Leave It: The Role of the Physical Anthropologist in the Field." We were all set for a major advance—Jamshed Mavalwala, a colleague on the American Anthropological Association Program Committee, was totally in favor of our endeavor and booked us into the largest ballroom in the hotel.

Walking into that huge ballroom a few minutes before the start of the session was at first exciting but then a little nerve-racking because we were all concerned with how good our work would be in comparison to other projects already going on, such as Tax's work in Action Anthropology. We waited, and then waited some more, for a few people to show up; after the first row of the huge room was mostly full and the second row somewhat occupied, we sheepishly decided to begin. After the shock of the poor attendance wore off, all of us participating realized that we were really onto something important as we listened to one another's papers, which explored how the knowledge that we were generating and/or that we brought in with us could be of significant benefit to the people whose lives and societies we were studying.

This experience was also a powerful revelation that I think none of us ever forgot—the broader membership of the American Anthropological Association wasn't quite ready to hear the field we represented or be concerned with what we were talking about at the time. Whether our message was important for the development of Action

Anthropology, or only our interests, remained to be seen. However, I certainly did not stop, and continued to push the issue of responsible exchange in many venues. So it was not surprising and was rather exciting to find that Sol Tax's earlier work paralleled and went much further than what we were proposing for physical anthropologists.

Vignette 4: The Chicago Opera

I will never forget the first time I met Sol Tax. It was later in the night after the international premiere of the opera *Tamu Tamu,* by composer and librettist Gian Carlo Menotti and commissioned by Sol Tax, himself,[8] for the Ninth International Congress of Anthropological and Ethnological Sciences (ICAES), the largest ever. The opera was performed at the Studebaker Theater on South Michigan Avenue in Chicago late in the summer of 1973, and for me, what transpired off the stage was as dramatic as what transpired on it. Imagine a huge audience filled with anthropologists from all over the world watching an opera that played out both first- and third-world perspectives on a contemporary life tragedy that was not so different from the encounters that many in the audience understood on a meta-experiential level that only anthropologists could identify with. Moreover, there—central in the audience, seated together—were Sol Tax, Margaret Mead, and Gian Carlo Menotti observing and participating like the rest of us. This mixture of opera, audience, and levels of meaning was theater at its grandest for anthropology.

But more than the grand opera, it was the sense that something like a truly important coming of age for a field was happening under the auspices of the highly successful *Current Anthropology* journal and the promise of many books of ICAES proceedings being generated by the overwhelming level of participation in the 1973 congress. For a relatively young assistant professor of physical anthropology in his early thirties, like myself, it was, the realization that anthropology was actually achieving the "world anthropology" status that Sol Tax had envisioned and which was already being brought to life through the many advances being shared on the pages of *Current Anthropology*, which Tax had founded about fourteen years before. I had worked hard preparing for these meetings, and by the evening of the opera I had presented three separate papers and was able to relax and be in the moment at its unfolding. Looking back, without remembering how it happened, I can remember attending a wonderful reception later that night in what I recall was a large, crowded and very noisy hotel suite where Sol Tax was hosting. When I came in, I recall, a graduate student asked me my name. When I said "Sol Katz," she went on incredulously, saying what a "wonderful occasion it was that you had invited Menotti to create an opera!" When I quickly figured out that she thought I was Sol Tax, I laughed and immediately corrected her—my name was not "Tax" but "Katz"! Her response was that it seemed incongruous to her that I (Tax) was "much younger than she expected," and I agreed!

A few minutes later, I introduced myself to Sol Tax as "Sol Katz" and in the noise he had a quizzical look on his face. I immediately said "Katz" and then relayed the story of my earlier meeting, and both of us had a good laugh. Tax was about thirty years older than I, with silver hair and a mustache; in my younger years, I had brown hair—and lots more of it than I do now. At the time, I had no idea if he knew anything more about me, and why should he? However, when we met again at one of the other meetings that week, I discovered that he did know about some of my work. In fact, not long after, I was delighted to open an invitation from Sol and Dimitri Shimkin (a close colleague of his) inviting me to be part of the planning for the Indian ICAES, planned for the New Delhi 1978 World Anthropology meetings. For the planning meeting in Champaign-Urbana at the University of Illinois, he and Dmitri organized five panels, each chaired by one or two people. Needless to say, I was delighted to be included and be partnered with Estelle Fuchs for organizing the bio-social division of the program.[9]

What I did not know at that time, and in fact did not understand until very recently, was that a relatively large grant proposal I subsequently wrote to fund the research being presented at the 1978 IUAES (International Union of Anthropological and Ethnological Sciences) New Delhi meetings on world food issues was funded through a resource connected to the Smithsonian Institution via Sam Stanley, who received a vote of confidence in the proposal from Sol Tax. (Sam Stanley was remarkably helpful to me in shepherding the proposal to fund the participants to come to India through the labyrinth of funding resources that were available[10]: it was a PL480 Eisenhower grant sponsored by food payment bonds from India during the Indian famine.) At the time, I thought it was important to have an Indian scholar from the U.S. on the project in order to help with the plans and connections in India; it so happened that the ideal person, Arjun Appadurai, had just joined the University of Pennsylvania anthropology department and was also very well connected to the University of Chicago!

Looking back at this occasion, I now realize how important my participation in the planning and presentation of the 1978 meetings was for my future career development with respect to world food issues. The New Delhi meetings led to the formation of an International Commission on the Anthropology of Food (ICAF) for the ICAES, headed by Igor deGarine and Mary Douglas. With the help of the Wenner Gren Foundation, I was invited to the Burg Wartenstein Conference Center to what turned out to be the Foundation's last scholarly meeting before the Center was closed in 1980. The work in New Delhi and elsewhere in India allowed me to solidify my thinking and position of intellectual leadership within the field. Furthermore, it exposed me to a much wider group of anthropologists interested in food than I ever would have been able to meet on my own.

Vignette 5: Post–Sol Tax Action Anthropology—The Task Force on the African Famine

Following the IUAES meetings in India and after conducting many other studies, especially in the areas of child health and welfare among poverty-stricken African American families in Philadelphia, I became increasingly concerned with the scientific investigation of the biocultural evolution of food systems. I continued to integrate anthropological studies into other venues, especially in the religion and science areas, that helped further sharpen the issues of ethics in my perspectives on science. After organizing a symposium on Religion and Food for the Toronto meetings of the American Association for the Advancement of Science in 1981, I became acutely aware of the role of religious traditions in Ethiopia in regulating fasting and its association with food rationing in times of food crises. This became particularly horrific in the context of the Ethiopian famine that began in 1984 and led to over one million people having starved to death by the end of 1985. It was late in 1984 with this famine in full disaster mode that I went to the American Anthropological Association meetings in Denver.

In anthropology by this time in 1984, the four-fields approach (keeping linguistics, archaeology, biological anthropology and cultural anthropology together as branches of a single field and being taught that way as the intellectual basis of the discipline) was starting to splinter. The AAA was deeply concerned with whether there would be a mass disintegration of the traditional discipline. In this context, the AAA decided to support a new division, called the General Anthropology division of the AAA, which was designed to preserve the four-fields approach. I attended the opening meeting of the new division with the idea of voicing concerns about the famine occurring in Ethiopia and elsewhere in Africa, while we anthropologists were busily discussing the latest results and politics of our work, almost unconcerned with the magnitude of this unfolding human tragedy. I believed that we, as anthropologists, could make a major contribution to understanding the basis of the famine, as well as mediate concerns and ideas that we could contribute to the general solutions that were being proposed at the time. So I proposed that a task force on the African famine be formed, with the idea that it could foster a new approach for the AAA to concern itself with problems of deep concern for humanity.

I was delighted that the proposal was voted upon and accepted at the end under "new business" of that first meeting of the General Anthropology division of the AAA. Sylvia Forman, who was elected first president of the General Anthropology division at that meeting, appointed me to chair the Task Force on the African Famine (Fleuret 1988) as a food expert, but I privately objected because I was not an Africanist and had no direct field experience there. Nevertheless, after further conversations with Dell Hymes who, as the newly elected president of the AAA, pointed out to me that leading the task force as a concerned "physical anthropologist outsider," I might also have an important role in helping to heal some of the splintering that had occurred in the 1970s between the theoretical academic anthropologists and the applied anthropologists by connecting them in a common partnership to help address this major human catastrophe. Hence, I agreed to head it up for the next year. Fortunately, I was able to partner with Dr. Rebecca Huss-Ashmore, who was a new assistant professor at the University of Pennsylvania and had conducted fieldwork in Africa. We immediately enlisted the help of a number of other experts (just as Dell Hymes predicted), including theoretical and applied anthropologists. Also, with the help and guidance of an old friend and colleague, Bob Netting of the University of Arizona, we enlisted a very substantial group of these anthropologists in a series of symposia on the African famine that were presented throughout the annual meeting.

These sessions, with the two camps of theory and practice not only talking to one another but working together to help solve a problem, went a long way—not only toward addressing the problems of famine in Africa but also the problems of the separation between the theoretical and the applied anthropologists. After all, who could deny that famine was going on in Africa; that anthropology had something to contribute to it; and that the knowledge about the issues had to come from the entire knowledge base and experience of those in the field. Finally, most importantly, it would take all of us working together to make a significant contribution. This was our goal and with the help of all those involved, it gave rise to an enormous groundswell of support so that for the first time in many years both sides of the controversy—applied and theoretical—were willing to sit on the same program. Unlike our previous experience with the "Take It *and* Leave It" symposium in the early 1970s, this time our four-session Task Force on the African Famine filled the largest rooms in the annual meetings of the AAA and resulted in one of the most successful conferences we have ever had on the exploration of world food problems.

Several years later, Dell Hymes reminded me of our earlier conversation that as a "physical anthropologist not connected to Africa" I had a better chance of uniting everyone on both sides of the divide between academic and applied circles than anyone inside those fields! While fully accepting Dell's interpretation, I responded that I preferred to reframe the success of the Task Force on the African Famine as a profound reminder that our compassionate concern for the "other" in all of anthropology transcended any of the intellectual boundaries that divided us.

This became a paradigm for how theoretical and applied anthropologists could work together in the future of the newly formed organization for the AAA that Roy Rappaport championed during his presidency of the AAA. Once again, based in part on the enormous success and its potential for continuing success under more knowledgeable leadership (I was not an Africanist), I retired as chair and recommended that the task force elect a chair with more direct experience. Anne Fleuret was elected chair[11] and Steve Reyna was elected to follow her two years later. In December 1992, Art Hansen issued a Position Statement on African Famine from the Task Force (whose expanded mission by 1992 was reflected in its being renamed the Task Force on Hunger, Famine and Food Security), representing the entire AAA that was published in *Anthropology Today* in 1993 (Hansen 1993). The Position Statement contained language that exactly reflected the kind of compassion and professional concern that is reflected earlier with Action Anthropology. The Task Force went on to many more successful years of meetings and publication of influential reports, and I went on to other venues.

This pointed to the kind of potential for resolution of the similar tension that seemed to be present for Sol Tax when he was implicitly criticized for going "outside" of anthropology when organizing the Chicago American Indian Conference.

Building on Action Anthropology for the Future

This is a book about several themes. First it is about Sol Tax and his life. It is also about the concept of Action Anthropology and how it developed and became a foundational element for much of the applied anthropological research that was done in the second half of the 20th century. However, it is more than this: it is also a synthesis of the paradigm of Action Anthropology and the people who created and developed it as well as the people who were the subjects of anthropological inquiry and the impact it had on their lives and traditions. This combination of factors may get at the essence of how Sol Tax believed Action Anthropology was a theoretical issue rather than an applied anthropology study. To Tax, Action Anthropology embodied a theoretical stance about how to interact with the subjects of anthropological fieldwork. Finally, this is a book about a period in the history of anthropology when the field was making a transition from being exclusively a "study *of people*" toward being a more open and inclusive approach that includes the "study *for people*." This is a critical distinction and its difficulty has concerned much of anthropology throughout the second half of the 20th century. *The point of this chapter is that the overwhelming evidence is that the future of anthropology tilts toward the latter without undermining the former.*

Anthropologists have historically built the science of humanity in all of its dimensions on the basis of a thorough knowledge of natural, cultural, and material history. Some of the original purposes for anthropologically studying the "primitive" and less "civilized" were predicated on gathering data to support a now disproven *scala naturae* theory,[12] in which the simpler subsistence modes like hunting and gathering were at the bottom of a ladder or scale and western civilization was at the top of this "evolutionary" scale. The same types of arguments were used for the biology of race and had by the late 20th century been thoroughly discredited.[13] In the late 19th century, this concept provided intellectual justification for the occupation and colonization of many regions, especially those with valuable natural resources, including most of sub-Saharan Africa and much of Asia. Along with presuming a hierarchy of the peoples of the world with those in economic and military power on top was a facade of benevolent paternalism that projected childlike behaviors onto those dominated, where their community beliefs, morals, insights, opinions, and traditions were gently dismissed or ignored unless, of course, there was a social disruption of any kind, which was always put down with brute force.

This system of belief permeated public culture of the West in the 19th century and through the first decade of the 20th century. By the end of World War I, this was no longer public policy but had crept into both popular belief and into the background of most every Western government agency. By this I mean it was implicit in the structure of how they functioned more than it was a stated policy. (In some cases, such as racial segregation or hostility to the other on the basis of national origin or religion, it was allowed by laws created earlier but still enforced.) By thirty years later, after World War

II, the great sacrifices of so many of the minority groups in the U.S. were so evident and the leveling of the playing fields associated with the staggering horrors of war challenged all of the previously accepted social rules that kept this kind of paternalism in place. And following the other great upheavals in the U.S., there were major social changes again, especially in the areas of civil rights and more recently increased recognition of the right to equality of economic opportunity. Looking back, it is important to note that Sol Tax was creating Action Anthropology well before many of these changes took place in the rest of society, and that, if the tenets of Action Anthropology had been fully accepted and integrated into practice, they were early enough in the history of anthropology to have protected the field from a number of ethical mistakes that were made. The problem was that they were not, even though they were being promoted by Sol Tax, arguably one of the most influential anthropologists of the time.

There were other factors going on at the time that may have partially eclipsed Action Anthropology from taking the position of significance it deserved. During the period when it was first introduced in the early 1950s by Tax, there was not much applied anthropology going on at least as indicated by the (admittedly incomplete) statistics that Bennett provides about the numbers of self-identified applied anthropologists during these times. Moreover, it seems as if Action Anthropology became identified with selling the field short. Academic anthropology looked down on applied anthropology and continued to do so in the mid 1980s when I was involved with the formation of the Task Force on the African Famine, which at the time was looked upon as an exemplar for breaking down this divide (although it still exists today). Also, as Sol Tax himself says in his definition of Action Anthropology in his 1975 *Current Anthropology* paper, "Action Anthropology," "...The first thing to make clear is we are theoretical anthropologists who are part of the tradition of cultural anthropology. Culture is our central concept, and everything else depends on it."…. This obviously means "we are not one of them." But it also calls into serious question the application of Action Anthropology to those who cross over from culture to biology and back again, as I do in much of my theoretical work. I choose to think Action Anthropology does apply to me, too. But as we shall see, maybe it does not. Does it apply to archaeology? Maybe not. Once again, I think it does—but it may not have applied when Tax first developed the concept because that was not what he was responding to. If we think about the implications of his 1975 statement 25 years after first coining the term, it is clear that he was trying to clear up misconceptions and in so doing may have excluded other dimensions that we can now examine along with evaluating the "tenets" for what they are worth in today's environment. We need to be reminded that Sol Tax never once claimed he was an applied anthropologist himself, even though he created the foundation and building blocks for the field to exist through his Action Anthropology concept.

How Tax did this is important to review because, without understanding it, we miss the opportunity to set the record straight and open a truly impartial evaluation of this important work for the future. In essence, until the early 1950s when Action Anthropology first emerged and for at least another couple of decades beyond, anthropologists were instructed in the classic idea (discussed in the introduction to this chapter) that they were doing a scientific investigation of the social traditions and cultural dimensions of a society and that as an "expert outside observer" they could make specific observations that were unfettered by the fact that they too were humans observing other humans. In other words, if the anthropologist could both participate and simultaneously observe the people, he or she might be able to make useful theoretical contributions to our understanding. On the other hand, if the anthropologist became too closely involved with the wants and needs of the population and maybe even satisfying them, he or she may be on a very slippery slope that would end up being unduly influenced by the people and by his or her involvement and concerns. This could lead to the corruption of the scientific knowledge and as a result might contaminate the generalizations being made by the conflict of interest between helping the people and studying the people. This is a real ethical problem whether it comes from being asked by the people or offering it to the people without being asked.

Without saying it directly, Tax came up with the idea in Action Anthropology that you do not intervene, you let the people make mistakes on their own but you do provide them with all the tools they need to answer questions critical to their needs and their concept of what ought to be, which is a very subtle but very important distinction. It's as if a fork in the road was developed that allowed the theoretical side of anthropology to be merged effectively with the side demanding concern and intervention. It was vastly different than the previous idea of a paternalistic approach where the outsider anthropologist perhaps knew better than the people on the inside because they had a vast amount of added experience about what the external world was all about and therefore could be very helpful for the "..poor downtrodden, submissive and naive childlike.." indigenous people. Of course, this is far from the truth that Tax had personally witnessed and worked with, and therefore a new bridge had to be established which allowed equality and subtle distinctions to be made. For example, even if the anthropologist thought he or she knew better, the fact remains that it was okay to be helpful if the people were allowed to make their own mistakes in carrying out their life's work. Parsing out the construct helps us to understand the significance of this important distinction.

At last Action Anthropology freed anthropology to follow a new path with possibilities that had not existed before, and gave new sources of freedom to those who were the subjects of their research to freely take advantage of the knowledge possessed by these anthropological outsiders. Of course, with freedom goes the responsibility, especially for the anthropologist, to act in an ethical manner in all of their interactions with the indigenous populations with whom they were working. This distinction was probably not always recognized by the rest of anthropology, which continued to look at Action Anthropology as merely another branch of applied anthropology.[14]

Over time these subtle distinctions of Action Anthropology became clearer, but it was not until the later part of the 20th century that much of this became resolved as the need for ethical foundations and tenets like those of Action Anthropology became essential tools to clarify the nature of being a professional in such a fast moving field. This is especially so when Action Anthropology ethics are examined in the broader context of the entire field of anthropology. Between the time that Action Anthropology was first formulated and today, anthropology truly underwent an enormous growth spurt in terms of the numbers of professionals in the field. However, this growth of the field came at a tremendous cost to those being trained. Most graduate students coming into the field were treated like and trained as if they too were going to be an academic like their professors. While many wonderful students obtained great academic positions, the vast majority for many years did not. For many years students were accepted into graduate programs to justify the academic size of the departments and to be teaching assistants. In no way were the numbers of graduate students being trained and the numbers of professional academic jobs available appropriately matched. In fact, at times it was in the order of perhaps a 10–50:1 ratio between the number being trained and the number of positions that were available in academia. The demographic implications of these employment numbers alone shifted the balance to favor the applied anthropology numbers. This huge excess of highly trained new PhDs and academically under- or unemployed has had a profound effect on the subsequent development of the field. It largely shifted thousands of anthropologists into more applied positions who were largely absorbed into various kinds of research communities that saw the benefit of an anthropological approach to problem solving. This shift is critically important in understanding what transpired throughout the late 20th century and helps explain the lack of understanding of Action Anthropology, since there were so relatively few who could either discuss/teach or exemplify the significance of Tax's contributions. Moreover, even if the unemployed and under-employed did understand the implications of Action Anthropology, many could not afford to risk offending their sponsoring agency with the level of ethics that Action Anthropology prescribed. Nevertheless this does not mean that Action Anthropology cannot have a place in the future. There is excellent evidence of a need and with the re-inauguration that this volume exemplifies intellectually and the success that it had in attracting such an overwhelmingly positive response from the indigenous American Indian community in the Northwest gives strong testimony about its lasting effectiveness and significance as a paradigm in the 21st century as well. However this does not mean that Action Anthropology can be taken wholly into the 21st century without careful and constructive new dialog about its limits and potentials.

If we look carefully at the tenets of Action Anthropology presented in the introduction to this memoir, they are all positive and laudable goals. However, they were formed before the field of applied anthropology became more complex and they have not been systematically updated to include the new frontiers of anthropological research and practice. For example, every line starts with "we" and appears to assume that "we" are cultural anthropologists. However, most anthropologists are rarely the only members of the cultural anthropology team as they were in the Fox Project. Today anthropologists in the applied field are more often than not members of a multidisciplinary team that may have some constraints on a wide range of issues that may not fit the Tenets of Action Anthropology, especially those that require short-term advice that may not fit with the ideals of "temper[ing] our bias for action by avoiding premature choices and responses." Often the deadlines are real and the needs for deliverable reports within a team framework are necessary. Added to this is the notion of how to judge when it is appropriate to respect the "right and ability of a community to make choices affecting its future, and the freedom to make its own mistakes," when in fact the mistakes made may be so costly as to jeopardize their future health, welfare and even their lives. As an example, it is amazing how long it has been for some African leaders to recognize the significance of the behaviors that led to HIV/AIDS in their countries. This example implicates those branches of applied medical and public health anthropology that are predicated on other ethical constraints, such as for medical professionals who could not explicitly follow this Action Anthropology ethic or such as the new President of the very influential World Bank, Doctor Kim, who is an HIV/AIDS specialist. For many in anthropology today an interventionist ethic motivates their professional identity and sense of responsibility. In these days of dual certification of careers such as psychology and anthropology or sociology and anthropology or any of the other subfields of anthropology not covered in Tax's concept, real issues with following the Action Anthropology tenets exist.

Furthermore, note that the tenets of Action Anthropology refer throughout to "community." Anthropologists in the past only worked with small and usually remote communities, and while the nature of what is done by many anthropologists today still involves communities, the fact is many anthropologists now work at other levels in terms of their advising and reporting. It is common that the levels of complexity, agencies within societies and nations and among national groups are all part of the contemporary process anthropologists deal with routinely. This kind of complexity was not part of the original configuration of Action Anthropology. While this brief analysis is not presented to diminish the power of the original statement, it does suggest that books like this one need to explore the potentials for expanding and updating this initial but profoundly important statement. Should a new statement be issued and if so, who should do it and how should it be called for?

While this book is not a Festschrift for Sol Tax, there are some very fine ones out there.[15] Nor is this book an analysis of the historic significance of Action Anthropology; there are already some excellent analyses out there, such as the very thoughtful one by Bennett in *Current Anthropology* (1988). Rather, it is more of a retrospective of a man and his theoretical stance that is provided to determine the degree to which the ideas embodied have stood the test of time. It is clear to me that Tax's ideas have, indeed, done this quite well and remain valuable in the 21st century. It is evident that Action Anthropology is not so much a theoretical stance as it is an ethical one, and by this standard it is as relevant today as it was the day it was first developed over 60 years ago. However, because it is an ethical stance generated by a remarkably perceptive person, Action Anthropology is almost inseparable from the persona of Sol Tax. And while I have no answer or any way to address the logistics of the question I raised in the paragraph above, I will once again return to the empirical as a means of adding a more complete current example: The Action Anthropology paradigm and what I see for its expansion in the future.

A Perspective for the Next Decade

I recently attended a session in Philadelphia to plan for the 250th anniversary of our nation and discovered that only a few people want to plan that far ahead, I suppose for good reason. No one knows what the future will bring; some are more interested in tomorrow than the day after; and, in the context of academics predicting the future, no one wants to be completely off-base. Fortunately, I have carried out many longitudinal studies, and some of the children who were born into it are now grandparents. So for me projecting a dozen years is not so far-fetched, even though the old rule of predicting the future still holds. So this final section is about the next dozen or so years and is mostly based on my current work with world food problems.

Looking backward is always a much easier way to predict how the future will emerge. However, it took anthropologists like Tax, whose experiences are so well documented in this book, to see so completely through the contemporary limitations of the governing social institutions of his time and invest enormous efforts to limit their effects on the people with whom he was working at the Fox site. In prospect, however, knowing historic antecedents to issues like institutional paternalism provides a complexity to Action Anthropology that helps us understand the present and the future possibilities. Action Anthropology, like nearly all of applied anthropology, has a structure oriented to the future, where our knowledge sphere will best serve, and also addresses humanity's needs in general. After all that Sol Tax has done in addition to this major work in Action Anthropology, he demonstrated as much as anyone in the field of 20th century anthropology that we do have something profound to say and that we should have some rules of engagement that are part of our foundation as a discipline.

The ethical underpinnings of Action Anthropology now have an elegant simplicity, but in their day Action Anthropology was as much a revolutionary shift from the scientific paternalism inherent in participant observer anthropology, as the early 20th century Boasian empiricism was from the empty speculation of 19th century armchair anthropology. In a sense, Sol Tax knew this when in 1975 he planned the 1978 world anthropology meetings in New Dehli. It was not a mistake on Tax's part that he selected six topic areas to lead into the future[16], almost any one of which would challenge the previous precepts of Action Anthropology. For example, the basics of the "biosocial dimension" that Sol and Dimitri asked me to address in 1977 were being developed in a biocultural approach I had outlined in a feature paper published in *Science* in 1974 (Katz, Hediger, and Valleroy 1974), and presented as one of the papers I gave at the

ICAES meetings Tax organized. Likewise, the important issues raised in the systems paper published in *Current Anthropology* already outstripped the logical calculus of the ethical dilemmas confronted by Action Anthropology. Certainly the original Action Anthropology precepts still hold water today, but the container has grown so large that only a small fraction of what the container held in the mid-century now appears to fit.

Furthermore, virtually none of the concepts developed for that next meeting in New Delhi (even though not all were realized) were part of the anthropological paradigm when Action Anthropology was first formulated. However, the principle of looking critically at the underlying value assumptions of how we treat and interact with "the other" is still highly relevant for every situation we address today. So the underlying question is valid, but the data to which it is to be applied has grown so great that it is nearly impossible to comprehend. It is so easy to miss what Sol Tax was doing at the time because it was so revolutionary on his part to challenge the basics of how anthropologists were supposed to behave, that for many it was easy to brush it off and wonder why Tax had gone off and become an "applied" anthropologist.

So what is its equivalent today? Can we anticipate what is and is not acceptable and what is likely to be implemented and what is not? It is possible that if we ask the right questions and get help with implementing our answers more effectively, we may be able to recommend improvements and revisions to Action Anthropology and/or paradigm changes in our models for how anthropology functions in the world that will hopefully have staying power equal to those Tax put in place over half a century ago.

Food Security, Safety, and Sustainability as an Impetus Toward a New Anthropology of Food Systems

I would like to suggest at least one paradigm shift that is already occurring and that could develop much further and have the kind of impact that Action Anthropology had in its origins and development. In order to address this look into the future I will develop three additional perspectives based on my experience in several areas with the AAA. They all involve the rapidly escalating concerns for the security, safety, and sustainability of the human food system from micro to macro levels throughout the world.

There are so many dimensions of the human food system[17] because it helps define who we are and how we live. Even when food resources are completely adequate, what we eat forms a critical dimension of our biology and culture. How does it fit with

Action Anthropology perspectives? Work on the many dimensions of the food system extends beyond the borders of Action Anthropology; it is universal and yet is deeply connected with ethnic identity. In one sense the anthropology of food is universal because it crosses global borders that Action Anthropology never crossed when dealing with issues of security, safety and sustainability. Food systems crosscut all regions of the world and if we combine issues about security, safety and sustainability, the food system involves all of humanity. If we visualize the magnitude of the problems that exist, then we have to make room for an expansion of the values that we need to consider to study and contribute to the potential solutions. How we will conduct the fundamental ethics of our work in the future needs to be planned now. For example, it is necessary, but not always sufficient, in the case of food systems to help solve a problem and learn something in the process; a trial and error learning process may work well when there is sufficient time, but depending on it alone may not yield a productive plan in enough time to meet the increased demands of our rapidly changing food system in the midst of a crisis.

The high levels of interest being expressed about food issues today require a significant expansion of the Action Anthropology ethos. Overall, food systems are a very important topic evident in the discussions and concerns of every population in the world today, and the ethics of food are at every intersection of the topic. In a sense this increased sensitivity about the future of food is what defined the interest in the Traditional Food Summit at the 2011 Society for Applied Anthropology meeting in Seattle, which was a direct prelude to the symposium that led to this book.[18] Although the Traditional Food Summit successfully highlighted innovative approaches to natural and cultural resource management through a traditional foods framework, it also did something more profound. The meeting unleashed an enormous well spring of interest from both the native communities of the Northwest region and many anthropologists from all over the U.S. and abroad who came together for the first time in recent memory to share deeply meaningful experiences and stories about their search for reestablishing an environment that would allow native people to have their first foods in greater abundance.

I did not attend the sessions that Sol Tax arranged in Chicago for American Indians; but at the 2011 Seattle meeting, I felt as if the Traditional Food Summit emphasizing the American Native "first foods" was a 21st-century reawakening of a movement like the one on indigenous peoples' rights Sol Tax unleashed about a half century earlier. The Seattle meeting witnessed the joining of the very widespread contemporary American yearnings for safe and healthy regional foods with the related yearnings of American Indians seeking to restore their traditional food systems. This common theme was made all the more powerful in the sense that all of this movement was occurring with the shared connections and partnership of the anthropological community in attendance. It was a very special occasion. If there was any question about how strong this movement was at the time of the 2011 conference or if it was just a passing interest stimulated by the unique opportunity of this 2011 meeting, the answer is becoming evident a year later. There is little doubt in my mind about its impact on the Northwest Coast tribes when I read that this year's Thirty-Sixth Annual National Indian Timber Symposium entitled "Expanding Roots: Cultivating Relationships & Opportunities," which is traditionally devoted to lumber issues, is now leading off its annual meeting almost precisely where the Traditional Food Summit left off with its emphasis on "first foods." The program for the sessions in May 2012 addressed a strong new sense of dedication emerging about the "first foods" issues so amply discussed in the 2011 Traditional Food Summit sessions.[19]

The broader social meaning of this movement among the Northwest Coast peoples involves seeking a voice for the restoration of their food system and the similar needs being expressed throughout the contemporary world points to the acute need for the development of conceptual frameworks to handle these concerns that are now lacking in our current understanding of the human food system. In this context it is increasingly apparent that the contemporary label of being an ***omnivore*** "who eats nearly everything" may lead us to overplay our potentials to eat so many types of food from so many nutrient sources. Being an omnivore is more of an abstraction about potentials than it is about the food that any specific people or society prescribes, proscribes and actually eats.

If we look at human food consumption more holistically over time, it appears that we are more likely to be programmed to become deeply involved in a particular food tradition that is the product of an evolutionary process that has taken many generations, centuries and even thousands of years to evolve. This aspect of the human food system needs a new terminology to integrate it into the meaningful continuum of abstractions that we are discovering about the origins of ethnic food traditions. While omnivore is the broadest term we can apply to the potential of humanity's diet, we are really *"ethnovores"*[20] in our individual, family, community and cultural values and behaviors. This shift in concept opens up a series of systematic questions. For example, we need to address how it is that until contemporary times, we were so deeply connected to our dietary traditions that we rarely, if ever, strayed away from them? What is the glue that holds us so tightly to the comfort of the ethnic cuisine that characterizes our childhood? To what extent is our current chronic and even infectious disease epidemiology associated with the contemporary loss of our *"ethnovoric"* predilections?

Action Anthropology in Supporting a Redefinition of Holistic Approaches to Human Food Systems

In addition to the critically important role that anthropology can play in the recognition of this worldwide movement toward re-establishing *"ethnovoric"* traditions,[21] it also has another major role to play at other levels that are equally important and provide new challenges for the continued transformation of Action Anthropology. For example, taking this concept of the ethnovore further suggests that the biological and ecological costs of playing as if we are *"poly-ethnovores"* (such as sampling from widely varying food traditions as if they are all equivalent foods that can be consumed without concern across their many evolved dimensions) are rapidly catching up with us. On the one hand, all kinds of food sensitivities that were never encountered before are flooding our emergency rooms and hospital beds, almost like some kind of infectious disease. In addition, over-consumption of easily obtained, calorically dense foods is leading to obesity and associated chronic diseases in epidemic proportions throughout the world and especially in the U.S. On the other hand, we are attempting to globalize food production at a tremendous ecological cost without considering the consequences of alternatives.

Moreover, carrying this *"ethnovore"* distinction a step further may provide insights into creating new ways of examining, diagnosing and treating people's nutritional deficiencies and disorders. It may be necessary to conceptualize foods in the diet from the "ethnovoric" perspective in order to understand their rich contextual meaning and to provide meaningful assistance. Making this kind of transitional move from concept to practice is an enormous challenge both to our intellect in testing its logical calculus and limitations, and to our ethical values. We need a revised Action Anthropology that is sensitive to this key new issue with an emphasis on anticipating the transition to a future world that will demand that we deal with these and related food system issues while maintaining sensitivity to the contemporary needs that still exist. The Action Anthropology tenets spelled out in the introduction to this book will in the future have to be built on contemporary values as well as adding many new subtleties to all we know now and need to know in the near future to be truly helpful to those in need of food security, safety and sustainability.

The challenges surrounding contemporary world food systems can also benefit from other key elements within the anthropological framework. As important as it is to view food in terms of the "ethnovoric" elements, anthropology has another strategic advantage in helping with these immensely important problems of food security, safety and sustainability. I strongly believe there is an enormous value to this conceptual investment in holistic synthesis. Our species and its environment are changing fast. Moreover, few, if any, of the other sciences attempting synthesis cover the general perspective with as much depth of understanding and insight about the time and cultural diversity dimensions as well as anthropologists do. Most scientists and policy makers accept the idea that human population is growing rapidly, in fact so rapidly that it is estimated that over the next 40 or so years population growth will be equivalent to adding a new city of a million people every six days over this 40-year period (by contrast in 2012 there were a total of nine U.S. cities with a million of more people).

Imagine for a moment what it would be like to plan to build and provide for a new city's population every 12 days for the next 38 years plus an additional million people every 12 days in rural areas (if we assume about half will still reside there given the needs for increased food production in the future!) However, this assumption about where people will live in the future illustrates one of the important points: 100 years ago less than 10 percent of humanity lived in cities, compared to today, when more than half live in cities. What is also clear about this enormous growth is that in the future, the population pressure and resource limitations will inevitably lead to mass migrations and attempted migrations. The point of this thought exercise is for Action Anthropology to open our thinking to the ramifications of these changes in the magnitude of population growth since Sol Tax first visited the Fox site that yielded the tenets of Action Anthropology. Human population has nearly tripled since that time—in other words, we have already been growing at phenomenal rates and the massive crowding, pollution, over-use of resources and developing scarcity are going to continue, along with massive growth of new technologies, like those that allow us, through the use of computers and the Internet, to know what is going on and stay in touch with the variables necessary for analysis through our anthropologically based models. Hence it is clear that Action Anthropology needs to build upon its previous dimensions and become open to including many new dimensions as well.

In essence, much of our contemporary world expertise is focused on the proverbial trees, whereas anthropology's depth of experience with conceptual models allows us to see the "forests" relatively clearly. Hence it is my contention that the future challenge for Action Anthropology is to renew the useful knowledge that underlies the principles and values of Tax's version of how to behave and relate to the people with whom we work. The need is not to reinvent the wheel and throw out an idea like Action Anthropology in order to call it a piece of our history, but rather to use Action Anthropology as an important building block to guide our future development as we take on new approaches and widen the way we integrate our knowledge sphere into the contemporary problems of humanity. Hence the challenge is to develop a continuous feedback process that engages our principles and expands the original philosophy to meet the needs of the present and the future. We cannot depend upon stagnant, historic approaches but need to develop a working resource of ethically principled models that continuously respond to and test whether we are remaining balanced in our approach and how we may need to change in order to keep from getting lost among the "trees" of new developments that may attractively throw us off the course (see Katz 1999). We need to move forward into the future with a strategic plan for how to proceed.

In order to begin to utilize and extend this ELSI-like feedback (ethical, legal, and social implications) effectively, Action Anthropology of the future will need updating to integrate within the scope and needs of many larger organizations that serve the kinds of communities and societies it has served in the past. Hence the need to work with NGOs within an enlarged future domain of Action Anthropology is now key, but also Action Anthropology needs to operate within the frameworks of international bodies like the World Health Organization, United Nations, Food and Agriculture Organization, UNESCO and regional organizations and cross national organizations like the Pan American Health Organization, Arab Nations, Pacific Rim, European Union, NATO, entire regions that share common trade routes, exchanges, traditions and other needs that were largely absent when Action Anthropology was being developed. In addition, economic agencies that develop policy decisions and mega foundations like the Gates Foundation have been formed since the founding of Action Anthropology. Regardless, the key questions are how and when can we contribute our individual and collective knowledge to assist with more humane solutions to the immense problems confronting human food systems? And how should we revise Action Anthropology and applied anthropology to consider these potentials?

Two paradigms have already been developed in applied anthropology: first, teams involving other disciplines often realize their lack of knowledge about the cultural system and values of the population with whom they are working and employ anthropologists to help solve specific problems. This approach has largely been the history of how applied anthropologists have gained entry into the NGO and governmental communities. However, a second approach is rapidly developing. This new approach stems directly from the work that we have been doing with food systems and global development in the current operation of our American Anthropological Association Presidential Task Force on World Food Problems.[22] It is inherent in the convergence of anthropological models of evolution at the biological and cultural levels, where the need for the combinations of other disciplines has become essential to the work of the field. For example, beginning with the leadership of archeologists such as Lewis Binford who stressed the need for a strong, scientific, anthropologically based evidentiary framework as a paradigm for testing archeological hypotheses and honing insights about the origins, development and even the collapse of ancient civilizations, archeologists have had to search out other disciplines and collaborate with elaborate teams to continue their work. This has led to new kinds of scientific integration with the archaeologist serving at the center for synthesizing the transdisciplinary efforts of a multidisciplinary team.

Like archaeology, biological anthropology has had to depend upon interdisciplinary efforts to develop and test hypotheses and to synthesize new theories about human origins and evolution over time periods of millions of years as well as over a single lifetime. In essence, these disciplines have had to develop a sense of the time dimension to make their efforts work effectively, and this has largely been successful with many spectacular scientific advances. However, these fields can also help us pose questions about the present as well. Of course, the present is complicated in two ways: there are already many other experts dealing with contemporary problems and secondly, the current training of anthropologists has not necessarily prepared them for this role. However, the potential need is so great that the rapid growth of food studies and the leading role of anthropology in it make it likely to be one of the fastest growing fields in the future. This is, in part, due to the fact that about one billion people are in hunger and in ill health and at least another billion people only earn enough each day to buy food and little else. Furthermore, there may be as many as another billion people who are suffering the effects of malnutrition from a poor mix of nutrients and/or issues of food safety.[23]

Anthropology has an admirable history of providing key insights on the micro problems associated with adjustments to food security. However, integrating contemporary food problems at the macro level by anthropologists has been limited by: 1) the daunting and fast changing complexity of the problems; and 2) a wariness to analyze the materialistic dimensions of world trade and financial markets on related global economic issues that directly impact food prices and therefore the hunger associated with poverty. This latter wariness is particularly understandable in light of the traditional focus anthropologists have had on the details of social life in small communities. However, even if we, who are advocates of Action Anthropology, are only interested in solving the dilemmas of hunger and poverty in these communities, it is increasingly evident that we also need to focus our understanding on the macroeconomic factors that tend to maintain poverty and hunger from one generation to the next. Similar arguments can be made for the types of training and expertise necessary to deal with food safety issues. Moreover, if anthropology as a whole is going to assume the kind of leadership that I am advocating in this future perspective for Action Anthropology, we anthropologists will need to integrate the key macro-economic variables more formally into our established capacity for working with a holistic, anthropologically based model of the food chain that maps out and explicates the leading causes of world food insecurity and declines in food safety and results in testable hypotheses about options for their solutions.

The American Anthropological Association Presidential Task Force on World Food Problems

There are staggering numbers of people living today in the shadow of too little, unsafe, and nutritionally unhealthy food. This has been a key area of my work on the American Anthropological Association (AAA) Task Force on World Food Problems (TFWFP) that was proposed and formed in an anticipatory response to the early evidence of a world food crisis that was developing in 2007.[24] A primary focus of our concern is how to bridge among these problems, and our initial steps have been to identify what they are and how they fit into the human food chain at local, national and international levels so that we can develop a comprehensive overview of what they are and how they interact with one another. Of course, macroeconomic issues are not the only specializations that need to be added to complete the models for the future of understanding food system problems. As a part of my efforts chairing the Task Force on World Food Problems, I have developed and listed below a dozen factors that are some of the primary causes of the food crises in 2007–2008 and 2011–2012 that will also need to be incorporated into our thinking in order to develop a more comprehensive heuristic model that may enable us to avert some of the problems that currently have plagued the attempts to solve this mega human problem[25]:

Factors Extrinsic to the Food System:

1. *Climate change,* including increased variation in temperature, rainfall, storm severity, other weather conditions, melting glaciers and rises in sea levels and salinization of river deltas;
2. *Major demographic change* increasing human population food demand by over two billion in less than three decades (with the prospect of another two billion over the next four decades) coupled with a massive migration from rural poverty to urban poverty throughout the world;
3. *Peak oil* production limitations and costs of shifts to alternative energy sources for farm fertilizer production, farm machinery, food preservation, transport, processing and home cooking;

Factors Intrinsic to the Food System:

1. *Unsustainable agricultural practices* that lead to depletion of aquifer agricultural irrigation sources accelerated by the last round of agricultural intensification associated with the increased water needs of "Green Revolution" plants and increased toxicity of ground water; also other agricultural practices leading to soil loss, increased desertification, and contamination of ground water and air from agricultural intensification;
2. *Use of plant foods consumed by humans as feed sources for animals* to increase meat and dairy production through feeding cereal grains and soy (particularly with the rise of incomes in China and increasingly in India);
3. *Food to fuels* and the diversion of agricultural resources (particularly in the United States, which shifts agricultural land and water with maize to ethanol);
4. *Loss of small farms and decreased food sovereignty* in many regions of the world with increased globalization of food trade through the World Trade Organization's Doha trade talks;

Regulatory Factors:

1. *Rapid globalization of world food trade*, industrialization of agriculture, and the increasing take-over of commodities markets by minimally regulated speculators;
2. *Commodity speculation and hoarding* that force up already elevated prices; national beggar thy neighbor and related arbitrary trade policies; currency fluctuation/ devaluations; and other economic factors (in addition to scarcity) that influence the price of food commodities;
3. *Land grabs* derived from large-scale foreign purchase, lease, and other controls of crop lands from central governments and/or agribusiness leading to the displacement of local populations who previously farmed the land with traditional rights to ownership but without contemporary property rights according to new laws passed at the central levels without regard to the local rights;
4. *Significant controversies about genetically modified organisms* (GMOs) the advantages and disadvantages of "unnatural" genetic modification for food enhancement, agribusiness advantage, and disease control;
5. *Inadequate oversight of food safety* includes use of inappropriate additives and antibiotics, chemical contamination of the soil and ground water, post-harvest handling and micro-organism contamination (such as aflotoxins), pest contamination, significant loss of food during harvesting, shipping, storage, processing, cooking, preservation, due to spoilage, loss during consumption, and metabolically due to genetic mismatch of constituents with consumers' ability to digest, metabolize or be otherwise affected by various food constituents (for example, chronic diseases such as obesity, cardiovascular disease and cancer, and/or specific genomic factors such as lactose intolerance, gluten sensitivity, metabolically active oxidants, isoflavones, sulfites, thiocyanates, polyphenols and so forth).

These issues represent many of the major factors that underlie the current crises and many are expected to be repeated over the next 40–50 years in new interactions with one another that lead to the kinds of unpredictable outcomes underlying the current food crises. However, with the assistance of the kinds of holistic models that anthropologists have been developing in archaeology and biological anthropology, together with the kinds of ethical guides that Action Anthropology represents, such as being inclusive about all of the social variables that need to be accounted for to assure people's rights to food are protected, there is the real possibility that new kinds of holistic models could be developed that will be truly helpful in solving some aspects of these problems. Together these conditions and problems have interacted in new ways to create a maze-like series of outcomes, the analysis of which will benefit from the kinds of holistic, ecologically based anthropological models of the human food chain that integrate macro-economic data to make them more useful in early prediction of similar problems. This will be particularly critical during the next 40–50 years, when population will continue to grow rapidly and climate change will reduce the productivity of many previously productive agricultural regions of the world.

To accomplish this goal, we need a global call for the development of a new position or proposition for addressing world food problems, perhaps by universalizing concern about food by showing the linkages between food security and food safety in order to demonstrate that food issues are everyone's business. The dimensions and levels of issues that would benefit from anthropological approaches are vast, complicated and numerous, and some of which I outlined in this section. There is a great need for better communications and coordination among experts and governments. This is happening but needs to be speeded up and catalyzed in new ways—especially using the tools of the Internet, and channeling the existing socioeconomic pressures for solving these problems (e.g., jobs, reductions in birth rates, waste due to loss, improved regulation, and accelerated technological development with free zones, and better education of those who want to transform the food system). However, without maintaining and enlarging an Action Anthropology-type of ethical stance, we will not be able to provide the contemporary moral leadership to accompany the increasingly sophisticated models with ELSI-like feedback that we are already beginning to develop to improve the sustainability of the human food system.

As we look forward into a world where adequate, safe and sustainable food for all humanity in terms of sheer numbers of people is at greater risk than ever before in human history, we need to be reminded of the challenge that Action Anthropology has laid down for anthropology. Our challenge is to enlarge our anthropological models synthetically while still keeping in touch with our humanistic perspective and bringing the ethical lessons of Action Anthropology to bear on how the future is encountered. In a more practical sense this challenge means paying close attention to who defines those in need, how we help those in need without representation, and actively selecting the role we play in being followers of the action or being the catalysts for sharing our understanding with other experts and creating the exemplary action for identifying the key big-picture issues. How anthropologists attend to these issues will be as challenging for us in much of the contemporary world going forward, as it was for Sol Tax when he created the remarkable new paradigm that Action Anthropology represented for the field more than 50 years ago.

References Cited

Bennett, John W.
1996 Applied and Action Anthropology: Ideological and Conceptual Aspects. Special issue: Anthropology in Public. *Current Anthropology,* 37(1):S23–S53.

Fleuret, Anne Fleuret A.
1988 The Task Force on the African Famine. *Disasters,* 12(1):19–20.

Hansen, Art
1993 AAA Position Statement on African Famine. *Anthropology Today,* 9(1):25.

Huss-Ashmore, Rebecca and Solomon H. Katz (editors)
1990 African Food Systems in Crisis, Part One: Microperspectives. Gordon and Breach Publishers, New York.
1991 African Food Systems in Crisis, Part Two: Contending with Change. Gordon and Breach Publishers, New York.

Katz S.H., M.L. Hediger, and L.A. Valleroy
1974 Traditional Maize Processing Techniques in the New World. *Science,* 184(4138):765–773.

Katz, Solomon H.
1999 Toward a New Concept of Global Morality. *Zygon,* 34(2):237–254.

Lurie, Nancy O.
1967 The Indian Claims Commission Act. *Annals of the American Academy of Political and Social Science,* 311: 56–70.
1972 The Indian Claims Commission. *Annals of the American Academy of Political and Social Science,* 436: 97–110.

Reyna, Stephen P., R. E. Downs and D. O. Kerner (editors)
1991 *The Political Economy of African Famine: The Class and Gender Basis of Hunger.* Gordon and Breach. Gordon and Breach, New York.

Smith, Joshua
2010 The Political Thought of Sol Tax: The Principles of Non-Assimilation and Self-Government in Action Anthropology. In *Histories of Anthropology Annual,* 6:129–170. University of Nebraska Press, Lincoln.

Stocking, George
2000 Do Good, Young Man: Sol Tax and the World Mission of Liberal Democratic Anthropology. In *Excluded Ancestors, Inventible Traditions: Essays Toward a More Inclusive History of Anthropology,* edited by Richard Handler. *History of Anthropology,* 9:171–264.

Notes

1. Although Boas did not go much beyond the science of understanding individual cultures, many other anthropologists did, and the Human Relation Area Files (HRAF) in 1949 became the resource that many anthropologists and now many other scientists have used to conduct research. The use of the HRAF was later criticized for its lack of longitudinal data, but it remains very useful for testing hypotheses with its more recent refinement of 60-culture Probability Sample Files and added random case selection procedures.
2. In the 19th century, government policy and action attempted to either wipe out or assimilate the Indians and destroy their ability to maintain their traditional cultural integrity, which centered on a deep spiritual connection to the land of their ancestors and a concept of communal or tribal ownership, as distinct from the Whites' concept of individual land ownership (largely based upon traditions of farming and agricultural experience). Furthermore, the 19th century Whites' expectation was that they would not long have to honor the treaties they signed with the Indians creating Tribal lands away from their traditional lands because they expected Indians to continue to disappear. (Note that the Indians, outnumbered and out armed, bargained as best they could for Tribal homelands.) The Jacksonian removal policy in the 1830s, for example, resulted in great loss of life of the South East tribes (the so called civilized tribes of the U.S. south consisting of the Cherokee, Chickasaw and Choctaw, Muscogee (Creek), and Seminole nations) when they were forced off their tribal lands and force marched on the infamous "trail of tears" to new homelands up to a thousand miles away in Oklahoma. The policy of mass removals to lands West of the Mississippi changed in 1848 to a policy of establishing reservations on the less desirable parts of old homelands, reserving the best land for farming by non-Indians. The "restored" tribal lands were broken up piecemeal to effect assimilation by preventing traditional tribal identity and subsistence. This policy also avoided a large Indian territory west of the Mississippi, with various tribes joining with one another and with the Plains Indians in opposition to the westward expansion of the Whites, whose wagon trains were already moving west. This divide, isolate, demoralize, and conquer through the reapportionment of lands was further exacerbated under the Dawes Act of 1887, under which the US unilaterally divided the reservations in severalty, transferring land from the tribes to individuals in order to hasten Indians away from tribal life to the life of individual farmers. Of course, these often inferior allotted lands would be further subdivided down the generations and lose all effective connections to the tribe. It also resulted in huge land losses overall for Indians, from about 150 million acres guaranteed by treaty or other legislation in 1887 to 50 million acres in 1930, much of it in small, scattered parcels within the old reservation boundaries. In 1896, the U.S. Commissioner of Indian Affairs reported in his annual report that a... "large majority of the Indians … on all … reservations are opposed to citizenship and a division of lands in severalty" and it was leading to great dissatisfaction. However, it was not until the middle of the depression in the 1930s that this was articulated to Sol Tax when he was working with the Fox Indians, who had quietly re-purchased land in Iowa that had been separated from them to supply the tribe with its traditional land resources. This very widespread dissatisfaction with the effects of the Dawes Act and the policies of the 1950s to further force the destruction of Tribal identity became the basis of the Chicago Conference that Tax organized in the 1960s, as the primary advisor on Indian Affairs for the Johnson administration in the mid to late 1960s (from personal correspondence with Nancy O. Lurie). For an excellent account of these issues see the important summaries of these policies and their effects see: Nancy O Lurie, "The Indian Claims Commission Act," Annals of the American Academy of Political and Social Science, 311:56–70,

1967. And, Nancy O Lurie, "The Indian Claims Commission," Annals of the American Academy of Political and Social Science, 436:97–110, (March) 1972.

3. Although Boas did not go much beyond the science of understanding individual cultures, many other anthropologists did, and the Human Relation Area Files (HRAF) in 1949 became the resource that many anthropologists and now many other scientists have used to conduct research. The use of the HRAF was later criticized for its lack of longitudinal data, but it remains very useful for testing hypotheses with its more recent refinement of 60-culture Probability Sample Files and added random case selection procedures.
4. I did not learn until later that Carleton Coon had a disastrous confrontation about race at the annual AAPA meeting in early 1963, before I arrived at the University of Pennsylvania, and both of my colleagues later told me they were "sure" I knew about it and were surprised that I would even suggest that we talk about "race" and our responsibility for public education at an AAPA annual meeting just a few years later in 1967 in North Carolina!
5. I chaired the Task Force of the American Association of Physical Anthropologists to revise and update the UNESCO Statement on the Biology of Race and also proposed the final completed statement to the IUAES in 1992 that was approved by their board for the work with Eric Sunderland when he was the Chair of the IUAES. The Race Statement became a permanent part of their internet website home page from 1994 until 2011 when it was revised to include more of the cultural dimensions. I also introduced the statement to President's Clinton's Cancer Commission for the National Institutes of Health in 1994. It resulted in a revision of the concept of race in the subsequent research guidelines for the NIH and other agencies of the U.S. government that was also adopted by many other governments and organizations throughout the world.
6. I also participated in two other congressional actions in the late 1960s and early 1970s, involving the lead paint ban authored by Senator Richard Schweiker of Pennsylvania and on issues of nutrition and aging with Representative Claude Pepper of Florida. In the mid-1970s, as a citizen, I also lobbied Senator Ted Stevens to establish a cultural center and museum for the borough of Barrow, Alaska.
7. According to the community, in addition to Caleb Pungowiyi's critical role in the early formation of the Norton Sound Health Corporation, he was also president and CEO of the Robert Aqqaluk Newlin Sr. Memorial Trust of Kotzebue and served on many important organizations and international panels, including the Bering Straits Regional Commission, the National Science Foundation Office of Polar Programs Advisory Committee (which originally sponsored our work in Barrow), the Alaska Native Science Commission, the Polar Research Board Committee on Bering Sea Ecosystems, the Inuit Circumpolar Conference, the international organization that advocates for indigenous people of the North, the Advisory Panel on Arctic Impacts from Soviet Nuclear Contamination and the special adviser on Native affairs to the federal Marine Mammal Commission. For more information on his life and his obituary see: http://community.adn.com/adn/node/157691 and also see his personal biographical statement.
8. A newspaper article in the *Abilene Reporter News* on September 9, 1973, about a "Today Morning TV Show" with Barbara Walters recounted a very humorous exchange between Barbara and Gian Carlo Menotti (Barbara had trouble pronouncing his name in Italian and finally settled on "John") about his new opera, Tamu Tamu, and how, much to Menotti's initial disbelief, this anthropologist by the name of Sol Tax had written him to invite him to compose an opera in the name of the International Union of Ethnological and Anthropological Sciences (IUAES)! Moreover Barbara's other two guests, Sol Tax and Margaret Mead, were going to explain how the opera, which is "set in an apartment in Chicago and that families of two races are represented … a couple from the United States and an Indonesian family" was altogether fitting for the Ninth International Congress that had just occurred in Chicago!

In essence, Margaret Mead apparently attempted to sum it up when she said, "We're thinking about the fact that mankind is one species [and] we are many cultures. It is important to preserve these varying cultures." Of course, this article leaves us with how Menotti achieved this, given the opera's reviews. Text Content on Page 108 of the *Abilene Reporter News*, September 9, 1973 http://newspaperarchive.com/the-abilene-reporter-news/1973-09-09/page-108

9. Six panels were invited for the 1977 World Anthropology Conference in preparation for the 1978 ICAES meetings in New Delhi. The topics and invited chairs were: Systems Analysis in Anthropology, Miriam Rodin and Gerald M Britain; The Lessons of Human Evolution, C. Owen Lovejoy and Gordon Willey; The Biosocial Interface, Estelle Fuchs and Solomon Katz; Human Ecology—Models for Human Survival, Thayr Scudder and John Bennett; Symbolic Anthropology and Pyscho-Social Interface, Margaret Mead and F. K. Lehman; and Public Policy Anthropology, Dorothy Wilner, David Madelbaum, and Sam Stanley.
10. These groups had broader participation than anthropology and in fact involved economics as well. One of the key recipients was Amartya Sen who at the time was in at Oxford (currently at Harvard) and subsequently was the recipient in 1988 of the Nobel Prize in Economic Sciences for his work on the causes and consequences of the Bengal Famine.
11. See http://onlinelibrary.wiley.com/doi/10.1111/j.1467-7717.1988.tb01150.x/abstract; Fleuret 1988; also Reyna, Downs, and Kerner (1991); Rebecca Huss-Ashmore and Solomon H. Katz *(1990 and 1991).*
12. See Arthur Owen Lovejoy's classic account in "The Great Chain of Being: A Study of The History on an Idea," Harper Torchbooks, 1960.
13. See the discussion of Race and also the footnote on the UNESCO Race Statement.
14. George Stocking in his history of Tax (2000) tends to give short shrift /gloss over this issue however the paper by Smith (2010; see footnote 3) presents a more substantial treatment of Action Anthropology and this volume goes much further.
15. See the summary of references pages 21–23 of the forward to this volume.
16. See the introductory discussion in Miriam Rodin, Karen Michaelson, and Gerald M Britain, "Systems Theory in Anthropology," *Current Anthroplogy,* Vol. 19 (4):747–761, 1978.
17. In creating the scope for the Encyclopedia of Food and Culture, I developed twenty-two dimensions about food that needed to be addressed in order to comprehensively cover the entire topic and today would probably enlarge the discussion by at least several more (see its appendix and introduction for more details).
18. This foreword to Drs. Harriet V. Kuhnlein and Nancy J. Turner's book (titled *Traditional Plant Foods of Canadian Indigenous Peoples: Nutrition, Botany and Use,* Gordon and Breach; 1991, Vol. 12 of *The History and Anthropology of Food and Nutrition,* Solomon H. Katz, series editor) was also listed in the Food and Agriculture Organization website highlighting indigenous peoples foods and appears to epitomize the needs that the Seattle Traditional Food Summit was addressing at its 2011 meetings.

    "While growing up on my reserve, I remember my parents, aunts, uncles, grandmothers and grandfathers telling me stories about the plants in our area. I would, in turn, explain the stories to my younger brothers, sisters and cousins, and invariably make up something along the way if I couldn't remember all the details. As kids, we would chomp on snake tongues, pilfer berries (we never made it home with enough for a pie), or gather milkweed to relieve our skin from endless mosquito bites. My grandmother had as much success as anyone giving awful-tasting medicine to a kid, especially when it was bitter roots to chew on for a sore throat. I never knew what a weed was, since I was taught that every plant has a purpose on this planet.

    "I am currently working at the Assembly of First Nations, a national Indian political organization, still pursuing my love of the outdoors as a policy analyst for environment and harvesting—hunting, fishing, trapping and gathering. During the past summer, I introduced this book to native communities in the course of my work. *If there is one way to get a native person talking, especially an elder, bring up the topic of traditional Native foods. The response was like a dam being opened—people would go into detail to describe some of their practices, or fondly remember what their parents or grandparents did a long time ago. They wanted to know if a certain plant or certain practice was included in the book. If it was, they checked the accuracy of it and felt good about it; if it wasn't included, they let me know about it.*

"If the enthusiasm and knowledge of the few native communities I visited are any indication, then this book will be a big hit. But we have to realize that it is only scratching the surface of Native knowledge about their plants. Sadly, though, there is also the realization that the foods themselves, and the skills and practices in using them, are slowly dying. There is a triple threat: the loss of knowledgeable elders, leaving no one to teach; the loss of culture, leaving little incentive to learn; and the loss of healthy ecosystems, leaving no foods available to take even if one wanted to. At this moment there are health advisories in some areas warning people of the potential risks to their health from consuming foods contaminated by industrial emissions and agricultural wastes. It has taken time for these things to be understood, and we are still hopeful that the situation can be turned around.

"That is where this book fits in. It can be used as a tool for First Nation People to change their situation. It is probably the first of its kind in Canada to document the literature on the nutrition, botany and use of our traditional plant foods. It describes in simple language not only technical information about the plants, but also how these plants are a part of our distinct culture. To retain this knowledge for succeeding generations is going to take the concerted efforts of people like Dr. Kuhnlein and Dr. Turner, along with academically trained Native youth and the elders and practitioners who maintain a vital link to Canada's environment.

"When Canada can no longer support the tiny percentage of people who depend directly on the land for sustenance, how can we expect this country to support an entire population? When Aboriginal People who live off the land in other countries can no longer support themselves with wholesome foods, what does that predict for global survival? Aboriginal People are, in my view, the best indicators of a healthy environment.

"As a biologist working with both Native People and non-Native scientists, I appreciate the usefulness of this book in its forthright writing style—it is easy to understand. The respect for the ways of life and foods of Aboriginal People is evident in the writing, which demonstrates the authors' integrity. In addition, the wealth and depth of the material gave me and my summer commentators a wonderful sense of pride in the extent of knowledge accumulated by our people in order to live healthy lives.

"We need to work hard together to preserve our knowledge and to protect the environments of the plant foods of the world's Indigenous People. This book is a good step along the way, *Ia wen*, Dr. Kuhnlein and Dr.Turner."

—Laurie Montour, Assembly of First Nations Ottawa, April 1991.

19. Thirty-Sixth Annual National Indian Timber Symposium, "Expanding Roots: Cultivating Relationships and Opportunities," May 14–17, 2012, at the Confederated Tribes of the Warms Springs Reservation of Oregon Kah-Nee-Ta High Desert Resort, Warm Springs, Oregon. The annual "Timber Symposium" program begins with the following sessions:

1) "**First Foods: A Cultural Approach to Management of Natural Resources.**" The Confederated Tribes of the Umatilla Indian Reservations Department of Natural Resources utilizes a cultural approach to manage its Natural Resources. This approach utilizes the Tribe's

First Foods order to relate ecology to the culture of the CTUIR in a tangible manner that demonstrates the need for First Foods for continuity of Tribal culture and to improve protection and fulfillment of the tribes' treaty-reserved rights. Wenix Red Elk, Education Outreach Specialist, Department of Natural Resources, Confederated Tribes of the Umatilla Indian Reservation, Pendleton, Oregon.

2) **"First Foods: The Significant Uses of First Foods on Warm Springs Reservation."** The Confederated Tribes of Warm Springs First Foods includes seven kinds of roots and berries. Discussion will include cultural use, share laws, treaties and declaration of sovereignty to protect natural native foods. Arlita Rhoan, Culture and Heritage Department, The Confederated Tribes of Warm Springs, Warm Springs, Oregon.

3) **"First Foods: Cultural Use Food Plants of the Confederated Salish and Kootenai People."** Discussion will include what staple food plants are used by the tribes (how they came to be and current feast days associated). Is there an integration of cultural use foods in our contemporary diet? Is there anything being done to help sustain important cultural use plant use (i.e., Education, restoration, etc.,)? Ira Matt, Crew Supervisor, Historic Preservation Office, Confederated Salish & Kootenai Tribes, Pablo, Montana.

4) "**The Return of the Wapato: Yakama Nation."** After a 70-year absence, the wapato (potato) returned to the reservation of The Confederated Tribes and Bands of the Yakama Nation. As a result of agricultural diversion, the water table was lowered and an imbalance in nature occurred. A shift in nature also contributed to a shift in the cultural foods and plants available. The Return of the Wapato provides an opportunity to learn how the Yakama Nation restores tribal land areas to historical conditions and ultimately protects the resources for future generations and those not yet born (see Emily Washines, Outreach Coordinator, Yakama Nation Fisheries, Toppenish, Washington).

20. More specifically, "*ethnovorism*" is a culturally distinctive and environmentally and geographically sensitive set of evolved food practices, behaviors and traditions that constitute a coherent food and dietary heritage. This heritage is transmitted culturally over many generations in an evolutionary process that balances the nutrient needs of the population with the social needs for maintaining a sustenance-based cultural identity from one generation to the next. This is in contrast to omnivorism, which refers to the full range of food consumption that is expressed across the human species. Because human populations occupy a very wide range of habitat and ecosystems, the use of the term "ethnovore" provides an important further distinction from the broader concept of omnivore that helps characterize the particular set of important dietary variations that have evolved as coherent food traditions within particular geographic ecosystems. In addition, the ethnovore distinction calls critical attention to the feedback effects of long-term food and dietary practices at the genomic level that have facilitated food traditions to become metabolically and digestively optimized within populations over time.
21. This has at least two other dimensions: (1) social movements like those espoused by the La Via Campesina movement currently based in Indonesia and the Declaration of Nyéléni in Sélingué, Mali in 2007 in Africa; and (2) national food sovereignty movements throughout the world unleashed in response to the great food crisis of 2007–2008 and its repetition in 2010–2011 that served to remind the world that food may not always be available through international trade routes when national policies subvert the sources and purposes of foods that were traditionally part of the human food chain.
22. http://www.aaanet.org/issues/press/upload/Advisory-The-Price-of-Hunger.pdf

23. If we assume that at least 3 billion contemporary people fall into these three categories (in hunger, at the edge of hunger and at serious risk of food safety hazards) and we assume there are about 500 anthropologists in food and nutritional anthropology, culture and agricultural studies and many ancillary sub-fields on anthropology who would be interested in working with problems like the ones mentioned above, then that would mean that each anthropologist would have to assume responsibility for overwhelming numbers of peoples in need. Suppose there were a thousand anthropologists in the world today who could do this work, it would still mean that each one may end up being responsible on average for three million lives with problems of food security, safety and sustainability. Even if there were 10,000 anthropologists directly involved, this would reduce the average numbers to 300,000 people at risk for serious food problems. Of course, these numbers are currently applicable and assume that the problems do not become worse or that the population remains constant, since both of these assumptions are very unlikely, the future need is for greater numbers of trained "food systems" anthropologists.
24. In 2006, I noted that a bill in the U.S. Congress was moving forward to shift a substantial portion of the U.S. corn (maize) crop from food production to fuel production (converting corn sugar to ethanol) and in order to benefit American farmers and cut off foreign sources of oil imports, a tariff would be established for imported ethanol sourced from Brazilian sugar and a reward would be established for gasoline blenders to incorporate this new source of fuel into gasoline. By the time of the fall 2006 meeting of the American Anthropological Association (AAA) meeting in San Francisco, it was a foregone conclusion that this bill would not only pass but also would be signed into law by President Bush as a way to stem the tide of U.S. balance of payments going to the Middle East where the U.S. was at war with both Iraq and Afghanistan. While U.S. farmers would benefit substantially from this new windfall profit from the already rising prices of the corn at market, it was evident that the planting of huge amounts of corn in the next season would occur and that this would have a major impact on the costs of both corn and soybeans that were often agriculturally cycled in the same fields. The international implications of this were enormous. The U.S. was both the largest producer and exporter of maize that was increasingly being used to feed mostly hogs for the increased animal protein consumption and this new move would drive up global maize prices and almost certainly lead to a lower level of soybean production from the U.S., which is also the largest exporter of soy, that would inevitably lead to increased soy prices as well. Hence, I decided to organize a symposium around a topic that looked like it would be important by the time we met again at the annual AAA meeting of November 2007 in Washington, D.C. This was a risky endeavor since there were no food problems at the time I entitled the symposium as, "Corn to Ethanol: A 'Perfect Storm' for Hunger by Thanksgiving 2007?" Unfortunately, my predictions were not only correct, but my worst fears became realized as it became completely clear by August 2007 that a global food crisis was developing. This large-scale U.S. food policy shift became the initial trigger for the global crisis. By the time of the annual AAA meeting I went to the business meeting much the same as I did in the mid-1980s for the Famine in Africa that resulted in the Task Force on the African Famine (discussed earlier in this article) and proposed under new business that a AAA wide Task Force be formed to look into the problem and provide anthropological leadership into the problems that were already developing. This motion carried unanimously with the amendment from Sethe Lowe, the president elect, that the Society for the Anthropology of Food and Nutrition and the Culture and Agriculture organizations of the AAA be requested to organize and staff it. While I thought it might be best for the proposed Presidential Task Force to have a broader representation, I decided not to oppose the friendly amendment since it was more important that it be formed and this represented an expeditious means of doing so that would not bog down on its primary mission. The presidents were

contacted and both agreed to appoint a Task Force and I was selected and elected to be chair. We were able to respond quickly and are continuing to do so.

25. Each one of these categories of factors, among others not included here, could use the help of hundreds and maybe even thousands of anthropologists integrating the results of each within the entire food system. The most recent presentation of these issues was at the annual AAA Meetings in Toronto in November 2011 and the Annual Meetings of the American Philosophical Society two days later in Philadelphia.

APPENDIX: PAPERS AND PUBLICATIONS OF SOL TAX

The following is a compilation of all known papers and publications authored and edited by Sol Tax; co-authored and co-edited works are also included and identified accordingly. The many books appearing in the Mouton Publishers World Anthropology Series, for which Sol Tax served as general editor, are not listed here.

1931 An Algerian Passover. *American Hebrew*, April 3, p. 548.

1931 The Interpretation of Culture. Unpublished undergraduate thesis, University of Wisconsin. Madison.

1932 The social organization of the Fox. Unpublished Master's thesis. University of Chicago, Chicago, Illinois.

1935 Primitive Social Organization with Some Description of the Social Organization of the Fox Indians. PhD dissertation, University of Chicago. University Microfilms International, Ann Arbor, Michigan.

1935 Folk Culture in Guatemala. *Bulletin of the Society for Social Research*, June, p. 6.

1936 Town and Country in Chichicastenango. *Three Americas*, 1(16):11–16.

1937 The Municipios of the Midwestern Highlands of Guatemala. *American Anthropologist*, 39(3):423–444.

1937 Some Problems of Social Organization. In *Social Anthropology of North American Tribes*, edited by Fred Eggan, pp. 3–32. University of Chicago Press, Chicago, Illinois.

1937 The Social Organization of the Fox Indians. In *Social Anthropology of North American Tribes*, edited by Fred Eggan, pp. 243–282. University of Chicago Press, Chicago, Illinois.

1937 Book Review. Epitomé de Culturologí, by J. Imbelloni. *American Anthropologist*, 39(3):546–547.

1939 Culture and Civilization in Guatemalan Societies. *The Scientific Monthly*, 48(5):463–467.

1939 World View and Social Relations in Guatemala. *Bulletin of the Society for Social Research*, June, p. 15.

1941 World View and Social Relations in Guatemala. *American Anthropologist*, 43(1):27–42.

1941 Social Anthropology and Linguistics. *Carnegie Institution of Washington Year Book*, 40:289–309. [Co-authors Robert Redfield, Sol Tax, and Alfonso Villa Rojas]

1942 Ethnic Relations in Guatemala. *American Indigena*, 2(4):43–47.

1943 Anthropological Research Problems with Reference to the Contemporary People of Mexico and Guatemala. *American Anthropologist*, 45(1):1–21. [Co-authors Ralph Beals, Robert Redfield, and Sol Tax].

1944 Information about the Municipio of Zinacantan, Chiapas. *Revista Mexicana de Estudios Anthropologicos*, 6:181–195.

1945 Anthropology and Administration. *American Indigenia*, 5:21–33.

1945 The Problem of Democracy in Middle America. *American Sociological Review*, 10(2):192–199.

1945 Democracy in Middle America. *America Indigena*, 5:4.

1945 Anthropology and Administration. *America Indigena*, 5:21–33.

1946 The Education of Underprivileged Peoples in Dependent and Independent Territories. *The Journal of Negro Education: The Problem of Education in Dependent Territories*, 15(3):336–345.

1947 *The Towns of Lake Atitlan. Microfilm Collection of Manuscripts on Middle American Cultural Anthropology*, No. 13. University of Chicago Library, Chicago, Illinois.

1947 *Notes on Santo Tomas Chichicastenango*. Microfilm Collection of Manuscripts on Middle American Cultural Anthropology, No. 16. University of Chicago Library, Chicago, Illinois.

1947 *Reconnaissance of Northern Guatemala*. Microfilm Collection of Manuscripts on Middle American Cultural Anthropology, No. 17. University of Chicago Library, Chicago, Illinois. [Co-authors Antonio Goubaud Carrera, Juan de Dios Rosales, and Sol Tax]

1947 *Miscellaneous Notes on Guatemala*. Microfilm Collection of Manuscripts on Middle American Cultural Anthropology, No. 118. University of Chicago Library, Chicago, Illinois.

1947 *Nota Sobre Zinacantan. Chiapas*. Microfilm Collection of Manuscripts on Middle American Cultural Anthropology, No. 20. University of Chicago Library, Chicago, Illinois.

1947 La Economia Regional de los Indigenas de Guatemala. *Boletin del Instituto Indigenista Nacional*, 2(3/4):167–168.

1947 *April Is this Afternoon*: *Report of a 3-Day Survey*. Microfilm Collection of Manuscripts on Middle American Cultural Anthropology, No. 19. University of Chicago Library, Chicago, Illinois. [Co-authors Robert Redfield and Sol Tax]

1947 *Reconnaissance of Northern Guatemala*. Microfilm Collection of Manuscripts on Middle American Cultural Anthropology, No. 17. University of Chicago Library, Chicago, Illinois. [Co-authors Antonio Goubaud Carrera, Juan de Dios Rosales, and Sol Tax]

1947 Book Review. A Primitive Mexican Economy, by George M. Foster. *American Anthropologist*, 47(1):150–152.

1948 Manuscripts on Middle American Languages and Cultures. *International Journal of American Linguistics*, 14(1):53–55.

1949 Folk Tales in Chichicastenango: An Unsolved Puzzle. *The Journal of America Folklore*, 62(244):125–135.

1949 *Panajachel: Field Notes*. Microfilm Collection of Manuscripts on Middle American Cultural Anthropology, No. 29. University of Chicago Library, Chicago, Illinois.

1949 Book Review. Rural Mexico, by Nathan L. Whitten. *American Anthropologist*, 51(4):636–637.

1951 Selective Culture Change. *The American Economic Review: Papers and Proceedings of the Sixty-third Annual Meeting of the American Economic Association*, 41(2):315–320.

1951 Statement on Peyote. *Science*, 114:582–583. [Co-authors Weston La Barre, David P. McAllester, J. S. Slotkin, Omer C. Stewart, and Sol Tax]

1951 Lacandon Nasal Ornaments. *American Anthropologist*, 53(1):148.

1951 *The Civilizations of Ancient America: Selected Papers of the XXIXth International Congress of Americanists*. University of Chicago Press, Chicago, Illinois. [Editor]

1952 Action Anthropology. *America Indigena*, 12(2):103–109.

1952 Book Review. Social Anthropology, by E. E. Evans-Pritchard. *American Anthropologist*, 54(3):388–390.

1952 *An Appraisal of Anthropology Today*. University of Chicago Press, Chicago, Illinois. [Co-editors Sol Tax, Loren C. Eiseley, Irving Rouse, and Carl F. Voegelin]

1952 *Heritage of Conquest*. Macmillan, New York. [Editor]

1952 *Acculturation in the Americas: Selected Papers of the XXIXth International Congress of Americanists* University of Chicago Press, Chicago, Illinois. [Editor]

1952 *Indians Tribes of Aboriginal America: Selected Papers of the XXIXth International Congress of Americanists* University of Chicago Press, Chicago, Illinois. [Editor]

1952 General Characteristics of Present-Day Mesoamerican Indian Society. In *Heritage of Conquest: The Ethnology of Middle America*, edited by Sol Tax, pp. 31-39. The Free Press, Glencoe, Illinois. [Co-authors Robert Redfield and Sol Tax]

1953 *Penny Capitalism: A Guatemalan Indian Economy*. Institute of Social Anthropology, Publication No. 6. Smithsonian Institution Press, Washington, D.C.

1953 Editorial. *American Anthropologist*, 55:1-3.

1953 *The Mesquakies of Iowa: A Summary of Findings of the First Five Years*. University of Chicago, State University of Iowa, Mesquakie Indian Project.

1954 Wenner-Gren Foundation Supper Conference. *American Anthropologist*, 56:387-388.

1954 A Report on the Behavioral Sciences at the University of Chicago. Chicago, Illinois.

1955 From Lafitau to Radcliffe-Brown: A Short History of the Study of Social Organization, in *Social Anthropology of North American Tribes*, enlarged edition, edited by Fred Eggan, pp. 445-481. University of Chicago Press, Chicago, Illinois.

1955 Some Problems of Social Organization, in *Social Anthropology of North American Tribes*, edited by Fred Eggan, pp. 3-32. Revised Edition (1937). University of Chicago Press, Chicago. Illinois.

1955 The Integration of Anthropology. *Yearbook of Anthropology*, pp. 313-328. The University of Chicago Press on behalf of the Wenner-Gren Foundation for Anthropological Research, Chicago, Illinois.

1955 The Indigenous Foundations of Latin American Culture: An Anthropological Approach. *Civilizations*, 5(4):499-508.

1956 Acculturation. In *Men and Cultures: Selected Papers of the Fifth International Congress of Anthropological and Ethnological Sciences*, edited by Anthony F. C. Wallace, pp. 192-196. University of Pennsylvania Press, Philadelphia.

1956 The Freedom to Make Mistakes. *America Indigena*, 16(3):171-177.

1956 Acculturation. Paper read at the Fifth International Congress of Anthropological and Ethnological Sciences. Philadelphia, Pennsylvania.

1956 Introduction. In *Workshop in American Indian Affairs*. Colorado Springs.

1956 The Integration of Anthropology. In *Current Anthropology: A Supplement to Anthropology Today*. Wenner-Gren Foundation, New York.

1956 No 'Crime' in SECC. *Chicago Maroon*, 30 March, p. 4.

1956 The North American Indians: 1950 Distribution of Descendants of the Aboriginal Population of Alaska, Canada, and the United States. University of Chicago, Department of Anthropology, Chicago, Illinois. [Co-authors Sol Tax, Sam Stanley, and Robert K. Thomas]

1957 Changing Consumption in Indian Guatemala. *Economic Development and Cultural Change*, 5(2):147-158.

1957 The Indians in the Economy of Guatemala. *Social and Economic Studies*, 6(3):413-424.

1957 The Fox Project. Paper presented at the symposium "Values in Action" at the Annual Meeting of the American Anthropological Association, Chicago, December.]

1957 Book Review. Dictionary of Anthropology, by Charles Winick. *American Anthropologist*, 59(5):898-900.

1958 Action Anthropology. *Current Anthropology*, 16:514-517.

1958 The Fox Project. *Human Organization*, 17(1):17-19.

1959 Residential Integration: The Case of Hyde Park in Chicago. *Human Organization*, 18:22-27.

1959 Current Anthropology: A World Journal of the Science of Man. Pre-issue.

1959 Obituary. James Sydney Slotkin, 1913-1958. *American Anthropologist*, 61(5):844-847.

1960 *The Evolution of Life: Its Origin, History, and Future. Volume 1 of Evolution after Darwin.* The University of Chicago Press, Chicago, Illinois. [Editor]

1960 *The Evolution of Man: Mind, Culture and Society. Volume 2 of Evolution after Darwin.* The University of Chicago Press, Chicago, Illinois. [Editor]

1960 *Issues in Evolution: The University of Chicago Centennial Discussions, Volume 3 of Evolution after Darwin.* The University of Chicago Press, Chicago, Illinois. [Co-editors Sol Tax and C. Callender]

1960 The Celebration: A Personal View. In *Issues in Evolution* (Vol 3.) of *Evolution After Darwin*, edited by Sol Tax and C. Callender, pp. 271-278. University of Chicago Press, Chicago, Illinois.

1960 Book Review. Man, Culture, Society, edited by Harry L. Shapiro. *American Anthropologist*, 60(2):379-380.

1960 Exhibits. In *Documentary History of the Fox Project 1948-1959: A Program in Action Anthropology*, edited by Fred Gearing, Robert McC. Netting, and Lisa R. Peattie. Department of Anthropology. University of Chicago.

- Exhibit 1. The Social Organization of the Fox Indians. Unpublished PhD Thesis, 1935, pp. 168-175 (pp. 3-7).
- Exhibit 3. Anthropology and Administration. From *America Indigne*, 5(1):21-33 (pp. 15-24).
- Exhibit 4. Letter—Sol Tax to John Province (pp. 27-28).
- Exhibit 8. Letter—Sol Tax to Lisa Peattie (pp. 32-24).
- Exhibit 16. Request for Support of the "Fox Project" (pp. 92-97).
- Exhibit 18. Letter—Sol Tax to Bob Merrill (pp. 121-122).
- Exhibit 20. Letter—Sol Tax to Bob Merrill (pp. 125-126).
- Exhibit 22. Action Anthropology (pp. 167-171)
- Exhibit 23. Acculturation (pp. 171-176).
- Exhibit 27. Letter—Sol Tax Sol Tax to George Willoughby (pp. 198-201).
- Exhibit 35. Letter—Sol Tax Sol Tax to Bert Stolpe (p. 229).
- Exhibit 41. Letter—Sol Tax to Glen Emmons (pp. 238-240).
- Exhibit 44. The Freedom to Make Mistakes (pp. 245-250).
- Exhibit 47. Proposal to Develop Professional Education among Indians by Means of a Ten-Year Scholarship Program for the Mesquakie Indians of Iowa (pp. 254-260).
- Exhibit 51. Termination Versus the Needs of a Positive Policy for American Indians (pp. 281-283)
- Exhibit 53. Symposium: The Fox Indian Project, a Program of Action Anthropology. Introduction (p. 284) and Learning through Action (pp. 304-307).
- Exhibit 55. Symposium: The Fox Project. Diagnosis for Action (pp. 312-316).
- Exhibit 87. Introduction to a Reader in Action Anthropology (extracts) (pp. 378-386).
- Exhibit 91. Letter—Steve Polgar to Sol Tax, May 4, 1958 (pp. 401-404).
- Exhibit 94. The Fox Project (*Human Organization*, 1958)(pp. 415-417).

1961 *Declaration of Indian Purpose.* University of Chicago Press, Chicago, Illinois. [Editor]

1962 *Anthropology Today: Selections.* University of Chicago Press, Chicago, Illinois. [Editor]

1962 Task Force on Indian Affairs: Implementing Change through Government. *Human Organization*, 21(2):125-136.

1963 The Importance of Preserving Indian Culture. University of Chicago Smithsonian Institution's Center for the Study of Man, Folder 1, Box 267, Series 8, Sol Tax Papers, Special Collections Research Center, Joseph Regenstein Library, University of Chicago.

1964 The Maya of the Midwestern Highlands, in *Handbook of Middle American Indians*, Chapter 8. University of Texas Press, Austin.

1964 *Horizons of Anthropology*. Aldine, Chicago, Illinois.

1964 The Setting of the Science of Man. In *Horizons of Anthropology*, edited by Sol Tax, pp. 15–24. Aldine, Chicago, Illinois.

1964 El Capitalismo del Centavo. Ministerio de Educaćion. Guatemala.

1965 The History and Philosophy of Current Anthropology. *Current Anthropology*, 6:238–269.

1965 The Origin of Man. Transcription of a Symposium by the Wenner-Gren Foundation. [Editor Paul DeVore]

1965 Los Municipios del Altiplano Meso occidental de Guatemala. Ministerio de Educaćion. Guatemala.

1966 The Importance of Preserving Indian Culture. *America Indigena*, 26(1):81–86.

1967 *The Draft: A Handbook of Facts and Alternatives*. University of Chicago Press, Chicago, Illinois. [Editor]

1967 *Acculturation in the Americas: Selected Papers of the XXIXth International Congress of Americanists* University of Chicago Press, Chicago, Illinois. [Editor]

1968 *The People vs. the System: A Dialogue in Urban Conflict*. University of Chicago Press, Chicago, Illinois. [Editor]

1968 Anthropologists: Are They the Modern Medicine Men? In *Anthropological Backgrounds of Adult Education*, edited by Clifford L. Winters, pp. 3–16. Center for the Study of Liberal Education of Adults, Boston University, Brookline.

1968 Society, the Individual, and National Service. *Current History*, August, pp. 78–83.

1968 Last on the Warpath: A Personalized Account of How an Anthropologist Learned from American Indians. University of Chicago Smithsonian Institution's Center for the Study of Man, Folder 2, Box 273, Series 8, Sol Tax Papers, Special Collections Research Center, Joseph Regenstein Library, University of Chicago.

1968 War and the Draft. In *War: The Anthropology of Armed Conflict and Aggression*, edited by M. Fried, M. Harris, and R. Murphy, pp. 195–207. Garden City, New York.

1968 The American Anthropological Association Symposium on American Indian Fishing and Hunting Rights. *Northwest Anthropological Research Notes*, 2(2):1–43.

1968 Discussion. In *Man the Hunter*, edited by Richard B. Lee and Irven DeVore, pp. 345–346. Aldine, Chicago, Illinois.

1968 Pueblos del Lago de Atitlan. Seminars de Integracion. Guatemala.

1969 Indian Identity and Economic Development. In *Toward Economic Development for Native American Communities: Papers Submitted to the Subcommittee on Economy in Government of the Joint Economic Committee*, 91st Congress, 1st Session, Vol. 1, Part 1, pp. 75–96. [Sol Tax and Sam Stanley]

1969 Linguistic-Cultural Differences and American Education. *Florida Reporter*, 7(1):15–19. [Co-authors Sol Tax and Robert K. Thomas]

1970 *Anthropology Today: Selections*. University of Chicago Press, Chicago, Illinois. [Editor]

1970 Letter to Robert Hinshaw, June 18, 1970. Center for Advanced Study of the Behavioral Sciences. Stanford, California.

1971 Cultural Differences in the Maya Area: A 20th Century Perspective. Sobretiro de Desarrollo Cultural de los Mayas. Mexico.

1971 Preface. In *Human Futuristics*, edited by M. Maruyama and J. Dator, pp. vii–ix. Honolulu, Hawaii.

1972 Foreword. In *This Land Was Ours*, Virgil J. Vogel, p. xxi–xxv. Harper and Row, New York.

1973 Serial Publications in Anthropology. University of Chicago Press, Chicago, Illinois. [Co-editors Sol Tax and Francis X. Grollig]
1973 ICAES Book Fair. *Anthropology News*, 14(5):2.
1974 Editors Report. *Current Anthropology*, 15:365–366.
1975 Action Anthropology. *Current Anthropology*, 16(4):514–517.
1975 The Bow and the Hoe: Reflections on Hunters, Villagers, and Anthropologists. *Current Anthropology*, 16(4):507-513.
1975 Preface. In *Fifth International Directory of Anthropologists*. University of Chicago Press, Chicago, Illinois.
1975 Afterword: The Inception of Extraterrestrial Anthropology. In *Cultures Beyond Earth*, edited by M. Maruyama and J. Dator, pp. 200–203. New York.
1975 History of *Current Anthropology*. Course Lecture by Sol Tax transcribed by Gay Neuberger. University of Chicago Smithsonian Institution's Center for the Study of Man, Folder 5, Box 247, Series 8, Sol Tax Papers, Special Collections Research Center, Joseph Regenstein Library, University of Chicago.
1976 Proposal for a New Institution: the Family as a Corporate Entity. *Center for the Study of Democratic Institutions Report*, 9(1):6–7.
1976 Self-Help Groups: Thoughts on Public Policy. *Journal of Applied Behavioral Science* 12(3):448–454.
1976 A Way to Begin. *Anthropology News*, 17(5):2.
1977 Anthropology for the World of the Future: Thirteen Professions and Three Proposals. *Human Organization*, 36(3):225–234.
1977 Horizons of Anthropology. 2nd edition. Aldine, Chicago, Illinois [Co-editors Sol Tax and Leslie G. Freeman]
1978 The Impact of Urbanization on American Indians. *Annals of the American Academy of Political and Social Science*, 436(1):121–136.
1978 General Editor's Preface. In *American Indian Economic Development*, edited by Sam Stanley, p. vi. Mouton Publishers, New York.
1979 The Autobiography of Santiago Yach, in *Currents in Anthropology*, edited by Robert Hinshaw, pp. 1–68. Mouton Publishers, New York.
1979 Anthropology for the Future: The Status and Prospects of a Program of International Cooperation. *Human Organization*, 38(3):326–330. [Co-authors Demitri B. Shimkin and Sol Tax]
1981 Jewish Life in the United States: Perspectives from Anthropology. In *Jewish Life in the United States: Perspectives from the Social Sciences*, edited by J. B. Gittler, pp. 297–313. New York.
1982 Creation and Evolution. Paper prepared for conference on 'Science, the Bible, and Darwin,' State University of New York at Buffalo, 16–17 April. University of Chicago Smithsonian Institution's Center for the Study of Man, Folder 10, Box 280, Series 8, Sol Tax Papers, Special Collections Research Center, Joseph Regenstein Library, University of Chicago.
1982 Planning Utopias. *Cultural Futures Research*, 7(1).
1983 Reconciling Evolution and Creation. *Society*, 20(2):36–39.
1986 *Archival History Program Videotaped Interview of Sol Tax*. Wenner-Gren Foundation for Anthropological Research. New York. [Interview conducted by Robert A. Rubinstein]
1988 Pride and Puzzlement A Retro-introspective Record of 60 Years of Anthropology. *Annual Review of Anthropology*, 17:1–21.

1988 *Practical Animism: The World of Panajachel.* Microfilm Collection of Manuscripts on Middle American Cultural Anthropology, No. 392. University of Chicago Library, Chicago, Illinois.

1990 Can World Views Mix? *Human Organization*, 49(3):280–286.

1991 A Conversation with Sol Tax. *Current Anthropology*, 32(2):175–183. [Co-authors Sol Tax and Charles Callender].

1991 *Fieldwork: The Correspondence of Robert Redfield and Sol Tax.* Westview Press, Boulder, Colorado. [Editor, Robert A. Rubinstein]

CONTRIBUTORS

Joan Ablon (PhD, Chicago, 1963) is Professor Emerita, Medical Anthropology Program, Department of Anthropology, History, and Social Medicine, School of Medicine, University of California, San Francisco. Ablon's earliest research documented the adaptations to urban life of American Indian relocatees and Samoan migrants in the San Francisco Bay Area. As the staff social scientist in a Community Mental Health Training Program at UCSF, she studied family interaction in a Catholic parish, alcoholism and the family, and Al-Anon Family Groups. In the mid-1970s she became a founding faculty member of the Medical Anthropology Program at UCSF, a joint doctoral program with UC Berkeley. Ablon's interests in stigmatized health conditions and support systems led to her analyses of psychosocial issues in genetic conditions, resulting in numerous articles and four books: *Little People in America: The Social Dimensions of Dwarfism; Living With Difference: Families with Dwarf Children; Living with Genetic Disorder: The Impact of Neurofibromatosis 1*; and *Brittle Bones, Stout Hearts and Minds: Adults with Osteogenesis Imperfecta.* ablonj@aol.com

John H. Bodley (PhD, Oregon, 1970) is the current Regents Professor at Washington State University in Pullman. He is a cultural anthropologist with research interests in indigenous peoples, cultural ecology, and contemporary issues. Dr. Bodley conducted field research with the Ashaninka, Conibo, and Shipibo indigenous groups in the Peruvian Amazon throughout his early career. He has visited other indigenous groups in Alaska, Australia, Ecuador, Guatemala, Mexico, and the Philippines. He has held visiting academic appointments at the University of Alaska, Fairbanks (1986), and the University of Uppsala, Sweden (1985). He was a visiting researcher at the International Work Group for Indigenous Affairs in Copenhagen (1980). In 1986, Dr. Bodley served on the Tasaday Commission for the University of the Philippines Department of Anthropology in Manila. He was a member (1991–94) of the advisory subcommittee for the human rights section of the American Association for the Advancement of Science's Committee on Scientific Freedom and Responsibility. He has taught at Washington State University for over 30 years. bodleyj@wsu.edu

Marianna Tax Choldin (PhD, Chicago, 1979) is Mortenson Distinguished Professor Emerita, University of Illinois at Urbana-Champaign. She was on the faculty of the University of Illinois-Urbana from 1969 through 2002, was an adjunct professor in the Graduate School of Library and Information Science, and served as director of the Russian and East European Center and head of the Slavic and East European Library. In 1991 she became the founding director of the Mortenson Center for International Library Programs, which she led until her retirement at the end of 2002. From 1997 to 2000 she chaired the multifaceted library program of the Soros Foundation, which has distributed millions of dollars to libraries and librarians in more than 30 countries. In her own research Professor Choldin studies censorship in Russia, the Soviet Union, and the post-Communist world. The author of numerous articles and books, she is best known for *A Fence Around the Empire: Russian Censorship of Western Ideas Under the Tsars* and *The Red Pencil: Artists, Scholars, and Censors in the USSR* (co-edited with Maurice Friedberg). In 1995 she was elected president of the American Association for the Advancement of Slavic Studies. In 2000 the government of Russia awarded her the Pushkin Gold Medal for contributions to culture. In 2001 she was the first recipient of the University of Illinois' Distinguished Faculty Award for International Achievement. In 2005 the American Library Association's International Relations Committee gave her the John Ames Humphry/OCLC/Forest Press Award for significant contributions to international librarianship. From 2004 through 2010 she was founding president of the Rudomino Library Council USA, an organization supporting projects that promoted tolerance in Russia. Professor Choldin received a public service award from the University of Chicago in 2011. mcholdin@me.com

Douglas E. Foley (PhD, Stanford, 1970) has been a Professor of Anthropology and of Education at the University of Texas at Austin since 1970. He is the former editor of the *Anthropology and Education Quarterly* and the *International Journal of Qualitative Studies in Education.* During his career, he specialized in cultural studies of schooling, social movements, and race relations in the United States. He published six books as well as sixty articles and chapters. His most recent ethnographies include *Learning Capitalist Culture: Deep in the Heart of Tejas* (2nd edition, 2010, University of Pennsylvania Press) and *The Heartland Chronicles* (expanded version, 2003, University of Pennsylvania Press). He retired to Guanajuato, Mexico, in May 2012. dfoley@mail.utexas.edu

Susan Tax Freeman (PhD, Harvard, 1965) is Professor Emerita of Anthropology at the University of Illinois at Chicago. She is a cultural anthropologist of Europe specialized in national ethnography and cultural marginality in Spain. She did pre-doctoral research in Chiapas, Mexico, and later comparative work on marginated groups in Japan and Appalachia in the United States. She is author of *Neighbors: The Social Contract in a Castilian Hamlet* and *The Pasiegos: Spaniards in No Man's Land.* She is also a scholar of Spanish culinary history and practice. As an undergraduate at the University of Chicago, she was staff assistant during the first two summers of Sol Tax's Workshop on American Indian Affairs, in 1956 and 1957, held at Colorado College and directed by Fred Gearing and Robert Thomas, respectively.

Robert E. Hinshaw (PhD, Chicago, 1966) currently divides time, writing, between Kansas City, the Colorado mountains, and a home in the rural community of Tzununa in Guatemala. Anthropological career involvements have included department chair at Beloit College and University of Colorado–Denver; faculty appointments at the University of Illinois–Normal, University of Kansas, and the national University of San Carlos in Guatemala. Interspersed with those appointments were a presidency of Wilmington College–Ohio, deanship at Bethel College–Kansas, and directorships of the Kansas Institute for Peace and Conflict Resolution as well as the Associated Colleges of Central Kansas consortium. Principal publications are referenced within this book. Research and writing in progress include a biography of Bolivia's recent president, Gonzalo Sanchez de Lozada, and a collection of essays comparing the evolution of consciousness of preliterate Maya neighbors in Tzununa with his own as a product of scientific literacy in a context of Quaker socialization. The Spanish version of the first of two companion historical novels set in Guatemala was released in 2012.

Solomon H. Katz (PhD, Pennsylvania, 1967) is Distinguished Professor of Anthropology at the University of Pennsylvania, where he has taught since 1968. He is Director of Penn's Krogman Center for Childhood Growth and Development, editor-in-chief of the Encyclopedia of Food and Culture, and has led the American Anthropological Association's special Task Force on World Food Problems since 2007. Dr. Katz has been studying the anthropology of food for over forty years and has conducted extensive research on African food systems in crisis: nutrition, culture, and evolution; the efficacy of genetically modified foods and organisms; and intersections between food and spirituality. In his current research and activism he hopes to highlight the magnitude of the crisis, and the potential solutions that are either available now or will be available in the near future to avert increasing the numbers in serious hunger to over a billion of the world's humanity. He also has expertise in the interface between secular and religious/spiritual communities at local and global levels especially as they are focused on the relief of food and hunger problems. He also has expertise in the interface between secular and religious/spiritual communities at local and global levels. skatz2011@aol.com

Jay Miller (PhD) holds degrees in anthropology, ethnohistory, and linguistics from the University of New Mexico and Rutgers, with allied coursework at Princeton. He has taught in the U.S. and Canada, at each of the four quarters (Southwest, Southeast, Northeast, and Northwest), as well as serving as an administrator in the heartland at the Newberry Library's Center for the American Indian History in Chicago. During his time in Chicago, he filled in at the University of Chicago and was befriended by Ray Fogelson, Fred Eggan, and Sol Tax. His co-teaching with Ojibwa and Menomini speakers at NAES, Native American Educational Services, became a kind of Action Anthropology for urban Indiens (for Indies not India). After a disastrous fire gutted the building, one of their refurbished classrooms was named in honor of Sol Tax. A dozen published books range over North America, with several on the Northwest Coast. Recent work has been concerned with current mound building, the 1830s' "ethnic cleansing" of Ohio, and the lifework of the late Vi Taqwsheblu Hilbert, a fluent elder, U.S. National Treasure, and traditional link to the lands and waters of Puget Sound.

Kevin Preister (PhD, University of California at Davis, 1994; Director, Center for Social Ecology and Public Policy, senior associate with James Kent Associates, and adjunct faculty, Southern Oregon University). Preister recognized early on that human change initiatives—projects, programs, and policies of governments or corporations—must fit within the culture of a geographic area and offer social, economic, and ecological benefits in order to be successful, effective, and sustainable. He has worked in a variety of settings on improved linkages between informal community systems and the institutions that serve them, including natural-resource management, human-service delivery, energy development and urban redevelopment. He worked with the Bureau of Land Management (BLM) for over 20 years, contributing through training programs and direct service to its management paradigm shift to incorporate community-based collaboration. Other clients have included the Oregon Department of Forestry; the County of Hawaii; and the Kootenai Tribe of Bonners-Ferry, Idaho, among many others. He has contributed to such publications as *Restoring and Sustaining Lands—*

Coordinating Science, Politics, and Community for Action and *Hastings West-Northwest Journal of Environmental Law and Policy.*

David G. Rice (PhD, Washington State University, 1972). Retired Native American Coordinator for Seattle District, U.S. Army Corps of Engineers (1984–2004), with responsibilities for relations with more than 40 federally recognized Indian tribes in Idaho, Montana, Oregon, Montana, and Washington. The focus of tribal interests was on Federal trust responsibilities, Indian treaty fishing rights, hazardous and toxic cleanup of Indian lands formerly used by the military, and habitat-restoration projects for fish, wildlife, and native plants. Upon request, Rice provided assistance to other federal agencies that lacked capability for similar work. From 1992 to retirement, he worked on traditional cultural property issues with more than 20 Pacific Northwest tribes regarding the effects of federally permitted projects, dam reservoir areas, and various military projects in the West. Prior to his government post, he was Associate Professor of Anthropology at University of Idaho (1969–79), with interests in contemporary Native Americans, treaty fishing rights, and the administration of a two-year University-Year-for-Action program (1972–74). windust1@yahoo.com

Sarah Anne (Sally) Robinson (PhD, University of Chicago, 1963). Sally Robinson is a retired anthropologist from Illinois. She attended graduate school at the University of Chicago during the 1950s, including one summer at the Fox Project field school. Among her interests are organizational structure, anomie and anomia, and the Salish Indians—in particular the Snuneymuxw First Nation with which she has worked for 50 years. She recently completed a term on the Society for Applied Anthropology Executive Board. Sarahar2@sbcglobal.net

Joshua Smith is a PhD student at the University of Western Ontario. His work in the critical study of the histories of anthropology focuses on the political philosophies and cultural (re)productions of engaged anthropological research with an emphasis on the political matrix particular to the colonial encounters of North America. Under the supervision of Dr. Regna Darnell, his work is looking at the historical and theoretical genealogies of contemporary engaged research methods such as community-based participatory research and collaborative ethnography, including their continuous and/or divergent relationships with the past anthropological engagements such as Sol Tax and Franz Boas, for example. Moreover, Joshua is working on settler and indigenous relations with a specific focus on the (mis)communication(s) that occur between what is often referred to as the "stakeholders" in collaborative research and community-based projects. This includes questions around knowledge production, transference, translation, and the political dynamics through which these are mediated and negotiated. He is a student associate with the Technoscience and Research Unit (Dalhousie University) and Intellectual Property Issues in Cultural Heritage (Simon Fraser University). actionanth@gmail.com

Darby C. Stapp (PhD, Pennsylvania, 1991) is the owner of Northwest Anthropology LLC, a small cultural-assessment business in Richland, Washington, which he started in 2009 following retirement from Battelle, Pacific Northwest National Laboratory. He has spent his professional career in the Pacific Northwest, where he has focused on American Indian ethnohistory and heritage management. Since 1991, he has worked with Plateau Tribes to address protection of sacred sites and traditional-use areas. He has published widely on tribal issues and coauthored two books: *Tribal Cultural Resource Management: the Full Circle to Stewardship* (2001), and *Avoiding Archaeological Disasters: A Risk Management Approach* (2009). He was program chair for the Society for Applied Anthropology Annual Meeting in Seattle in 2011 and has served as co-editor of the *Journal of Northwest Anthropology* since 2007. dstapp@pocketinet.com

Albert L. Wahrhaftig (PhD, Chicago, 1975) is Professor Emeritus, Department of Anthropology, Sonoma State University. A summer in Mexico during his undergraduate years at Stanford converted him from a career in architecture to a love for Mexico, a commitment to anthropology, and a vague sense that it could be used to improve human situations. Throughout his graduate career at the University of Chicago and thereafter, Sol Tax served as his model and lifelong mentor; he has always been an Action Anthropologist at heart. His varied involvements started with fieldwork in Chiapas, Mexico, continued with a tenure as Assistant to the Coordinators of the American Indian Chicago Project, followed by two years of rural community development in Colombia as a member of the Peace Corps' first group of volunteers, and then fieldwork in traditional Cherokee Indian communities in eastern Oklahoma as part of the University of Chicago's Carnegie Corporation Cross Cultural Education Project. Thereafter he taught for 35 years at Sonoma State University, directing undergraduate students in a variety of local-action projects while also continuing with varied brief field trips, most of them to Mexico. In the past several years, his interest has turned to visual anthropology. As an ethnographer in partnership with videographer Bruce "Pacho" Lane, the two have completed videos in Tepoztlan, Mexico, and in the

Totonac Indian community of Huehuetla, Puebla, Mexico, the latter at the request of members of the community. wahrhaft@sonic.net

Tim Wallace (PhD, Indiana, 1975) Tim Wallace is an Associate Professor and applied anthropologist in the Department of Sociology and Anthropology at North Carolina State University. Since 1994, he has been the Director of the NCSU Ethnographic Field School, now in its 20th year and located in Lake Atitlán, Guatemala. He is currently the President of the National Association for the Practice of Anthropology (NAPA) (2010–2012) and Editor of the *SfAA News* (2007–2013). He was the editor of the *NAPA Bulletin* (2003–2009). He has published on tourism and heritage-related projects in Madagascar, Hungary, Costa Rica, Guatemala, and North Carolina. He is currently working on a tourism-development project, called People First Tourism, in Warren County, North Carolina, and is writing an anthropology of tourism heritage in the Lake Atitlán region of Guatemala. tim_wallace@ncsu.edu

INDEX

Journal of Northwest Anthropology *Memoir Series*

The *Journal of Northwest Anthropology* publishes occasional monographs and multi-author collections under the *Memoir* series. Those issued prior to 2005 appear as *Northwest Anthropological Research Notes Memoirs.* Authors interested in publishing through this series should contact the *Journal of Northwest Anthropology* editors at the Richland, Washington, office. The following are titles of the memoirs published to date:

Memoir 1 (1967)
An Examination of American Indian Reaction to Proposals of the Commissioner of Indian Affairs for General Legislation, 1967
Deward E. Walker, Jr.

Memoir 2 (1973)
Influences of the Hudson's Bay Company on the Native Cultures of the Colville District
David H. Chance

Memoir 3 (1976)
Quileute Dictionary
J.V. Powell and Fred Woodruff, Sr.

Memoir 4 (1978)
Flat Glass: Its Use as a Dating Tool for Nineteenth-Century Archaeological Sites in the Pacific Northwest and Elsewhere
Karl G. Roenke

Memoir 5 (1979)
A Bibliography of Idaho Archaeology, 1889–1976
Max G. Pavesic, Mark G. Plew, and Roderick Sprague

Memoir 6 (2002)
It's About Time (híiwes wiyéewts'etki), It's About Them (paamiláyk'ay), It's About Us (naamiláyk'ay): A Decade of Papers, 1988–1998
Michael S. Burney and Jeff Van Pelt, editors

Memoir 7 (2012)
Festschrift in Honor of Max G. Pavesic
Kenneth C. Reid and Jerry R. Galm, editors

To purchase Memoirs 1 through 6, contact Coyote Press, P.O. Box 3377, Salinas, CA 93912.
http://www.californiaprehistory.com